Before a Bad Goodbye

Tim Clinton

WORD PUBLISHING

NASHVILLE

A Thomas Nelson Company

This book is affectionately dedicated to the memory of my mother, Mildred Faye Mowrey Clinton (1925–1996). Her life taught me of God's rich love and the beauty of a life well lived.

Published by Word Publishing
Nashville, TN

Unless otherwise marked, Scripture quotations used in this book are from the New King James Version of the Bible (NKJV).

Scriptures marked NIV are from the New International Version.

ISBN: 0-8499-3743-4

Printed in the United States of America
99 00 01 02 03 QPV 9 8 7 6 5 4 3 2 1

ACKNOWLEDGMENTS

*A*t last, this book. Crafting the pages of this manuscript has been one of the most challenging and painful exercises of my life. The cost has seemed exceeding at times; however, if even one child is able to continue to wake up to both mom's and dad's loving voices, it will have served its purpose.

A special note to:

My wife, Julie: I love you. You make my life so blessed. I am simply amazed at the way you love me all the time.

My children, Megan and Zachary: God could not have given me two more precious souls to call me Daddy. Your embraces give me life.

My father, Pastor James E. Clinton: Dad, thank you for being such a godly example and for loving my mother.

Our families: Julie and I believe that even though geographically the distance is great between many of us, the strength and love that we draw from God and one another gives a special bond that few families ever experience. We love you all.

I am deeply grateful to so many who helped along the way:

Bill Kritlow, Janet Reed, and Dawn Emeigh helped sculpt and give life to the manuscript.

Heidi Brizendine and Shannon White gave countless hours of technical support facilitating revision after revision. A special thank you to Sealy Yates, Tom Thompson, Lee Gessner, and my new friends at Word Publishing for setting my feet to a path and having confidence in this work. To Scott Titus and the entire AACC staff for standing by and tolerating me through this journey. And, finally, to so many marital experts whose writings and, in many cases, personal interactions have enriched my life, marriage, counseling ministry, and this work.

The case studies set forth in this work are crafted carefully to protect the confidentiality of each client and broadly represent the themes, issues, and interactions of numerous clients I have worked with over the years.

CONTENTS

Part 1. Reframe

How Couples Lose at Love

Part 2. Reclaim/Release

Part 3. Reconcile

Part 4. Refashion

Reframe

WORLDS APART

God never wastes a wound.
—*Unknown*

*I*t's a horrible moment when rage turns to emptiness—when all its power vanishes and nothing is left but an unfillable, hopeless void and a deep ache in the heart.

Carla had gotten all the way to the airport before it happened to her, past the ticket counter, at the gate where she found herself surrounded by other travelers. *They look like all travelers—either blank-faced or completely self-absorbed. Look people. Isn't it obvious I'm on emotional fire here? Don't you know what I'm going through? Do I have to fall apart before you'll care? But you wouldn't care.* After all, if her husband, John, didn't, why should they?

As Carla sat in the corner of the gate area, her heart suddenly burned with that indifference—from them, from John. Oh, how had her marriage crumbled like this?

He *had* loved her once. She knew he had.

Eyes aflame with tears, she remembered the weekend barely two years earlier when he'd kidnapped her and they'd stolen away to a quaint, rose-laced country inn where they'd watched the crimson sunset in a magic embrace. He'd been so tender. So attentive. Now that wonderful weekend looked more like an aberration, an oddity. It seemed he'd had the one moment of being Dr. Jekyll as he'd worked himself into being a truly evil Mr. Hyde.

This had been the worse fight ever. He'd really gotten in her face; he'd called her stupid and worthless, a blight on his precious career. She'd screamed back at him and battered his chest with her fists. He'd shoved her back, and when she'd come at him again he'd slapped her. He could probably call it an accident but she wasn't sure. The rage in his eyes was volcanic. So this time she left. She just couldn't take it anymore. The pain in her heart was just too excruciating, too all-consuming. With every moment, she saw her very core burn—the fire inside turning to ashes everything that made her who she was. She was becoming a charred, hollow shell—the ruins of war. When all was said and done, she just couldn't take being married to someone who obviously didn't love her anymore.

But it hadn't always been like that.

When they were dating, they had shared special times, walked in the park, attended Bible studies together, and learned about life and love. They never seemed to get enough of one another.

They also had fun in the first few years of their marriage. Carla embraced married life and took responsibility for the home while John began working an entry-level position with a large manufacturing company. As it is for most young couples, money was tight. But that didn't matter; for Carla these were the best of times. They were madly in love.

When John received his first promotion, life began to change. Since John had to spend more and more time at the office, Carla found herself feeling increasingly lonely. It became common for her to share important personal thoughts and feelings with friends rather than John. Ironically, though they finally had money, they couldn't find the time to get away for a quiet weekend together. That's why the weekend he'd kidnapped her had been so precious. But it had only been a speck of light in a very dark room.

Eventually, Carla's loneliness and insecurity turned to nagging, insisting John pay more attention to her and her unmet needs. "I just want your undivided attention once in a while," she'd say. Who could blame her? But in striving for his attention, she began demanding that he stop seeing his friends, cut down on the time he spent at the gym, and stop playing sports on the weekends so he could be home more. John, weary of her incessant demands, began to play on Carla's insecurities and withdraw. His coworkers soon became his only escape, and he started staying at work even later to "catch up on projects."

Carla quickly became resentful, depressed, and jealous. She began neglecting the dishes and laundry, sometimes for days at a time. She constantly thought about her marriage and how John was forcing it to go wrong. In John's eyes, she became lazy, nagging, and hateful. "She just doesn't understand how much I do for her," he said.

So now her marriage seems to have ended with her escaping from the house clutching a small overnight bag and a breaking heart. Would she ever go back? *Was* her marriage over? Were all the struggles, the battles, the hurts—and all the hope—simply gone? If her marriage were a movie, would she be watching the final credits roll by? Would the theater be going dark soon?

How could the Lord let this happen? They were Christians, or at least she was. She wasn't so sure about John anymore. But God had once been in their marriage, and at church they seemed like the perfect couple. They were successful, lived in a beautiful neighborhood, and always bought the best. But for all those friends she had at church, Carla had found no one to confide her secret heartache and disappointment to. She was just too ashamed to admit that her life was in shambles, too afraid that word would get around that her marriage was in shambles.

Like so many I've counseled, loneliness, anger, and resentment had invaded her heart and begun breaking it in two.

Marriages like Carla's, and the institution of marriage itself, are on the front line, and I believe we're at war for the very heart and soul of this intimate bond as couples struggle to make sense of their marriages. This struggle leaves them physically, emotionally, and spiritually battered as they try to hold on to some level of closeness and commitment to the one they've vowed to love.

Another such marriage is Larry and Holly's.

Larry is in advertising, a clever job for clever people, and Larry takes a lot of pride in the fact that he is good at it. But all that pride vanished one evening when he came home from work and found a note on the microwave:

> We've left. There's no love here anymore. I don't think we'll ever come back. We've tried. Sorry to leave you like this.
>
> Bye,
>
> Me

Their separation shocked everyone. Raised in solid, Christian families, both had parents who were prominent leaders in their Christian communities. When they met in college, everyone christened it a match made in heaven.

But made there or not, the first year was tough. After graduating, Larry took a job several hundred miles away from their roots, and Holly had a difficult time being so far away from her mom—something Larry had trouble understanding. "We're talking about a parent here. You're supposed to break free of parents. That's what life's all about." He, of course, seemed to be dealing with his own family issues pretty well, and he never failed to point this out. All that changed when his mother suddenly passed away. Even though she and Larry hadn't been very close, Larry had problems dealing with the loss, and since he'd been less than understanding with Holly, he had trouble going to her for support. Of course, Holly wasn't in the mood to give him much support, anyway. The two began distancing themselves from one another. Then Holly discovered that she was pregnant. Although the birth of their first child was a happy occasion and initially seemed to pull them together, by the following year, arguments over money and the division of responsibility for the baby's care began wedging between them. Larry and Holly often found themselves in separate corners, living in separate worlds. Rather than talking openly with one another about their hurts, their main goal was simply to "keep the peace." But avoiding conflict wasn't enough to keep the hearth fires burning. Soon there was the note on the microwave, and soon after that Larry sat in my office, tears flowing freely. "I miss her, and I've failed her. All I ever wanted to do was have a family and be a godly man. And now I'm neither." He brushed tears from red-rimmed eyes, then said something I'll never forget: "The scary thing is, she doesn't think God expects her to stay anymore."

Those words seemed so final to Larry. "She can't mean that, Tim. She can't really be gone for good; so many of her things are still at the house. Her favorite pillow, her clothes. She has to be coming back." There was so much hope in those last words—and so much sadness. For at the center of his heart, he believed there *was* no hope.

What's Forever For?

If you have chosen to read this book, chances are you or someone you love has a marriage that's in trouble. So much trouble, in fact, that you may feel there is little or no hope. You may even be wondering if it is worth the effort to try again to make things better. Well, you're not alone. And if your marriage is in trouble, conventional wisdom tells you there are two places you'll go.

The first place is divorce.

Despite what we know about how to strengthen marital relationships, about half of the marriages occurring this year will eventually end in divorce. And most people who have divorced will move on to another relationship, eager to fill the emotional void. Sadly, second marriages show an even higher incidence of divorce, and most of these relationships encounter the same problems that plagued the first.

The second is pain.

Divorce statistics don't do justice to the true number of couples suffering the heartbreak of marital division. You see, for all the people who are counted as statistics, there are many millions more who are living in their own "private worlds" of pain.

As one client recently said, "I'm not married, just un-divorced." And as another said, "He's not a husband—he just lives here."

These people live together behind closed doors, simply existing. They virtually hate each other and treat one another with poisonous contempt. They remain married for the sake of the children or because of religious beliefs, but whatever the reason, love is no longer a part of their marital equation. Down deep, they feel trapped inside a painful prison. Of those marrying today, another significant percentage will end up in marriages like these.

But how do they get there? Failing at love just doesn't fit into the dreams of the young girl who, throughout her life, hopes to meet her very own Prince Charming and have a fairy-tale marriage. And failing at love is the last thing the young man thinks about when he sees his bride walking toward him to take his hand forever. No couple stands at the altar planning to end up in such a union. So what happens?

Some couples fall prey to job stress, problems with children, or financial struggles, compounded by communication problems that keep them from talking things out and understanding each other. Others may be hit hard by tragedy—the loss of a child, a financial disaster, illness, infidelity, or sexual dysfunction—something that devastates, even destroys, one or both partners. These couples find their pain is so overpowering that their marital bond is literally crushed beneath the weight of it.

Still other couples lead normal lives yet find it is all they can do to keep love alive. These couples read every marriage book they can find, attend weekend marriage seminars, and cry torrents of tears, all to find love and genuine fulfillment.

You've Tried Everything

Maybe one of these paths sounds uncomfortably similar to yours. Or maybe you got here by a different route. But however you arrived, you've probably been hurt, and the pain and disappointment are searing. What's more, you've probably begged God to intervene, to make things better, to make your marriage work again. Maybe God's seeming lack of response has added even more bitterness to your situation. You probably feel as if you've tried everything, like there is nothing left in you to give. As sad as it sounds, this describes most hurting couples and individuals I have worked with in my counseling practice.

By the time these souls reach the counseling office, most are tired, angry, frustrated, and numb. Some question whether their love can be saved or whether their marriage was really "made in heaven." Marriage isn't supposed to be that way. It *should* be filled with more joy than sorrow, more warmth than indifference, more love than anger. Marriage is supposed to be filled with touching, holding, and tenderness. But instead, it's all many couples can do to just hang on, and frankly, they'll do just about anything for the tiniest glimmer of hope.

I wish I could promise you that your marriage will become everything you ever hoped it would be. I can't. But I know the hope God offers in Luke 1:37: "For with God nothing will be impossible." And in Isaiah 41:10: "Fear not, for I am with you; be not dismayed, for I am your God. I will strengthen you, yes I will help you, I will uphold you with My righteous right hand." And this hope is not only the possibility of regaining what you once had but also the hope of having a higher kind of love together.

A Higher Love

"Set me as a seal upon your heart, as a seal on your arm; for love is as strong as death, jealousy as cruel as the grave; its flames are flames of fire, a most vehement flame. Many waters cannot quench love, nor can the floods drown it. If a man would give for love all the wealth of his house, it would be utterly despised" (Song of Sol. 8:6–7).

Near our home in Virginia are the Peaks of Otter in the Blue Ridge Mountains. The hike to the top of the most-climbed peak, Sharptop, is exhausting, and along the way I stop now and again. The higher I get, the more expansive and beautiful the view becomes—rolling purple hills; patchwork farms carved from rich, green forests; a glistening church steeple. When I finally reach the peak, the sight is even more arresting, more magnetic. I see something holy, a beauty for the moment God has made only for me.

But as beautiful and special as that glimpse of God's creation can be, it doesn't hold a candle to the sight of a couple who has achieved a higher kind of love: a love built on strong affection and deep commitment; a free-embracing, tender love; a love that proclaims 1 Corinthians 13 loudly and clearly, purely and faithfully.

I want your reading of this book to be like joining me on the trek up the Peaks of Otter. I'm not going to ask you to "give in" or "hang in there." Rather, I want you to journey with me on that high trail. Just as I have seen the beautiful world in new and exciting ways, I want you to see your marriage with new eyes. I want you to see how you can turn a painful struggle or loss at love into a strong union, as in the couple on the beach, hand in hand at age seventy. For their effort and commitment to one another, God has given them a higher, richer love—the type God, your loving Father, desires for you.

Our Journey Together

What, then, is this journey we're going to be taking? It will cover four countries with distinct borders and different terrains but with one very important destination—the potential restoration of your marriage, a restoration that promises even greater satisfaction than before with even greater love and intimacy between you.

The first country we'll work our way through, or part one in this book, is Reframe. While there we'll discover where your marriage is right now and what pressures it faces. We'll take a hard look at the alternatives you're facing: divorce, with all its tortures; "giving up," with its emotional deadness; or commitment and work, with its vulnerability and promise for the future. Then we'll take a hard look at the journey you took to get here, a journey whose every step you will not only recognize but will also learn to avoid in the future.

In part two, Reclaim/Release, we'll begin the process of reclaiming your marriage for yourselves and the Lord, of releasing you to love again. We'll work to remove the obstacles that stand in your way and build the structures that will help bridge the gaps between you, to make it safe for you to love and be *one* with each other again.

Part three, Reconcile, will help you put your hearts together again and see love in new and exciting ways. You'll begin to achieve what you may have never achieved before, a higher love built on a foundation of forgiveness and trust.

And, finally, we'll travel to the fourth country, our destination. Part four is Refashion. Here you'll discover how to maintain what you've achieved and remain on the road to greater relational intimacy—emotional, physical, and spiritual—a oneness with healthy separateness.

Making Some Changes

According to *Time* reporter Janice Castro, many Americans are embracing simpler pleasures and homier values in place of materialism. "They've been thinking hard about what really matters in their lives, and they've decided to make some changes. What matters is having time for family and friends, rest and recreation, good deeds and spirituality."[1]

In a recent *Time*/CNN poll, 69 percent of those questioned said they would like to "slow down and live a more relaxed life," and 89 percent indicated that it was more important these days to spend time with the family.[2]

The tragedy, however, is that most don't believe they will ever get the freedom or opportunity to do so. "There's just no time and we're too far under financially to recover." The demands and pressures of life are beating us, and most are settling for less than they should in their relationships and life. Many couples spend as little as four minutes a day in meaningful conversations.[3] No wonder our relationships seem so empty.

"I Can't Love Again."

I know some of you are thinking that Carla's and Larry's stories don't even come close to hinting at the pain and betrayal that you have been subjected to. Many of you may say, "You don't understand. He's so mean and hurtful." Or, "She has done things that I don't think I can forgive her for." Or, "I can't love again. . . . I just can't."

It is only natural to feel this way when your spirit has been destroyed and you are weary from your efforts at restoration, but ultimately the "I can't love again" mentality must be overcome.

Before Jesus was betrayed, He knelt in a garden and spent time with the heavenly Father. Do you remember what He prayed that night? "Father, if it is Your will, take this cup away from me" (Luke 22:42a). Jesus was struggling because He saw a hell-deserving humankind that was not worthy of the love of God, and He knew that His Father would turn His back on Him. Yet, He yielded and said, "Not My will, but Yours be done" (v. 42b). The result was divine love.

This kind of sacrificial and unconditional love will not be easy. In fact, it may be the most difficult thing that you ever do. But God has given the perfect example, through Jesus Christ, of how you can search your heart and God to find the strength and courage to try again. Even if you are struggling alone, you *can* feel optimistic. Quite often, one person acting alone in marriage can trigger new responses in a relationship.

I realize that if you have been torn apart by pain and feel that something irreplaceable has gone from your marriage, you cannot be expected to, nor will you want to, commit to a long effort or complicated process of recovery. And I am not going to ask you to do that. All I want you to do for now is to determine that you will take a simple and small step toward healing your marriage.

To agree to follow the model presented here is to resolve that the only thing you can be guilty of is the willingness to clear the decks, be open and honest before God, and love your partner. Even though you may be facing seemingly insurmountable grief, this is a gift you can give to yourself. For it holds the promise of being true to God, to your marriage, and to yourself, no matter what the outcome.

The idea of again reaching intimacy with your partner may sound like an impossible dream. Worse yet, you may not even want your partner anymore, let alone want to risk allowing him or her to hurt you again. But there was a time when you did love your spouse, when the thought of *not* being intimate was just as abhorrent. I believe positive change is possible and can be achieved in new and far-reaching ways. The destructive cycles that have hopelessly enmeshed you can be interrupted and the downward spiral halted. This is the message of God who, in the midst of Hosea's deep marital distress and abandonment turned the "for worse" into "for better." And how does He do that? By being "our refuge and strength, an ever-present help in trouble" (Ps. 46:1).

In the next chapter we'll look at how you should prepare to take the first step on your journey.

Two

A Closed Spirit

"Be angry, and do not sin":
do not let the sun go down on your wrath.
—*Ephesians 4:26*

*L*et me present a concern I always share early in my work counseling new couples. Pain, especially a lot of it, *closes the spirit.* It goes deep and blinds our internal eyes. Closed spirits often assign evil motives to perfectly innocent acts and blind us to love and intimate relationships.[1]

By the time a couple reaches the counseling office, each spouse is exhausted, frustrated, and empty. Some question whether their love can be saved; others are just hanging on, waiting for that glimmer of hope. Some want to let go—and some do. It's extremely difficult to love when you have been hurt deeply.

Confusion

Carla sat in my office, obviously uncomfortable. Not only was she about to discuss things that seemed too far out of control to understand, but by just being in that chair, she was also admitting that her marriage was dying. That admission is tough for anyone.

"Carla," I began. Her eyes came up. "I've read your chart, and I know you're in a lot of pain right now. Help me to understand more about what happened to your marriage."

That simple directive was all it took. Carla opened up.

If *you* were to open up right now—if you were sitting in my office with the door closed and you could say anything you wanted about how you felt—what would you say? As you read Carla's process of discovery, explore your own emotions as well.

"I'm so confused," she began. "I really thought we loved each other, and now I can't see how we can. Tim, we've said a lot of hateful, hurtful words to each other. How can people love each other and say those kinds of things?" She went on for a while, desperately trying to make sense out of her failing relationship.

Most married partners I see begin by voicing their confusion—they simply can't understand what has happened. "It was supposed to be so different. I'd prayed for God to give me him (or her) since I was little. But the person I thought I married has changed."

Are You Confused Too?

Do you feel this kind of confusion? If you do, may I offer some suggestions? First and foremost, remind yourself that if you are a Christian, everything you are going through right now will work together for your good (Rom. 8:28). Realize God's hand is in it. Now we may never know all of what He's doing, but one thing we can be sure of: He is near, and He's working things out (despite our actions) for His purposes—and one of His purposes is to love and comfort you.

Another of God's purposes is to reveal Himself to others through you. Those others include your spouse, your children, and your friends and acquaintances. You're going through a deep trial right now, and He'll be reflected both in the grace you display while you work your way through it and in the eventual comfort you'll give others because of the comfort He gives you (2 Cor. 1:3–5). As you see God as your refuge, as your strength, and a present help in this time of trouble (Ps. 46:1), those around you will see that He would be there for them as well if they called upon Him. This trial will allow you to become God's living truth.

So as you make decisions, as you respond to what is taking place, no matter how confused you might be, remember you are God's witness. Behave in such a way as to bring Him glory.

"So I guess I should be careful how I talk about John to my friends," Carla finally said. "I'm no witness when I talk him down."

"He *is* your husband."

"So I need to start behaving myself."

"You're traveling along a difficult path. As you negotiate each twist and turn, first seek the Lord. Get His help in determining your next step. It's okay to be confused. But remember, God isn't. He knows exactly where you're going and the best way to get there. Lean on Him."

"Okay, I'll try not to be confused anymore, but, Tim, what am I going to do with my anger? I'm in knots with it. John makes me so very mad."

Have you asked yourself the same question?

What to Do with Anger

We're not going to heal all your anger here. And the truth is that it may not be necessary. You do need to contain this God-given emotion, though, and not let your anger gain a foothold and build to a sinful reaction like revenge or resentment.

"Is John the only one you're angry at?" I asked Carla.

"He's the major one."

"What about your family? Are they doing everything you want?"

"My mom's being really supportive. My dad's acting like a jerk. He's blaming it all on me. Calls me a nag. Although he hasn't said it in so many words, he believes John has a right to treat me like this."

"Anyone else?"

Carla thought hard, then her eyes filled with tears. "God," she finally said. "I'm really mad at God. It's hard for me to say, but I feel betrayed by Him. I mean really *betrayed*—and abandoned by Him."

I nodded. "He's big enough to take it," I told her. "And He knows you're angry at Him. The best thing you can do right now is just admit it, realize He loves you anyway, and start dealing with your anger in general. Anger can be very corrosive—emotionally, physically, and spiritually. It boils up when we think we've been threatened, hurt, or wronged. And if it's not handled properly, it can tie you in real knots."

"But I can't help being angry."

"But you can help how you respond in your anger."

Responding in Anger

How about you? I would be very surprised if you're not angry as well. Anger is an emotion from God that speaks to a state of preparedness to deal with mistreatment. Anger in itself isn't wrong. Ephesians 4:26 tells us that we can be angry yet not sin. The difference between sinning or not in anger is, therefore, simply an act of the will. Sometimes a tough act of the will. Why? Because anger is a powerful, deeply rooted emotion that can also lead to some real destruction. And sometimes we get angry without all the facts.

The Consequences of Uncontrolled Anger

Uncontrolled anger can be terribly destructive—jails are full of those who were unable to control their anger. I doubt if yours will lead you there. But it can lead you to those terrible moments when you explode or act irrationally, particularly in public, or do things you later regret. Worse still, ruminating on your anger or taking revenge can destroy you right along with your target.

Unchecked, anger can wreck your ability to be objective—to see what forces are working on you. Nursed, it can turn quickly into resentment or bitterness. Repressed or suppressed, it can lead to such negative expressions as being impatient, overly critical, or domineering. It can even cause a deep depression.

Who are you angry at? Search your heart right now. Perhaps your list is like Carla's: your spouse, a parent or two, friends who've let you down. Maybe your list includes yourself. Carla didn't mention it at the time, but she was very angry at herself for allowing her marriage to get into such a state. "I must have done something—maybe most of it," she said a few sessions later. "Maybe my dad is right. Maybe I am a nag. And there were so many times I just let John down." Is God on your list as He was on Carla's? If He is, don't try to avoid it. Tell Him so. He already knows anyway, and by voicing it, you begin to heal your anger.

Dealing with Anger

We'll cover several aspects of dealing with anger as our journey together progresses, but for now allow me to give you some suggestions on how you might begin to set your anger aside.

Consider the Source and Empathize

It's very possible the targets of your anger are in pain too. Perhaps the stresses that have played a part in bringing you to this place have also been at work on them. Perhaps that stress has distorted their view of you and what they did was a reaction to a *you* that doesn't really exist. It helps to take a moment to put yourself in their shoes. Look around at their world for a moment and feel the pain they might be feeling. Perhaps you'll understand their motives a little better, maybe even determine that they were at least partially justified in doing what they did. This exercise can give you a little more understanding of what they're going through. Anger begins to dissolve in understanding.

Make a List

As Carla did, make a list of those you're angry at. Be complete. And leave a little room after each name.

Next, write down why you're angry at each person. Now this might be a little tricky. Sometimes we're angry at someone and we're not sure why. Maybe it's just the person's attitude. Or maybe you've had a long-running feud and right now, when you're going through this difficult time, you find you're angrier at him or her than you've ever been. Just be as specific as you can.

Okay. Now you have a list of people and their transgressions; what's next? We are not to react badly in our anger, to be vindictive or hateful, or to turn it inside. So, what *are* we to do? Proverbs 16:32 tells us to be slow to anger. Seneca tells us "The greatest response to anger is delay"[2]— jogging, taking a walk, counting to ten. And while you're delaying, don't react, rather think about your response. A large part of your response should be to take responsibility for your anger: "This is my anger. No one else's. Mine." And though you delay, do not let anger linger.

All that's well and good and to be remembered the next time anger emerges, but what are you going to do with that list? The first is to commit yourself to not being vengeful. Then tell yourself convincingly that whatever the reasons for your anger—toward mom, your mate, or Susan at work, or even God—there are appropriate ways to deal with them and the anger. Let's take a look at what those ways are.

Get Confident in God

"Repay no one evil for evil. Have regard for good things in the sight of all men. If it is possible, as much as depends on you, live peaceably with all men. Beloved, do not avenge yourselves, but rather give place to wrath; for it is written, 'Vengeance is Mine, I will repay,' says the Lord" (Rom. 12:17–19).

Anger is an emotion that demands change. When you've been slighted or demeaned or handed an injustice or hurt intentionally, anger mobilizes you for a response. It focuses your attention, pumps up the adrenaline, and gets you prepared for war. Of course, war is not what we want. Therefore, the first thing you need to do is realize that God is taking care of you. Whatever the injustice or the slight, if God is for you, who can be against you? Of course, that doesn't mean that you want whatever happened to you to happen again. Nor does it mean you want the person who wronged you to remain ignorant of your plight.

Release and Confess Sinful Anger

If your anger is sinful—based on selfishness or something you've caused—then release your anger. Let it go. And, as necessary, confess and repent of your anger to God and anyone who may have been injured by it.

Discuss Your Anger with the Target Person

If your anger is legitimate—if you have been treated unjustly or intentionally hurt—dispassionately tell the wrongdoer how you feel about what he or she did. Be as specific as you can about your anger and what produced it: "When you said those things to me, it really hurt. I came to you as a friend, as someone who would listen. And instead you treated me with real contempt. That made me angry."

Then listen to the response. If it's a sincere apology, accept it in love. If it's not, don't get angry again. Continue the discussion and understand where the other person is coming from. Since we often read too much negative into things, take what's being said out of the realm of *emotion* and place it into the realm of *information*.

For example, when Carla and John came to counseling, Carla told John that when he'd implied that she was lazy and a burden to his career, she'd been hurt; she'd felt totally put down. That, when added to everything else, caused her to leave.

"I didn't say you were lazy," he'd replied. "Frankly, you're the least lazy person I know. You're just busy doing things that don't help me."

"Like what?" she'd asked. She'd expected an apology. Not getting one threw her a little off balance. But she remained calm, working hard not to be put down by what John was saying but to see it as information to respond to later.

"You're busy doing your crafts or going to meetings instead of having my boss over for dinner or helping me entertain my management team. I could use your help that way. But you don't do that."

She had to agree. She didn't do that.

Now Carla has a choice to make. She can either spend less time doing crafts and more time helping John, or she can keep things as they are. She received information and she understands. And although she easily could have, she didn't get angry.

If the Person Remains a Thorn

If, after discussing the situation with the person you're angry at, the person still continues to treat you poorly, Proverbs 22:24 tells us to "make no friendship with an angry man, and with a furious man do not go." If you don't have to deal with the person anymore, don't. If you do, be polite, but be careful "lest you learn his ways and set a snare for your soul" (v. 25). This person has proven to be dangerous to you emotionally.

But what if that hurtful person is your spouse? For now, love and pray for your spouse and set realistic boundaries so you don't destroy each other. Don't allow unrealistic expectations to hurt you. Be loving but not foolish. Be giving and expect nothing in return. Doing this, of course, can be difficult, for there's nothing more precious to us than appreciation from the ones we love and to whom we have given so much. And a spouse, even a hurtful one, certainly falls into that category.

A Call to Love and Prayer

As a final step in dealing with anger, remember that, above all else, you are called to love. "Beloved, let us love one another, for love is of God; and everyone who loves is born of God and knows God" (1 John 4:7). No matter how legitimate your anger, no matter how great the injustice, you're called to love. And we're to pray for our enemies, to bring them and their needs before the Lord. So whatever you do in response to your anger, do it in love. Matthew 5:44b reminds us to "do good to those who hate you, and pray for those who spitefully use you and persecute you." Be careful to repay evil with good.

Just as there's usually a great deal of confusion and anger during times of marital trial, there's also a great deal of searing pain. Let's deal with some of that now.

Dealing with Pain

Pain rushes at you from so many places during these times of difficulty. There's the pain of rejection, of injustice, of watching your marriage die. There's the pain of betrayal, of abandonment, of the prospect of being alone. And unlike scraping your knee or breaking your arm, the pain doesn't just go away. It seems as if every morning the pain is renewed and perhaps even made more severe as your marital situation worsens. Unfortunately, the pain is appropriate. These are horribly painful experiences to be going through. The problem, of course, is that pain is emotionally debilitating and sad. And acknowledging the pain somehow makes the source of it real. It says your concerns about your marriage have validity, and you're going to have to do something about it, which can only mean more pain. So many try to deny the pain.

If you have been rejected, if you feel the pain of abandonment, if pain is rushing at you from all directions, denying it doesn't help. If you repress your anger, eventually it will do a lot of damage, just as denying you have a broken arm will do a lot of damage.

So acknowledge the truth. If you've been rejected by your spouse, admit it: "Yes, she's rejected me. It hurts. I hate it. But it's true. My marriage is in real trouble."

If this is true for you, admit it right now—no matter how hard the admission.

Then mourn your loss. Cry, put on a black armband, wear widow's weeds, do something, but allow yourself the luxury of mourning. By doing so you're going to release some of that pain. Probably not all of it, but some.

Later in this book I'll help you work through even more. Hopefully you'll get to the point where your pain is turned completely around and you experience true joy in your marriage again. But for now, let's just release what we can. I know that things may look pretty hopeless. But always remember, *looking* hopeless, when you're walking with God, is a far cry from *being* hopeless.

The next step in our preparation goes hand in hand with our initial steps in dealing with pain. It's forgiveness.

Forgiving

We'll go into greater detail later about forgiveness. For now, allow me to say that not only are we called to love all those who hurt us, but we're also called to forgive them. It's never easy to forgive; revenge always seems easier and certainly sweeter. But in our heart of hearts we know that's not true. The better course (although it might not be easy) is to lay our desire for retribution at the foot of the cross and allow God to deal with keeping us whole. With forgiveness comes peace, and peace may be what you long for most right now.

If you continue on this journey to a higher love and a more fulfilling marriage, there will come a time when I'll ask you to make yourself vulnerable again. But we will take steps to minimize your risk. For now, if you've been hurt, be careful not to put yourself into a position to be hurt again. There are some simple rules to follow to help make sure that doesn't happen. Don't give of yourself with the expectation of a positive return. Be careful not to put a lot of confidence in someone who's let you down before. And don't gauge your worth by someone else's evaluation. You're God's child, and there's no greater worth anywhere. And, finally, if you do get hurt again, go to the Lord for His warm, healing salve.

So far, we've made some important preparations for your journey. It's hard to prioritize them, but one of the more important steps follows—it concerns beginning to just be yourself.

Removing the Masks

My daughter Megan once loved to play the "monster game." Usually, I'd pretend to be a mean lion and chase her around the room. She'd run and scream with delight, but part of her at times was honestly frightened of me. When the fear became too much, she'd yell, "Don't be monster! Don't be monster! Be Daddy again."

How many times have you played this same game? You parade around with a mask on, pretending to be someone you're not. Many of us carry around hidden hurts, grievances, disappointments, and unpleasant, even debilitating, memories. Unfortunately, in many cases, more time is spent hiding these wounds than healing them. We walk around wearing "I'm just fine" or "we're making it" or "honey, I love you so much" masks when reality couldn't be farther away. What a relief it is when you can simply take off your mask, be yourself, get honest, and be loved for who you are.

But, of course, that's easier said than done; you might not like who you believe you are. Perhaps as a child you received messages that said you weren't lovable, maybe even not likable. Or perhaps the mask hides some hidden wound, something that might cause you embarrassment, shame, or fear.

In any case, I admire your strength for keeping the mask in place, but the time has come to be honest with yourself and those around you. As best you're able, take off the mask. Be yourself.

Getting the life and love God desires for you and your marriage takes work, grace, and the willingness to remove masks and be honest, even vulnerable, again. Healing, both personally and relationally, will take time and effort.

Redirect all the energy that goes into creating and preserving masks toward finding a way out of the pain. In the long run, you'll find that course far less taxing and far more fulfilling.

Your Journey Continues

No matter what path you choose, there is a future ahead of you. If your marriage truly is in trouble, the best course is to admit it and begin to determine what to do about it. As it turns out, your choices are not that many, or that complex. In the next chapter we'll begin taking a hard look at what they are.

THREE

A ROOM
WITHOUT EXITS

Honesty is the first chapter of the book of wisdom.
—*Thomas Jefferson*

As you continue your journey, be careful that you are not dominated by your emotions—because *everything* is at stake. It's also critical to honestly and carefully consider the options that lay before you while being judicious in your responses to new situations and in all things you choose to do.

Doug didn't.

"She Called Him Daddy."

I'd been working with Doug off and on for about two years. His last visit had been several months earlier, so it was a surprise to hear his voice on the other end of the phone line. Doug's a bulldog of a man— short and intense with committed dark eyes and a set jaw. One would hardly expect him to have an emotional breakdown. But if his voice was any indication, that's exactly what he was having.

"She called him Daddy," he kept saying. "My little blue-eyed, angel-faced four-year-old called him Daddy."

"Who'd she call Daddy?" I asked.

"This guy Melissa's dating. My daughter called him Daddy." And then he broke down and started crying. "I just can't stop," he said, trying to suck back a wild flurry of tears. "Just one more chance, God. That's all I want. Just one more chance to save my family. Please?"

In many ways, divorce is like a room that soon proves to have no exits. After being married eight years, Doug and Melissa entered that room just after Doug first came to see me.

He was angry that afternoon he entered my office. His bulldoggedness gave his anger a fierce quality, but there was more boiling inside of him than just anger. He also seemed racked by bitterness and searing emotional pain.

That session started with me asking him to describe his relationship with Melissa.

"We were only seventeen when we met," he'd started. "We dated a year then got married. I was eighteen and thought I knew it all. We wanted to build a different kind of family. We didn't know then that our families were dysfunctional. We just thought they were mean. They yelled a lot, called each other names. We didn't want that. But I guess wanting to build a good family and actually doing it are two different things. We started fighting right off—about money, how we liked the house kept. I was a stickler, and she didn't mind the laundry strewn all over. We got just as loud as our families had, and then I shoved her once or twice—and she whacked me back. I hated that in my old family. And I hated it more in my new one."

Nodding, I felt the hopelessness that clung to the top of his words. I glanced at his fact sheet. "You have children," I said.

"She got pregnant after we were married about a year. Shoot, within three years we had two in diapers. Two screaming for supper. When we had the first, we thought it was bringing us together. That's why we went and had the second. Figured after two we'd be joined at the hip." Doug sighed. "It was more like hitting us with an ax."

"What did you argue about then?"

"How to raise them. They seemed to prevent us from ever having a good time. We used to at least get out on a date now and again, but figuring in a baby-sitter, you gotta take out a second mortgage just to go to a movie. And making love—well, that became something for the Smithsonian. After five years she split with the kids."

"How'd you take that?"

He winced hard. "It was like getting kicked in the stomach. I pleaded for her to come back. Even cried—and I don't cry."

I believed him. Bulldogs rarely cry.

"She'd started seeing a counselor. And wanted me to go too."

"Did you?"

He shook his head. "I figured we could solve our own problems. After all, we made them by ourselves. Why couldn't we solve them?"

"Making problems, Doug, is different from solving them."

He pushed a hand at his chest. "I know that now. But then—I was younger. Stupid."

"Did she come back?"

"After six months she couldn't stand living in an apartment about the size of a storage bin, so she came home. But reluctantly. We had a heart-to-heart talk. I mean a *real* heart-to-heart, and she finally agreed to take another shot at it. Of course, she didn't give up wanting me to go to counseling with her."

"Good."

"But I didn't give up, either. No counseling for this guy. No sir-*ee*."

"How'd things go?"

"O.K. Melissa decided things were so good that she didn't need the counselor anymore. And I suppose things would have stayed good if I hadn't lost my job—then another. It was pretty tough."

"How'd you handle it?"

"Got mad. At everybody. And she got mad back. Pushing, shoving on both sides. Smashing things against the walls. After a real knock-down-drag-out, she threw the kids in the car and left again. She came back after I pleaded with her. We sort of got in the habit of doing that. We'd fight, she'd leave, I'd plead, she'd insist on me going to counseling with her, I'd refuse and plead some more, and she'd come back. It was like a script to a bad movie. For years we did that. You'd think we'd catch on after a while. But I'm one thick dude."

Thick dude or not, Doug finally got the message when Melissa left and told him she wouldn't be coming back. In an effort to prove that he really wanted her back, Doug decided to come for counseling. For Melissa, his gesture was too little, too late. Even after he started coming for help, Melissa filed for divorce. That hit Doug so hard that we continued the counseling process through-out the divorce and child-custody proceedings. Doug never gave up hope that his relationship could be healed. To his credit, even though his progress was slow, he did begin to show improvement. Wanting to share that good news with Melissa, Doug begged her to come to a counseling session with him. Finally she relented and came. Seeing this as an opportunity to reconcile with her, Doug was thrilled.

Maybe too thrilled.

Their session began by giving Melissa an opportunity to talk. The years of hurt began pouring out of her in a river of accusations. Faced with that onslaught, Doug suddenly lost sight of his desire to rebuild their marriage and reverted back to his old habits. He became angrily defensive. Unable to refute anything she said, his frustration took over and he began shouting and blaming. He finally stormed from the office. Melissa remained for a moment to cry, "He'll never understand, Tim. He'll never change." Then, heartbroken and sure that divorce was her only option, she left.

There's No Easy Way Out

The tragedy of Doug and Melissa's story is that it happens every day. Of course, the names and the arguments are different, but the ultimate decision remains the same—to leave the spouse you vowed to love. Although painful, it seems to be the right decision.

Perhaps you're facing that decision right now. Perhaps you see yourself on a fast road to divorce. Well, by picking up this book, you've entered a rest stop where you can catch your breath and consider alternative solutions. Of course, you can merely slow down, give it a glance, then get back on the freeway. Or you can stop and make use of the time to carefully consider your options.

Stepping Back, Not Out

Allow me to explain why I suggest you stop and step back from instead of out of your marriage. When there's severe pain, you and your partner react to one another out of that pain. Those reactions can be quite hurtful—even brutal. Allowing yourself to step back from the situation gives you the opportunity to see more of it and allows you to better understand what's really going on. That perspective lets you see where you're headed, what decisions you might be facing in the future.

So, let's take a look at your options. There are three for couples in this kind of distress, and in the next three chapters we'll examine them.

FOUR

DOOR #1:
THE BIG "D" (DIVORCE)

We have been poisoned by fairy tales.

—*Anaïs Nin*

Some might refer to divorce as "getting out and getting on with your life." Saying it that way actually makes it sound appealing. After all, divorce, in many cases, seems like the easy way out. Although everyone knows divorce is traumatic, emotionally wearing, and painful, making the decision to just stop trying often looks a whole lot easier than getting back in the ring and continuing to slug it out. Staying seems to require a deep well of time and energy, and great personal sacrifice and risk that even Job couldn't endure. Cutting and running just seems like the only viable alternative. If you're lucky, maybe your troubles will remain "back there" somewhere. And if you're *really* lucky, the divorce will allow you to quit feeling defeated, ashamed, angry, bitter. Even if those negative emotions follow you, they have to be less *after* leaving than they would be if you stayed.

Is that true? Are the consequences of divorce more tolerable than doing your best to work things out? Obviously more than 50 percent of those married for the first time think so. But are they right?

Let's take a look at why couples divorce. In that way we'll also learn what difficulties those couples would have had to overcome to stay together. In 1992, Lynn Gigy and Joan B. Kelly did a study that gave the top ten reasons why couples divorce.

Reasons	Males (%)	Females (%)	Total (%)
1. Growing apart; losing a sense of closeness	79	78	79
2. Not feeling loved and appreciated by spouse	60	73	67
3. Sexual intimacy problems	65	64	64
4. Serious difference in values or lifestyles	57	63	60
5. Spouse unwilling/unable to meet partner's needs	48	64	56*
6. Frequently felt put down/belittled by spouse	37	59	49*
7. Emotional problems of spouse	44	52	48
8. Conflict about spending and handling money	44	50	47
9. Severe and intense conflict and frequent fighting	35	44	40
10. Conflicts about roles (e.g., division of labor)	33	47	40*

* Denotes statistically significant male-female difference on an item.[1]

Traditionally, divorce has been based on fault. In the old days, adultery or severe marital cruelty had to plague a marriage before divorce was legal. Not so anymore. Christians, of course, are to use the biblical standard for divorce. To determine what that is, most Bible scholars reference Matthew 5:32, 19:9, and 1 Corinthians 7:15. It's certainly much closer to the old days. But in spite of God granting His people a way out of marriage, most would agree that God's ideal is for couples to be united in marriage for life (Gen. 2:24; Matt. 19:5–6; 1 Cor. 7:39). While I believe there are valid biblical grounds for divorce, and certainly some of you may not have a choice but to divorce, God's Word never demands it. In fact, the Bible consistently presents a message of forgiveness and reconciliation.

Of course, God's desire that marriage endure didn't stop the divorce reforms of the 1970s when most states instituted "no-fault" divorce laws. These laws threw the doors for divorce wide open, allowing the number one reason for divorce to flourish: "We've just grown apart." As a result, instead of being committed to one another for "better or worse," many couples today *try* marriage, and if it's not what they'd hoped, they hit the speed-dial button labeled *attorney* and start discussing community property. But don't confuse divorce being "convenient" or "simple" with "easy" or "painless."

Divorce is always a *lose/lose* proposition, and looking at it metaphorically, it's a *room without an exit.* According to Dr. Judith Wallerstein and Sandra Blakeslee, the couple and children involved often do not outlive the scars of divorce. Her findings are listed in the classic study *Second Chances: Men, Women and Children a Decade after Divorce.*

> Whatever the reasons behind the decision, most people ending a marriage hope to improve the quality of life for themselves and for their children. They hope to find a new love, a more enriching relationship, a more responsive sexual partner, a more supportive companion, a better provider. Failing that, they hope to establish a single life that will provide greater opportunity for self-respect, contentment, and serenity, or at the least, less turbulence, intrusiveness, and hurt. People want to believe that divorce will relieve all their stresses— back we go to square one and begin our lives anew. But divorce does not wipe the slate clean. . . . Few adults anticipate accurately what lies ahead when they decide to divorce. Life is almost always more arduous and more complicated than they expect.[2]

You may waltz right into divorce, but you'll never leave it. Literally, closing the divorce door behind you gives a whole new meaning to the once-hopeful saying, "This is the first day of the rest of your life."

And for all the trouble that exists in that room, entering it isn't free.

The Cost of Divorce

Divorce lawyers bill from $250 to $500 per hour—and often double that with more charged for courtroom time. It is not unusual for the best-paid divorce lawyers to submit bills well into six figures to America's wealthiest clients. Marriages with assets and incomes in the six-figure range will normally spend $20,000 to $50,000 to get divorced. If the divorce is conflicted and messy, involving much court time, it will easily approach $100,000 in costs. Middle-income families will spend from $2,500 to $25,000 for a modern divorce, which cuts America's poor and low-income families off from legal representation in divorces.[3]

Starting Over

Although leaving your marriage may sound like the best thing, there will probably come a time when you'll want to get back into circulation. Picture yourself reentering the dating scene. Of course, everyone's situation is different, but few of my divorced clients have found much reward in dating again. In fact, the opposite is far closer to the truth. When you were dating before, you may have been in high school or college. There were young, eager, reasonably balanced people splashing around in the dating pool. Now, though, you're older, and many of those who make good life partners—people who are faithful, firmly grounded, and able to commit strongly to a relationship even during the difficult times—are probably married. Many of those your age who now populate the dating pool have already failed at least once at marriage. And, like their ex-spouses, they were at least partially at fault for the divorce and carry those faults along with them. With great frequency the issues that plagued the first marriage surface again in a second marriage.

So there are a lot of less than satisfactory dates, a lot of relationships that start out promising but quickly fade as selfishness, or hidden anger, or moodiness bubbles to the surface. There are also many nights that end with wishing you could finally find Mr. or Ms. Right. But there are few Mr. or Ms. Rights and a lot of Mr. and Ms. Good-enoughs. And over time, lonely evenings become acceptable alternatives to bad dates. And often preferable. A client recently said to me as she was working to patch up a pretty bad relationship: "It sure is easy for everyone to throw in their two-cent's worth on what I should do, but Tim, they all have someone to hold onto each night. It's sad being alone."

So not only do you find yourself very much alone, but you also find yourself alone with the destructive effects of the divorce. You're left with deep scars that affect both partners, all the involved children, and family and friends.

Partners' Scars

One family expert characterized the process of divorce negotiations as "one of the more demanding tasks that rational beings are expected to perform."[4] And based on what I've seen, he's right. And there's little wonder why. In some form or another, the battle over the things of divorce brings together a rush of boiling emotions—including abandonment, anxiety, betrayal, inadequacy, loneliness, rage.

Let's take a closer look at some of the emotions my hurting clients have discussed.

Abandonment: Suddenly all the plans and hopes for the future, all the ties, the memories, the happiness, and real joy are simply tossed over the side in favor of some other course or some other person. All has come to nothing, and nothing's what I have left.

Anxiety: What happens next? Everything's set up for the two of us. Having enough money to pay the bills, Christmas parties, evenings with friends or relatives. Everything changes. What about the kids? How am I going to be able to afford schooling and college? Who has time to figure all this out? My ship's going to sink before I figure out how to steer it or plug up the leaks.

Betrayal: I gave everything to him. Everything. I worked for him. I made sure his life was a good life, that he always had a place to come home to, a hot meal, a warm bed. I was always there for him. When work was falling apart, he could always count on me. He could count on my encouragement, my smile. And this is what I get. It's not fair. He stole the best years of my life!

Or: I never missed a day of work so he could have this home. I worked hard. Took all that nonsense at work to make sure the kids had everything they wanted. I took them on nice vacations. And he ups and does this to me. Why, Tim?

Inadequacy: I couldn't make it work. I tried. I did everything I knew how to do, but it just wasn't good enough. I wasn't smart enough, sexy enough, sensitive enough. What's wrong inside me? Others manage to get through the years. There are couples at church who've been married fifty years, and we couldn't even make it to twenty. I'm inadequate to the task. Worthless.

Loneliness: The silence is awful—deafening. We used to sit here on a Saturday night just the two of us. We'd make popcorn, rent a movie, and just sit here holding hands. Now the house is so quiet. It's as though my life has huge holes in it—holes I'm forced to rattle around in. It's easy for friends to tell me what to do, but they have someone to go home to, someone to hold. Only when you're alone do you understand.

Rage: How dare he treat me like this? How dare he? How dare he hurt me like this—abandon me to do all this by myself? How dare he?!

And these emotions don't just disappear overnight. In fact, some linger for life. Others fade only to reappear, and when they do, they come back in driving waves.

But there are other struggles too. Often a continued attachment to the lost partner forces long periods of intense grief and mourning, sometimes even cloudy gray depressions. Some of my most difficult counseling sessions have been with clients going through such periods.

Dr. Wallerstein also wrote:

> Incredibly, one-half of the women and one-third of the men are still intensely angry at their former spouses, despite the passage of years. . . . To our astonishment, divorce continues to occupy a central, emotional position in the lives of many adults, ten and fifteen years later. . . . A third of the women and a quarter of the men feel that life is unfair, disappointing, and lonely. I knew that divorce is not an event that can be gotten over if one simply waits long enough, but even I was surprised at the staying power of feelings after divorce. . . . There is no evidence that time automatically diminishes feelings or memories; that hurt and depression are overcome; or that jealousy, anger, and outrage will vanish. . . . People go on living, but just because they have lived ten more years does not mean they have recovered from the hurt.[5]

The Stages of Change

But you'll be going through more than just emotions. You'll be going through change—the change from living in a two-parent family and having a spouse to living in a single-parent family and being single. And this is not simple. In fact, the changes are so dramatic that sociologist Paul Bohannon proposed that this emotionally complex experience requires six overlapping stages to finally put it behind you.[6]

Emotional: We've just taken a look at the emotions involved and what they'll bring. As you go through the following list of stages, imagine what it would be like to navigate each while all of those emotions are at a full boil.

Legal: Every state is different. Each has its own process for dissolving a marriage. Property needs to be divided. Custody must be decided. Income and retirements (even if the partners are young) need to be split. Child support and college tuition (even if the kids are babies) need to be calculated. And holidays—who gets to wake up with the kids on Christmas morning?—need to be decided. A host of decrees and papers must be negotiated and signed. There are lawyers and judges and negotiators to be seen. And it's all to unravel what you once so rapturously tied together.

Economic: The economic toll on most people going through divorce needs to be experienced to be believed. Although we touched on it earlier, there's another way to look at it. What was bad before is worse now, particularly if one partner stayed home with the kids. The income that supported one household must now support two. Stress soars as everybody suffers, particularly if the partner who stayed home with the kids must go out and work. Suddenly there will be child-care expenses where none existed before. Often the house must be sold and each, alone, must try to qualify for another.

Co-parental: Two separate people, living and working in different worlds, trying to raise the same set of kids is at best an impossible situation. Now throw in the emotions and see what happens. Even when each has the kids' best interests at heart, the conflicts are impossible to avoid. Wars can easily erupt over holiday divisions, over whose weekend is whose, and over unforeseen time conflicts that force custody renegotiation. Then add such subtleties as choosing the best schools—when perhaps the most expensive alternative is the most convenient for the poorer partner—and you see how out of control it can all become.

Community: Friends are divided up. Areas of the community—shopping malls, grocery stores, movie theaters, cultural centers—become off limits to one of you so you don't accidentally meet. Even the choice of churches becomes affected. I have a client whose husband left her for another woman. Although my client lives less than a mile from a church she could easily attend, she goes all the way across town to another because her ex and his new wife attend the closer church. Partners will often do anything and everything to avoid that chance meeting.

Psychic: Probably the most difficult aspect to divorce involves getting your ex out of your mind and life. You don't just move on. Attachment to a spouse often continues for some great amount of time. Negative thoughts and feelings can also linger.

Each of these stages may be characterized by intense anguish and seemingly immobilizing tasks before any level of well-being can be achieved by either partner. For some, I think, well-being literally takes a lifetime to achieve.

Kids' Scars

Divorce hurts kids. Period. Child psychologist Dr. Lee Salk believes "the trauma of divorce is second only to death" and that "children sense a deep loss and feel they are suddenly vulnerable to forces beyond their control."[7]

It is the rare child indeed who is prepared for divorce when it happens. "The first reaction is one of pure terror," writes Dr. Wallerstein in her fifteen-year follow-up on 130 children of divorce.[8] And that terror leaves considerable damage in its wake. Children suffer from intense fear, insecurity, depression, detachment, loneliness, abandonment, and withdrawal, which all lead to a jumble of problems. And, of course, children inevitably blame themselves for Mom and Dad splitting up. So we add guilt to that list. It's no wonder many kids go on to suffer severe emotional problems as they battle deeply buried anxiety, discouragement, and insecurity.

Dr. Tom Whiteman, president of Fresh Start Ministries, has dedicated his life to helping broken families. If "recovery" defines the point where divorce no longer has a daily impact on how those affected by it view or live their lives, Dr. Whiteman's research has found that about a third of the kids recover within two years of the divorce, about a third will recover at some time in their lives, and about a third never recover.[9]

There's little wonder how these statistics, particularly regarding the latter two-thirds, came to be. Parents, at times, take such a selfish, cavalier attitude toward the child-casualties of divorce. That attitude is never so clear as it is in the following dialogue. It comes by way of Dr. James Dobson, widely known author, speaker, and founder of Focus on the Family, and will help us understand how children are often left hanging in the breech, forced to interpret the most devastating event in their young lives—the rending of their homes, the shattering of their parental fortress—terribly alone.

That's the Way It Goes Sometimes

When I was ten, my parents got a divorce. Naturally, my father told me about it because he was my favorite.

"Honey, I know it's been kind of hard for you these past few days, and I don't want to make it worse. But there's something I have to tell you. Honey, your mother and I got a divorce."

"But Daddy . . ."

"I know you don't want this, but it has to be done. You mother I just don't get along like we used to. I'm already packed and my plane is leaving in half an hour."

"But Daddy, why do you have to leave?"

"Well, honey, you mother and I can't live together anymore."

"I know that, but I mean why do you have to leave town?"

"Oh. Well, I got someone waiting for me in New Jersey."

"But, Daddy, will I ever see you again?"

"Sure you will, honey. We'll work something out."

"But what? I mean, you'll be living in New Jersey, and I'll be living in Washington."

"Maybe your mother will agree to you spending two weeks in the summer and two in the winter with me."

"Why not more?"

"I don't think she'll agree to two weeks in the summer and two in the winter, much less more."

"Well, it can't hurt to try."

"I know, honey, but we'll have to work it out later. My plane leaves in twenty minutes and I've got to get to the airport. Now I'm going to get my luggage, and I want you to go to your room so you don't have to watch me. And no long goodbyes, either."

"Okay, Daddy. Goodbye. Don't forget to write."

"I won't. Goodbye. Now go to your room."

"Okay, Daddy. I don't want you to go!"

"I know, honey. But I have to."

"Why?"

"You wouldn't understand, honey."

"Yes, I would."

"No, you wouldn't."

"Oh well. Goodbye."

"Goodbye. Now go to your room. Hurry up."

"Okay. Well, I guess that's the way life goes sometimes."

"Yes, honey. That's the way life goes sometimes."

After my father walked out that door, I never heard from him again.[10]

Do you have kids? Are you on that fast train heading for divorce? The odds are pretty poor for them, aren't they? Their world will be torn apart; foundations they thought were granite strong will turn to sand and clay. They will become convinced that everything, even God, can eventually crumble before their eyes. It's a terrible reality for children to live with.

And all that's caused by just the breakup. What about life for them afterward? Their pain is made even more severe by the stress of living in a single-parent family—something shared by about thirteen million kids in this country.

I truly admire the men and women who take on the responsibility of raising their kids alone. But often it's difficult to make ends meet and juggle the day-to-day responsibilities of being both Mom and

Dad. Regardless of their heroics, clear evidence remains that kids from single-parent families tend to get less parental attention, have less love and supervision, and as a result, struggle more often with feelings of inadequacy and insecurity. They are also more prone to delinquency than children in two-parent families.[11]

You may say, "But I know kids who have made it through a divorce." Maybe so, but the statistics indicate that those kids made it in *spite* of the divorce, not because of it. And the question remains, "Is it really worth the risk?"

She's My Girl Friday Till Sunday Afternoon

Is it really worth the risk not only to the children but also to your own heart, when, as Doug experienced, you find yourself slowly and inevitably eased out of your children's lives? "She called him Daddy," Doug told me, and although his daughter would always deny it, for that instant in time, that other man was more her daddy than Doug was. Are you prepared for that eventuality? If your heart is still coming up with excuses and crying, "Tim—I understand that, but . . ." Please stay with me. Read on.

In the next chapter we'll take a look at another of your options: being married in name only.

FIVE

DOOR #2:
IN NAME ONLY

The bitterest tears shed over graves are for
words left unsaid and deeds left undone.
—*Harriet Beecher Stowe*

*I*n chapter 4 we looked at the ramifications of divorce. They aren't pretty, especially if there are children involved. But that doesn't stop millions of people from opting for it. For some, however, divorce is not an option, and many of those choose to live in what I've come to call "in name only." And with this choice comes the sacrifice of their existence—their hearts and their chances to ever experience true love with another.

Why do people make such a choice?

There are probably as many reasons as there are those who choose it. Maybe they're remaining together for the kids, or they can't afford to get a divorce, or they've found that staying married is too lucrative to give up. Perhaps they're embarrassed or feel their social or Christian standing wouldn't tolerate a divorce. Perhaps they just can't bear to fail at marriage or to be alone again. For whatever reason, here they are—in a marriage that weighs them down and douses every good feeling in oppressive emotional tar.

Who hasn't seen such a marriage? When you come in contact with one, you may see an occasional flicker of light but never a flame, perhaps a heartbeat but no life. Instead of enjoying the beautiful covenant that God desires, the couple shares an emotional chill, even open hostility. The marriage has become nothing more than an ink stain on a stale legal document, an obligation no one wants to fulfill.

And no matter how hard they try, they can't hide it. Julie and I had lunch with friends recently who have been struggling with their marriage for several years—their problems are known by most of their close friends. During the lunch conversation, one of them announced that they'd really been working hard on building their relationship. But you couldn't see it. Tension, anger, and disgust were stamped on their every communication—every word they said, every look between them, every intolerant sigh.

You cannot hide persistent pain. These two people were simply existing together. Even as I write this, they remain under the same roof, continuing to build the barriers that plague their marriage and keep them apart. They're not alone. In my work, I see couples each week who haven't touched, kissed, or slept in the same bed for years. A client of mine said it best when she blurted out, "You just learn to live with it." If you can call that *living*.

Time Heals *No* Wounds

We've already identified some of the reasons unhappy couples stay together. Well, there's another—a persistent belief that says, "If I endure and ride this out, all will work out in the end." I admire the courage, effort, and determination that goes into "riding it out," but the belief is 180 degrees out of phase. Time rarely heals a wound. In fact, the older this type of relationship, the more disengaged a couple becomes and the more difficult it is to help them. They fall into an acceptable level of pain. They begin to lie to each other and to themselves that they've achieved "peace." And the alternative—rocking a painful but steady boat—is more than they want to risk.

They've convinced themselves that love is just not important enough. Or, worse yet, they've convinced themselves that this is the inevitable outcome—final resting place—of love.

Staying and living unhappily with your spouse may seem noble, or even like the less painful option; but when the situation is examined objectively, existing in a loveless marriage is much like stealing. It robs both partners of love, of mutual respect, of joy, and of whole trunkfuls and albums full of warm, happy family memories.

If you're living in a prison of pain, please realize that it's not what God ordained and desires for a marriage. God's desire is for marriage and the resulting family to be special. It's the place where little hearts and hands are fashioned and you are at the center of a circle of influence. There is very little in this life that justifies hanging on to a marriage in name only—where you endure and just exist, where a burning love has become stoic acceptance and dead tolerance. You end up enabling the very indifference you hate.

Doesn't it need to stop somehow? Doesn't it *have* to stop—somehow?

Partners' Scars

According to leading marital authorities James Cordova and Neil Jacobson, when couples have been disengaged for a long time, they are increasingly difficult to help.[1] As the years drag on, marital distress builds upon itself, creating profound suffering and sorrow. The need to protect oneself creates a distance between spouses, which then solidifies. What was once the flame of love cools, then burns out and turns to the polar opposite of love, *indifference*. Turning indifference back into a loving, vulnerable relationship is very difficult.

Megan, one of my clients, summarizes her journey this way. "It's April; looking back on last summer, it all seems like a bad dream now.

Like it was someone else whose life was falling apart. Like many couples, we're opposites in so many ways, but we'd learned to deal with it because we loved each other. But that didn't last. Before long we really began being hateful and hurtful to one another. So much so that by last August, I was going through some severe physical and emotional turmoil—stress headaches, sleeplessness. Either I couldn't go to sleep or I'd wake up in the middle of the night and lay there, restless. I felt like life was out of control, and, frankly, I couldn't handle that. Keeping a stiff upper lip and pulling myself up by the bootstraps wasn't working anymore.

"My heart was broken and I felt as if I were one raw, exposed nerve. I couldn't control my crying, for one thing. Just asking me how I was doing would bring on tears. Hopelessness took up residence and followed me everywhere. I pondered death—mine, his, it didn't matter. It was a way out. But I couldn't do it; I wanted to live. I also wanted the agony to go away. But I couldn't rise above my life. I thought of little besides my own pain. I was a basket case, and I *hated* that. And since all my prayers had gone unanswered, I thought even God had deserted me. I felt alone.

"Remembering what I went through then brings tears to my eyes even now. I had to get on medication to fight the depression and to help me sleep better. I resented that. And I also resented that fact that it seemed I was the only one being affected. Why didn't he have trouble sleeping? Why wasn't he devastated? I'll tell you why. Because he didn't care about me. I remember asking, 'Why, God, do you hate divorce? Don't you know how painful marriage can be? Do you really want me to suffer like this for the rest of my life?'" [2]

In a situation like this, despair comes easily. Most partners feel hopelessly trapped in such an emotionally corrosive situation. The inevitable distress brings perpetual heartache. Since it never goes away, there's never closure—never relief. As a result, most eventually exhibit signs of decreased immunity and are more susceptible to bouts of depression. [3]

They are in what amounts to never-ending mourning.

Nina Donnelly captures the essence of this quite well. "The trouble with trying to mourn loss when death isn't involved is that there is no body, no funeral and no public shoulder to cry on. There is no traditional, socially sanctioned outlet for mourning when the loss isn't death. Loss of function, relationship or financial resources for example, bring no printed obituary, no 'remains' laid to rest, no public gathering to cement the fact and focus love on the mourners."[4]

On the day I wrote this, a young man came for counsel. He was emotionally overwhelmed because his wife had told him she wasn't sure she wanted him anymore. After hearing this, he had sat in a closet holding a shotgun to his temple. His pager going off finally yanked him back from the brink. "I came to my senses. But Tim, I felt so alone. Ending it all seemed like the right thing to do."

The wounds go deep. And living in denial, ignoring the obvious, hoping that someday it will all become the way it should be only makes the wounds deeper.

But, of course, adults aren't the only ones scarred by the marriage in name only.

Kids' Scars

Only five out of a hundred spouses interviewed in a major marital study desired a marriage like their parents'.[5] Just five. Why? There were a number of reasons given, but I ultimately believe it's because your kids are watching. You may think you're hiding the anguish produced by your inability to connect and love, but you're only kidding yourself. They hear it in your every word to each other and see it in your lack of contact. It charges the air. Believe me, you cannot *not* communicate.

Your words and actions are powerful—and your children observe and interpret them, often accurately. They know, because of the way you feel about each other, that their world is vulnerable and might crumble at any moment. This sense of temporariness can create in them the same level of distress and pain that you are going through—

maybe even more. And they're far less prepared to deal with it. So they'll be dealing with it for a very long time.

An example of the imprint that an in-name-only couple can make on their children was given to me by one of my clients. One day she was watching her young children play in the backyard. Suddenly their play erupted into a battle. Her seven-year-old son was screaming at his six-year-old sister, shaking his finger at her and pacing back and forth in the sandbox as he did. And her daughter wasn't just taking it. She fired back salvo for salvo, her voice every bit as angry and animated. Being a concerned mother, she was about to open the window and call out to them to stop when she recognized what they were shouting at one another. It sounded very much like the battle that had erupted between her and her husband the night before. They'd both thought the children were asleep. Her heart sank as she realized they'd obviously been mistaken.

Don't let your children be scarred by your prison of pain. Please don't make the mistake of assuming that they won't understand or are too young to be hurt. They do understand. And they will be hurt. Remember, you're not making memories, you *are* the memories. You cannot *not* communicate. Your words and actions have real power. Don't underestimate them.

In the next chapter we'll discuss the final option—the option I hope you'll choose. It's the option I also hope will bring your marriage back from the brink.

Six

Door #3: Staying Power and the Power of Staying

The love we give away is the only love we keep.
—*Elbert Hubbard*

The most devastating assault on any marriage is adultery. Jane found this out the hard way—when Tom left her for another woman. You might expect Jane to have been enraged, but in fact, she was far more shocked and confused. And when she discovered that the other woman was her best friend, her confusion turned to a deep sense of betrayal and abandonment. Finally, as all of those feelings came together, she was visited by an unfathomable brokenness. Sure, she and Tom had had their share of problems and heartaches; they'd even had years when they could hardly communicate. But none of that had prepared her for this kind of emotional earthquake.

And although she had expected Tom to ask her for a divorce, hearing him actually say the words was nearly more than she could take. Even after such a betrayal, she had a very difficult time accepting the fact that her marriage was over. Only then did the rage come—pure and white-hot, heated by all the shattered dreams and the unfairness.

And as the heat grew volcanic, the thought of opposing the divorce became increasingly remote.

But when the divorce papers actually arrived, Jane suddenly had a whole host of reasons not to sign them. She was too busy to read them over. She needed to rethink the property settlement, and there might be something more to consider in setting the child support payments. The mere thought of dealing with all that legalese gave her a headache. There were other reasons, but even she knew they were only excuses. The plain truth was she just couldn't bring herself to sign those papers and admit that her marriage was dead. As long as her pen remained somewhere other than touching that page, there was still a chance her marriage could be saved.

Although Jane didn't realize it at the time, she was making the best decision she could possibly make for herself and her marriage. And for her children. She and Tom have two, Jill at three and Brandon at five. And for everyone's sake, she was keeping her marriage and family alive—no matter how thready its heartbeat.

After having the papers for a couple days, she finally told Tom that she wasn't going to sign. Of course, he went ballistic, shouting and intimidating and threatening to take the divorce forward without her. She remained surprisingly calm and told him he could if he wanted, but she still had hope for their marriage and she wasn't yet prepared to snuff it out.

To add spiritual weight to her decision, she began going to a Bible study with a friend and earnestly praying for Tom. But her focus wasn't just outward. She looked inward too. With the help of God's Word, she saw the mistakes she'd made and the sin inside herself—sin and mistakes that had contributed to the poison in her marriage. She sought forgiveness and began seeing a Christian counselor. She came to the conclusion that if her marriage was going to have a fighting chance, saving it had to start with her. That realization took her from a vague sense of mission to a fully-defined commitment. Sure she had every right to leave Tom and no one would blame her, but now that option hardly existed for her. She was fully committed to God's example of love and forgiveness.

However, as these things sometimes work out, Jane's new commitment didn't start out all that well. The day she made it, Tom moved in with her old best friend. But a commitment is a commitment, and Jane was determined to stick by hers.

She was able to talk to Tom only occasionally—generally when he picked up the kids—and when she did, he was still angry with her. But she never let his anger get to her. She spoke lovingly and firmly in return, always doing what was best for her and the kids. She never belittled Tom or called him names or presented any weakness. With God's help, she became a strong, loving, Christian woman—one Tom could respect.

Throughout their separation, Jane never stopped caring for Tom. She never stopped praying for him, and she never stopped sharing Christ with him—when not in word, always in deed. And the greatest deed of all was to never give up hope that God could, and eventually Tom would, honor their marital union.

Don't think for a minute that any of this was easy for Jane. Although that upper lip of hers remained stiff, her heart was in constant pain. She was able to comfort it though by continually reminding herself that she was doing what she wanted to do. That knowledge allowed her to withstand the emotional onslaught and dig deep inside to find forgiveness for her wayward husband.

As the months dragged on, her strength began to ebb. She was seriously thinking about giving up and restarting her life from ground zero when Tom showed up at her front door. Head hung low, he told her how terrible things had become for him and that he'd finally realized that he'd made a terrible mistake in leaving her and the kids. His sincerity was written all over his face in his tears.

But his realization went further. He wanted to come back and try to mend their relationship. "I want to know the Lord like you do. I want to see the same changes in my life that you've made in yours."

These things are always easier said than done. Reconciliation takes difficult change—a lot of open and honest discussion, a lot of compromise. But eventually, as wounds began to heal and trust began to build, Jane invited Tom to move back into their home. They made more progress as their relationship solidified, and there actually came a moment—one they recognized together—when their new relationship became stronger and more intimate than before.

Last year Tom and Jane celebrated their twentieth anniversary. Looking back, Jane can see how easy it would have been to just give up, to just throw in the towel and walk away, to take the kids and move on with her life. Many would have applauded her courage. And far fewer people would have called her a fool for sticking it out. But today, she knows she made the right choice. God used that painful process to refine, polish, and strengthen Jane and Tom as individuals and as a couple. Hard work? Lots of it. But with the Lord's help, they weathered the storm and landed on a far more beautiful shore than they'd left.

What am I saying here? That you should stand firm and maybe, just maybe, your spouse will come to his or her senses and want to come back? No.

I'm saying two things. First, no matter how far down you think your marriage has gone, it still might be worth saving. The greatest marital tragedy *can* be overcome, and God can take the bad and use it for His good. Second, your marriage can be rebuilt; it can be more beautiful and exciting than ever before. How? By following God's plans for love and life. By resolving to stay and try to work it out. God can bring beauty from ashes.

Of course this may be the most difficult decision you'll ever make. So don't hesitate to pray earnestly and lean on your heavenly Father. After all, marriage is very important to God—not just marriage in general, but *your* marriage. It's literally sacred ground.

Sacred Ground

Throughout the Old Testament, beginning with Genesis 2:18ff, God defines marriage as special to Him (and to us) then solidifies that notion by creating laws, both moral and civil, to govern and protect it. It's no accident that two of the Ten Commandments deal specifically with marriage. In Proverbs 18:22, the Holy Spirit speaking through Solomon reconfirms that marriage is a good thing and is looked upon with favor by God. And in the New Testament, the Holy Spirit speaking through Paul presents marriage as the one union that symbolizes our relationship with Jesus (Eph. 5:25). And this relationship, above all others, is cloaked in beauty and purity. It is a relationship of shared, unconditional love, of mutual servanthood and sacrifice, one truly blessed by God above all others.

And *your* marriage is defined by that ideal.

If you would like to bathe yourself in God's Word about marriage, here are a few places to start: Malachi 2:14–16; Matthew 5:31–32; Mark 10:2–12; 1 Corinthians 7:10–11.

While you're reading, think about the fact that your marriage is sacred ground. It's a union God has sanctioned, not just because you were determined to come together but also for His purpose (Matt. 19:6).

What does all this mean to the marriage struggling for survival? It means God can and wants to work in your marriage, no matter how desperate it has become. He wants to bring you and your spouse to higher levels of spiritual development, joy, and peace.

You might cry out, "But look at us! We're one step from the cliff. We're teetering right on the edge. How can He or anyone, particularly how can *we*, keep us from toppling over?" In Jeremiah 32:27, God said that there was nothing too hard for Him. It is often difficult to say just how God will work or how we will respond. Hardness often darkens and closes the heart. Jane certainly couldn't have predicted that Tom would end up back on her doorstep. But God worked.

Why? Because He can.

When considering God's ways, we can only speculate, but part of it had to be His commitment to marriage, His particular commitment to Jane and Tom's marriage, certainly Jane's commitment to work on the marriage, and, eventually, Tom's recommitment to do the same.

By deciding to stay, you are deciding to work hard. It takes work to start over, to create a new opportunity for the marriage to succeed, to cultivate and nurture a better love, to discard all the excuses and deal only in reality. And by staying you're committing to change.

Change

Change Starts Inside You

You are the only person over which you can exercise true control. Although we may want to control our kids, our mates, or our coworkers, we know we can't. At least we always seem to fail when we try. So when it comes to making changes around us, we must start with what we *can* change—ourselves. And the greatest and most important change you can make is to seek God's leading and blessing. While we long to have happy marital relationships and we should work toward that goal, true happiness is intensely personal and deeply spiritual. True joy only comes from God through a personal relationship with Jesus. No man or woman can ever satisfy the real longing that lies deep in the human heart; only He will. Get alone with God and, through His Word and Spirit, let Him have control.

Change the Way You Look at Your Past

Your past is many things—a mosaic of memories, experiences, lessons, heartaches, and triumphs—but above all else it's a foundation upon which to build. We all have things in our past we would just as soon forget, things we wished had never happened. Perhaps they are things that have scared us and scarred us. Maybe we've spent a good deal of our conscious lives trying to overcome them. It's important to continue doing that work. But never look back on your past with fear. Rather, look on it as something from which you can learn.

Change Means Relating Completely Differently

First, study how *you* relate to your mate. People in troubled marriages often spend a lot of time focusing on how their mates relate to them—the contempt in their mates' voices, their choice of words, whether they're listening. Each time words or actions point to a cooling love, that mate's in real trouble, and the wall between the two grows higher and thicker. Second, don't worry so much about how your spouse relates to you. Rather think about what you're bringing to the relationship. Focus on the contempt in your voice, your choice of words, and so forth. Then make a conscious choice to be kind, polite, and loving.

Change Requires Investment

Nothing is free. Everything requires an investment. When rebuilding a relationship, as with many things in life, the payback is not immediate. There may be days, weeks, maybe even months when you'll be investing your kindness, love, generosity, selflessness, genuine caring, trust, and laughter—and getting very little, if anything, back. But if you're faithful in making your deposits, that faithfulness will hopefully be rewarded. In all probability, you'll get your investment back from your spouse with full interest. Remember, God sees your faithfulness; He sees what you think goes unnoticed.

Understand that there are risks. As you take responsibility for changing yourself, you'll be making sacrifices and taking risks. And often it will get worse before it gets better.

"Back When We Were Beautiful"

What was your relationship like when you and your partner first met, when you realized you were crazy for each other? Singer Matraca Berg's song, "Back When We Were Beautiful," recalls the sweet beginnings of a couple's life together. How were those sweet beginnings for you? Remember how she looked in jeans and a crisp cotton blouse? Or the heady aroma of her hair when she got close? Remember how he laughed over the silly little things you did? Or those things you did together? Remember the when-can-we-be-alone glances across the room at family gatherings or the stolen kiss in the kitchen when you were supposed to be washing dishes or checking the turkey? Or how your heart filled and floated around the room when you first thought of marriage and spending your whole lives together?

These are not dead dreams.

They could very will be a glimpse at your future, if you're willing to make them so.

One client came to this conclusion about her relationship: "I know what I need to do. I need to change, and I want to. But right now all I can do is cry." It's okay to cry. And if you feel like crying now, go ahead. But don't let them be tears of mourning. Let them be tears of cleansing and renewal.

Options Quickly Become Paths

Life goes on. Time passes. Situations develop and choices are made. And before you know it, options become paths, paths become set, and destinations that may have been best for you become unattainable. You don't want that. It makes sense, then, to clear out the obstacles to making the best choices. In my work, one obstacle seems to pop up quite often. Many couples have difficulty committing to working on their marriages because one spouse feels that in doing so, he or she is in some way excusing the other's role in destroying the marriage.

If this is true for you, both you and your mate need to take responsibility for the marriage's trouble. It's also worth considering the pressures that assault a modern marriage. It's only by God's grace that any marriage remains standing tall.

In the next chapter we will discuss those pressures. By better understanding them, you will see how your marriage came to be where it is and, thereby, make it easier to work on reclaiming what you and your spouse once had.

Of course, I hope you choose to stay in your marriage, take the risks, and make your marriage work. But whatever you do, the time is nearing when you should do something while you're still able to positively affect your marriage's outcome.

How Couples
Lose at Love

SEVEN

EVERYDAY PRESSURES
THAT TEAR AT LOVE

*We can chart our future clearly and wisely only when we
know the path which has led to the present.*

—*Adlai Stevenson*

ere are some quotes from a few of my clients.

Carla (to her mother in 1984): "John is the sweetest,
most loving man I've ever met. I can't imagine him
ever being mean."

(To me in 1998): "When he decides—no when he *proves* to me—
that he loves me, then I'll consider working on this relationship . . ."

Bill (to his sister in 1986): "Carol just has a way of making me
happy. Even when I'm just sitting in the living room with her and we're
not saying a word to each other, I just feel her love for me. Just feel it."

(In my office in 1997): "I would give you a medal of honor if you
could live with her for one week. She's the most hateful, mean, and
nagging person I know . . ."

Donna (to a college classmate in 1985): "He brought me flowers
the other night. Just out of the blue. He said it was just because he was
thinking about me on the way home. He does that sort of thing, and
it's so endearing to me."

(To me in 1998): "He's a sick man and needs a lot of help. I don't even think he is capable of loving someone else. You should meet his family . . ."

Curtis (to his friend in 1988): "She made my favorite dinner last night, and then we ate it by candlelight. I've never felt so special. Never."

(To me in 1997): "She is the most selfish person I have ever met. I had no idea that she would be this nasty once we got married . . ."

As you probably guessed, these statements were made by people describing their feelings at the beginning of their marriages and later, when they came in for counseling. It's hard to believe the same people made the paired comments, but it's even harder to believe they were making them about the same spouse. Obviously something happened between the first statement and the next.

In this chapter I want to share with you how couples begin to make such shifts—how they start to lose at love. Specifically, I'll discuss the pressures that tear at marriages and unfortunately often succeed at destroying them.

Barriers to Intimacy

In all my research I've found no one who has come up with a simple reason why couples lose at love. But I have found a number of factors that clearly tear at the marriage bond and erode the love that acts as marital cement. Every couple experiences them to one degree or another.

As you read the following, and as I give examples from people I've counseled, take a critical look at your own marriage and determine how your marriage has been affected by these pressures.

Barrier #1: Everyday Stress

Who today isn't stressed out? One definition of stress is, "a state which arises from an actual or perceived imbalance between demand (e.g., challenge, threat) and capability (e.g., resources and coping)."[1] In short, you've got to do something and you don't know how, or you don't have the tools, or you don't have the time.

It's like we are "hyper-living." We are pulled in every direction, busy going nowhere fast, and having to do more with less. Before long tempers flare, stomachs ache, hearts break. Hurried decisions become bad decisions. And bad decisions make people hurt. And our hurt makes us irritable, discouraged, and very difficult to live with.

On the average, six out of ten Americans report feeling "great stress" at least once a week. I'd like to meet the four who don't. Richard Swenson, in his book *Margin,* suggests that we live in a marginless society.[2] He's right. Our days are filled. If someone calls to reschedule something, the likelihood is we won't be able to. There's no room for error, no time to rest, no room to turn around.

We've all heard how devastating stress can be on our physical health. By affecting our immune system, stress opens us up for any number of illnesses—colds, flu, heart disease. By pushing our emotions to their limits, stress magnifies any predisposition we might have to emotional struggles as well. Blend into the mix an attempt to maintain a healthy marital relationship, and you can easily see the overwhelming impact that stress can have on a marriage. Retirement, job loss, a prolonged illness, the loss of a loved one, an adolescent out of control, even moving to a new home or community can balloon into major stress.

Mary and Bob had only been married for two years. They had met during their freshman orientation at college and from that moment on had been inseparable.

Eight months after their wedding, their perfect world was shattered when a drunk driver crossed the median and hit Bob's vehicle head-on, instantly killing his best friend who was riding in the passenger seat. Bob suffered critical injuries that left him with severe physical limitations. Immediately, Mary began the long process of helping him recover from his physical injuries while allowing him space to deal with the emotional trauma of losing his best friend.

Even with their insurance coverage, the bills from Bob's physical therapy soon became overwhelming, and Mary began to work several evening shifts as a waitress in addition to her job as an administrative assistant at a local utilities company. Bob began to slip deep into depression as he became unable to cope with his injuries and his inability to provide for his wife. He resented her work at the restaurant but felt powerless to change their situation.

In the evenings, Mary was exhausted and in need of some TLC. Instead, she had to cater to Bob and his unrelenting needs. By the time she stopped long enough to realize she required help, she was physically and emotionally drained. Too exhausted to even cry, she explained her situation to me, then hurriedly added, "I still love him. I know I do. I know we can make our relationship work despite all this. But I'm so tired. So very tired."

Can we say that their love was too weak to withstand the challenges life handed them? No. Their love seemed strong enough. But with constant battering by their physical limitations—Bob's injuries, their exhaustion—the financial strains, and a general lack of communication brought on by the strain, their relationship simply began to buckle under the pressure. If something's not done soon, extended periods of disaffection will likely occur.

Although this case study is extreme, it's not atypical. As you read it, did you see parallels in your own relationship? Does one of you have any special needs the other must work hard to satisfy? Are there financial worries, or are you working very hard to make sure there are no financial issues? Although Mary and Bob didn't have children, maybe you do. As wonderful as they are, kids add stress.

One of the most important things I do with couples during their counseling experience is to get them to identify the "stresses" that have had a profound effect on their relationship. More often than not, when the couples have finished their lists, they are astounded at the assault they've endured. Under this kind of pressure it's common to see one partner attacking the other simply because the pain he or she is in leads to lashing out at somebody. I'm not excusing hurtful behavior, nor am I trying to relieve the responsibility both partners have to treat each other lovingly, but stress can definitely bring out the worst in us. Anger and frustration certainly come much easier. And when they come, the marriage can often become a war zone.

Let's find out about the stresses assaulting your relationship. Do your own inventory. Take a sheet of paper and, using the format here, start writing.

What Stressors Have Been Tearing at Your Marriage?

Put down the lost jobs, the missed bills, the loss of parents, the recent move, the family situations, the kids misbehaving—everything and anything that caused a sleepless night or a cross word. Keep your list simple and be honest.

1. _____

2. _____

3. _____

4. _____

5. _____

6. _____

7. _____

8. _____

Now that you have a list, determine what about each situation causes stress and look for a solution. For instance, Mary found that a demanding work schedule made it difficult for her to spend enough time helping Bob in his therapy. That caused stress in a number of ways. First, Mary felt stress because Bob wasn't getting as much therapy as he needed, and it was her fault. She also felt stress because she felt she shouldn't put her job before Bob, but their money problems dictated that she had to. Bob was stressed because missing therapy was delaying his recovery and making a full recovery less likely.

What were their options? Mary could tell her boss that she couldn't work the extra hours, but she felt that might impact her job. Besides, they really needed the extra money. They could see there might be some relief if Bob could do a portion of his therapy without help. A call to Bob's doctor turned them on to a physical therapist who devised a new regimen for Bob. That freed Mary up enough to take advantage of the overtime and keep Bob on the road to recovery.

Most stress also results in worry. The ultimate cure is to realize that God is in this with you and He loves you with an all-consuming love. That love allows Him to tell us to "be anxious for nothing" (Phil. 4:6).

Don't be too quick to completely condemn stress. It can bring opportunity with it. Stress can allow you to work problems out together. So instead of seeing stress as just a destructive force, see it as an opportunity to support and love one another. This strengthens a relationship, for dealing with stress shapes character and character shapes love.

Barrier #2: Satanic Assault

During one of Carla and John's early sessions, as we explored the issue of satanic assaults on marriages, Carla related a curious episode. She and John had been married about two years and were still very much in love. It was a Friday and they both looked forward to John getting off work a little early. They planned to have a nice dinner at home then go out to a late movie. At the appropriate time, Carla lit the barbecue. But John didn't come home. He called about when she'd expected him and told her he'd be late, saying, "The boss is leaving for a business trip, and he wants this presentation done tonight so he can take it with him."

Although Carla had no reason to doubt John—after all, his boss had done this to him before—this Friday was different. She developed an eerie feeling. Her mind raced with the thought that John wasn't telling her the truth, that he hadn't stayed at work to finish a presentation. He was out somewhere. She was sure. And he wasn't just out with the guys. He was out with a woman. She had no idea where this intrusive thought came from, but it kept playing over and over in her head. After about an hour, she called his office, but the switchboard was closed and there was no way to ring John's office. By the time John came home, she was not only frantic, but she was also furious at him and attacked him the moment he stepped through the door. "Where were you? You liar. You weren't at work. You were out with somebody." He didn't know what to say. He ended up getting angry, and the two of them spent the evening separated by walls.

I am not a "demon under every rock" type of person, but I do believe that Satan is alive, powerful, and working to destroy marriages today. He is the great confuser and the ultimate liar. Peter described him as a "roaring lion, seeking whom he may devour" (1 Pet. 5:8b). Since the Garden of Eden, he has set out to destroy anything and everything ordained by God—especially marriage. Who are we to believe we are exempt from his assault? (See also 1 Thess. 3:5.)

Scripture tells us that the path of marriage has been forged by God, and He can provide direction and inspiration that cannot be found through other means. Since the beginning of creation, God has always intended marriage to be a bastion of honor, companionship, and love.

But despite God's desire, Ephesians 6:12 reminds us that "we do not wrestle against flesh and blood, but against principalities, against powers, against the rulers of the darkness of this age, against spiritual hosts of wickedness in the heavenly places." Throughout Scripture, we are given examples of Satan's unmerciful attacks on relationships. Perhaps none is as popular and well known as the story of Adam and Eve. Imagine living in paradise with a partner created just for you. Imagine knowing no stress, no dishonesty, no unhappiness, none of the patterns that characterize many of today's relationships. Rather, you know only a pure, unadulterated, and perfect love. This was the paradise created for Adam and Eve. Yet, Satan still found a place where he could penetrate the perfection, and he destroyed their paradise. Now, instead of knowing only a pure love, Adam and Eve were faced with a tainted relationship that would require work, sacrifice, and forgiveness. If Satan could penetrate paradise, imagine how easy it is for him to attack your less-than-perfect marriage.

How, then, does he attack?

He knows our Achilles heel and sends his fiery darts right at it. If we feel distant from one another, he finds a way to force an even thicker wedge between us. If we're feeling betrayed, he might help tempt us to feel abandoned. If we're angry, he might help tempt us to feel enraged. Whatever the negative, he magnifies it, particularly when we're discouraged. And if anything beautiful is about to happen, like Carla and John's date, he can help turn it very ugly.

So how do you fend off such attacks? By being "strong in the Lord and in the power of His might" (Eph. 6:10) and staying close to God's Word. By reading it and meditating on it daily and surrounding yourself with godly influences in your daily walk. And whenever possible, by engaging in evangelistic ministries. Do all this, whenever possible, as a twosome.

Most couples I work with have sparse or nonexistent spiritual lives. They don't practice the spiritual disciplines like praying together, sharing God's Word, or attending church. This scarcity of God's influence in their lives opens them up to the forces of darkness. And these forces mean them no good. They war in every way possible against spiritual intimacy between mates. You have a powerful enemy, and trying to make marriage work without God is foolhardy. I believe Satan knows that if he can get into your marriage, he can shake your world and everyone who's a part of it. He can deeply trouble your children, shake the faith of your parents and relatives, and negatively impact your witness and your church.

Don't underestimate him. He's got a quiver full of some pretty sharp arrows—foolish pride, lust, temptation, lies, hurt—and he fires them with deadly accuracy, keeping you from building a strong marriage and enjoying your mate's love. Your only hope is to diligently wear the full armor of God (Eph. 6:13ff) and repel those arrows.

If you falter, or if the assault is too overwhelming, don't try to fight the battle by yourselves. Give your defense over to the Lord. Trust Him to bring His solutions to your problems, and in all things seek God's purpose and rejoice in it. If God is for you who can be against you? He sustains you when you seek after Him and His truth, when you can no longer sustain yourself.

There's another barrier to intimacy that adds to the possibility of satanic assault and creates additional avenues for day-to-day stress. It's going into the marriage with unrealistic expectations.

Barrier #3: Unrealistic Expectations

One reason Carla found it easy to believe that John was out with another woman was the expectations about married relationships that she developed as a teenager—when she was fourteen to be exact. She'd been at a skating party with friends and had come home to a cold silence between her mother and father. This was unusual. They were both outgoing, gregarious people, and life at home was characterized by warm laughter rather than this icy quiet. Instantly sensing something was wrong, Carla asked her mother what. But she only got a very chilling stare. Carla went to her room and worried most of the night. The next morning she learned that her father had gone to stay the night at a local motel. "He's been cheating on me," her mother told her. "Some woman at work."

Of course, Carla was devastated. Here was the one man in all the world she trusted, and he was being proved a fraud. Well, as it turned out, her parents were able to work things out and her father came home again. But one way her mother justified taking him back was to tell Carla, "All men do it. They all cheat on their wives at one time or another. It's not right that they do, but they do."

All men, she'd said. Not some men. Not most men. But all men. And since Carla's father was so pure and wonderful, if he did it, then, indeed, all men must do it. That expectation followed Carla through several relationships in high school, then in college. And sure enough, if someone broke up with her, it was to see another girl. Of course, in high school and college, that's why people break up. But that didn't matter; her expectations for relationships were confirmed. So, when John was late that night, the evil one had a foothold. Her inner tape kept playing the thought that John was no different from all other men; he was late because of his cheating.

It wasn't true. When they later talked about the incident, Carla discovered why she had this tendency to be jealous. Well, Carla had another expectation and that was that a husband would never make a decision that would intentionally cause his wife distress. John now knew that when he was late, Carla would become deeply worried. So Carla now expected him never to be late again, certainly not for trivial reasons.

But he *was* late again and often for trivial reasons. And Carla's worries burned for two reasons: one for her expectations that she would be cheated on, which she fought; and one for her feelings of betrayal. These were fed by her expectation that her husband would alter his way of doing things to accommodate her fears. As it turned out, John was always faithful, but he was not as considerate as Carla expected. There are other expectations we bring to marriage that are often too high as well. Some of the more conspicuous ones include:

A marriage will complete me. Perhaps you grew up in a difficult environment, maybe with parents who didn't care like they should or with siblings who stole the limelight. In any case, you reached marrying age plagued by hurts and wounds. Now you have the opportunity to build your own family—where love reigns, where you feel whole. At the first sign of trouble, disappointment can literally cripple such a marriage.

Love won't hurt me. This expectation sees marriage as the ultimate safe haven. After all, your spouse loves you while your parents didn't. Again, the first hurt can devastate such a marriage.

Life will be easy. This is the "happily ever after" expectation of which fairy tales are made. Every unhappy moment brings disappointment and concern to the marriage. Job 14:1 reminds us, "Man who is born of woman is of few days and full of trouble." As the hurts pile up—and as the disappointments pile up because there are hurts—this expectation bites the dust.

Love will keep us together. As the song goes: "All you need is love." Well, not so. And because we need more than our love, this expectation produces the greatest disappointment by far, for it batters the very thing that is supposed to hold us together—love. Love is supposed to be strong enough to shield us from hurt and, of course, restrain our mates from hurting us in the first place. But we get bruised, angry, hurt; and because hurt people hurt people back, in the end, when we see love as not strong enough, we can easily say our relationship just wasn't meant to be. Human love does *not* conquer all, only divine love does. Human love does, on the other hand, give us the reason to work on conquering our hurts and anger.

How do you combat unrealistic expectations? With realistic ones. No one is perfect, including your spouse. No one person can fulfill all of your needs, nor will you supply all of your spouse's needs. No marriage is free from discord, and no spouse is completely unselfish. Marriage brings two people together who have a good number of human frailties, and puts them in such close proximity that those frailties will hopefully, in Christ, develop muscle.

Barrier #4: Selfishness/Sin

The resounding theme of the day is "I" or "me." Through selfishness, marriages, designed to be a team effort, have been reduced to prenuptial agreements, occasional intimacy or none at all, and quickie divorces. Counseling offices across the nation are filled with people who have been hurt or shattered by a loved one in pursuit of "personal gratification."

My wife, Julie, and I know a husband who insists on "going out with the guys" every Thursday evening for dinner. Recently, one of his children became seriously sick, and his wife desperately needed some help at home. Did he heed her request that he stay home on a Thursday evening? No. "That's just the way it is. That's my night." As you can imagine, his wife was very hurt. She now had proof that he thought his night of fun was more important than her need for help. What this man was failing to understand was that marriage, his included, is a "we" business. Couples' therapy expert, Mark Karpel makes a beautiful statement that illustrates this: "In the state of 'I' there is a boundary between us; in the state of 'we' there is a boundary around us."[3] And for any marriage to grow strong, deep sacrifice and selfless effort must be made.

Julie and I see that in our own marriage. There have been times we both have given up activities or put aside feelings to honor our commitment to one another and our relationship. And there have been times when the sacrifice wasn't pleasant. But it's always right. Honoring your spouse is a fulfilling element to marriage, and it can be quite romantic. In fact, I dare say nothing is more romantic than selfless acts of love and kindness.

Growing up, a dear friend told me: "Tim, the greatest struggle you'll ever have in life is *you*." He was right. *Me* and *I* are the most poisonous words in a marriage. When *me* takes over from *us*, the needs of the marriage relationship are tossed aside. But it's easy to do, isn't it? The Saturday golf game takes over and suddenly weekends together dissolve. Watching your favorite television programs at night becomes more important than communicating. Dinners with clients leave a spouse groping for companionship. *Me* becomes operative and *us* diminishes. The moment you see that happening—and believe me you will—stop, think about what you're doing and about the intimacy you're losing, and return to loving your spouse unselfishly.

How? You might just think back to the "dating years" when everything was so other-oriented that you couldn't get enough of each other. God's admonitions in 1 Peter 3:7–8 and Ephesians 5:28–29 to put your mate ahead of yourself was no sacrifice at all. The demands, arguments, and uncaring comments were nonexistent. Wouldn't it be great to live with that kind of selfless love each day? But more than just selflessly, love your spouse as one who is very valuable, one who is *honored*.

In an article titled "Treat Her Like a Queen," Gary Smalley gave this advice regarding honor in relationships: "At the heart of all loving relationships—with God, your spouse and kids, your boss and coworkers—is honor. To honor someone is to attach high value to that person. It is a *decision* we make, regardless of our *feelings*. When we decide to honor someone, we are saying that they are extremely valuable and important to us."[4]

And part of honoring your spouse is not only to put him or her first, not only to see your mate as valuable, but also to help perfect your partner in his or her relationship with God in Christ. Dan Allender, in the book *Intimate Allies,* says that we are to "cultivate Christ in our partner at every opportunity."[5] And how do you do that? By being a spiritual partner. By helping your spouse put on the full armor of God, by helping your mate to see God in your marriage and in him- or herself, by helping your spouse make the right choices—and by showing Jesus, reflected in you—by your unconditional, selfless love. Of course this is no easy task. Paul said as much about his walk with the Lord in Romans 7:15b, "For what I will to do, that I do not practice; but what I hate, that do I." But life is not given us to be easy. With the Lord's help, we're here to discipline ourselves to righteousness and to approach God with a spirit of expectancy.

Each marriage relationship is different—its strengths, weaknesses, triumphs, and problems are unique—but one thing is universally true. The surest way to split any relationship apart is for one partner to pursue his or her own "personal gratification." Invariably such a pursuit comes at the expense of the other's well-being, and it often leaves the other partner behind, picking up the pieces of shattered promises. Don't allow yourself to be fooled; your selfishness, actually any sin, will have an adverse effect.

Barrier #5: Childhood Scripts

We've already discussed Carla's "script" or expectation: that all men cheat on their wives. Many counselors believe that most of what drives us as adults has a basis in our early years. Families tend to reproduce themselves. Look back, find those unresolved elements of your life that end up governing large areas of your life now, and deal with them. Such areas may be physical, emotional, or sexual abuse; parental divorce; abandonment; gross failure; loss; or any number of other painful memories. These memories speak to attachment issues and how we give and receive love. And these patterns tend to be deeply ingrained, not easily broken. If left to fester, they'll one day rear their heads and tear your relationship apart.

If your spouse has experienced any childhood trauma, take time to understand his or her childhood script—what his or her preservation tendencies might be—then help your spouse to resolve those back issues of life. At the same time, monitor your actions so you don't aggravate an already difficult situation for your mate. Some patterns are not easily broken. As necessary, see your pastor or a professional Christian counselor. It may be one of the most precious gifts you could give yourself and your marriage.

Barrier #6: Speed

We're the "microwave" generation. And it's easy to think a quick change this coming weekend will "patch" everything up from the week. But relationships take time. You need time to understand one another, time to enjoy and respond to one another, time to recognize each other's needs and help satisfy them. Couples need time to build intimacy, and time is the one thing couples don't have much of anymore. Things are moving too fast. Careers run in no other gear than high. Activities and information crowd our lives until we're rationing our minutes and seconds and giving nothing our undivided attention. And when bosses and children and committees need more and more of our time, the only one left to steal the time from is our mate. Even when trouble comes up between us, we want to fix it quickly so that we can go on to other things.

How do you keep from letting this happen?

Realize that your mate is, indeed, the most important person in your life—more important than your boss, your children, and everyone but your God. More important than the kids? Yes. One of the most precious gifts any parent can give to a child is to love the other parent. And just as you wouldn't neglect your children, neither should you neglect your spouse. Set aside time—enough time—for your spouse. An hour a night, a Friday night date—you know what makes sense. And during that time, talk to each other, and care and love and never forget the wonder of your mate, especially the love you share.

A Final Word

Largely because of the pressures on modern marriage and, of course, human sinfulness, spouses who swore to love one another, people who began by only differing from one another in subtle ways, slowly, even unintentionally sever their loving ties and find themselves sulking, nagging, and spilling all over everything.[6] But I hope you'll see that there's no reason to just blame each other for the deterioration of your marriage. It's happening to couples everywhere.

As Wallerstein and Blakeslee put it, "All happy marriages are not carefree. There are good times and bad times, and certainly partners may face serious crises together or separately. Happily married husbands and wives get depressed, fight, and lose jobs, struggle with demands in the workplace, and crisis of infants and teenagers, and confront sexual problems. They cry and yell and get frustrated. They come from sad, and abusive and neglectful backgrounds, as well as from more stable families. All marriages are haunted by ghosts of the past, but every good marriage must adapt to developmental changes in each partner."[7]

So, if your marriage is in trouble, it is so for many reasons. And there are many reasons for you to make a conscious decision to step back and work to save your marriage—to take it to higher, safer ground.

I trust you'll make that decision now.

EIGHT

THE PATH OF DISAFFECTION

We are slaves to what we don't understand.
—*Vernon Howard*

Remember Larry and Holly from the first chapter? They grew apart because, in Larry's eyes, Holly couldn't handle the four-hundred-mile separation from her mother, and, in Holly's eyes, Larry was insensitive to her needs as a woman and mother. They grew apart because they didn't communicate very well and as a result began living separate lives.

But growing apart didn't just happen. They didn't wake up one morning to find themselves at opposite ends of the house with lives that seldom touched. What divided them was a gradual, very subtle, even sometimes unintentional, but still definable process of disaffection. They began to "lose at love."

Isn't that a horrible way to put it? Yet that's what has happened, and by understanding the process that causes this loss, the hope is that you can turn the process around and begin to win at love again.

But there's another reason to explore this. By seeing the process, you'll also see how the outcome is often a reasonable response to an unreasonable situation. You'll see that the process began to unfold, and in a certain sense—possibly because you didn't sense it was unfolding—you were at its mercy. Even though you can point to some very destructive things happening to your marriage, and even though you both have to share responsibility for where your marriage is, neither of you is totally to blame. In fact, you are both faced with a paradox.

The Paradox of the Two Rights

In the last chapter we discussed the six barriers to intimacy that exert pressure on a marriage. And they are formidable—satanic pressure alone is chilling. Both partners in a marriage succumb to these pressures to varying degrees at various times. But if you're honest, in order to blame your mate for the trouble in your marriage, you must ignore the contributions you have made. In each marital case I have dealt with, there is always the dilemma of two rights. He has his reasons, and she has hers, and usually the "I'm not moving" syndrome is firmly in place. I want you to stop for a moment and consider the folly. As you learn about the process that brought you to this place, stop blaming each other for a moment. Step back and start with a clean slate. Then go forward and explore the problems in your marriage without accusations.

"I Don't Want Your Stupid Flowers!"

After finding the goodbye note on the microwave, several months passed before Larry had the nerve to try to visit Holly. They had talked, but not face-to-face. And when they met, it was so Larry could see the kids. But he also wanted to let Holly know how much he still cared for her. He took her flowers—her favorites—a spray of white and pink carnations surrounded by baby's breath and ferns. It wasn't original, but she had loved them when they were dating.

But the moment Holly opened the door and saw the bouquet, her expression soured and she said, "Those better not be for me. I don't want your stupid flowers, Larry, or your boxes of candy, or your sweet notes. I don't want any of that stuff. You understand me? Do you? All I've ever wanted was you. Not your gifts—*you!*"

His love gesture didn't connect. Totally blown away, he began to regret everything all over again. But, of course, there were no words to express his feelings. He only nodded and dropped the flowers on the ground beside the porch. "I'll toss them later," he mumbled.

Gestures like Larry's *can* help, but don't expect them to cover a multitude of offenses. Anybody can bring flowers; anybody can look at someone with cow eyes and recite poetry and say meaningless things about love—anyone. As a counselor, I can train a spouse to do nice things, but it's a different process altogether to get a heart to love someone again.

In order to bring a *higher love* into your marriage, we need to go deeper—right to the heart of your relationship—and begin rebuilding there. Love gestures, if rejected, will become acceptable again when they come wrapped in sincerity that the heart knows and understands.

But right now you're operating from a very different place. I believe we're all built with a natural sense of self-preservation. When we sense danger, we do what we have to do to improve our situations and increase our chances of "staying alive." It's human. It's natural. Self-preservation is a reasonable response to an unreasonable situation.

The process of disaffection is predicated on this need to survive— to minimize the hurts and put ourselves where we will suffer the least damage. The problem, of course, is that it ends up doing great damage.

The Process of Disaffection

As its name implies, disaffection is a process. Step by step, day by day, emotion by emotion, this process of one thing leading inexorably to another at times looks very much like a downward spiral that ends at the deepest and most pervasive pain. And it begins with the smallest step away from one another—distancing.

Distancing

Larry and Holly returned from their honeymoon to find the letter. It had been a wonderful trip filled with all the things a honeymoon should be filled with. And they'd planned for the euphoria to continue. And why shouldn't it? They'd been dating for nearly two years. They'd grown so close to one another some said it was hard to see daylight between them. They loved each other—totally, unswervingly. Surely whatever the future held for them, love could smooth every bump and quiet any storm. The letter changed all that.

At least for Holly.

Larry had been worried about finding a job in Springvale. He'd majored in advertising and the only position in town was with the local newspaper—circulation 10,000. Larry saw that as advertising in name only. So he'd sent his resume and portfolio off to a firm in Richmond. The letter said he'd gotten the job.

"Of course we're going," Larry told Holly.

"I'm a small town girl," Holly said, panic stabbing at her. "You know I'm a small town girl. And my family's here."

"But the job's there. You'll be fine." His tone was dismissive. "You'd better get packing. I'm supposed to be there the day after tomorrow, and it'll take us a day to get there."

And he left her to get ready to pull up every root she'd ever had.

That night she tried again—in bed. "Larry, sweetie," she began, "God's been good to you, and I believe you're going to do very well. If you stay around here, you'll end up owning this town in ten years."

"In ten years I'll end up owning Richmond," he said, a satisfied grin on his face. "Now which would you rather have in your back pocket? Richmond or Podunk-ville?"

And that's when it began. Less than two days after the most wonderful honeymoon two people could have, Holly suddenly came to the realization that she was not the most important thing in Larry's life, and she stepped back. Not far at first, but just far enough to call her mother and tell her how insensitive Larry was.

"But you can't blame him, dear. He's a man and men need to conquer things—careers and new lands and people."

"But if he loved me, he'd care what I think," she protested. "It's not so much that he's making the decision but that he doesn't even think what I have to say has any value. It'd be different if he really considered what I wanted and tried to accommodate me in some way. The way you'd do if you really valued what the other person had to say. But he doesn't do that."

When they got to Richmond, the first month was very difficult for Holly. Larry reveled in his new job and the fact that his new coworkers loved his ideas, and even though he spent most of his evenings at home, he spent them trying to think up new ideas for the people at work to admire. Holly suddenly found herself second fiddle to a fast food hamburger joint that needed a new slogan—"They sizzle when it drizzles"? Nope. "Ketchup to our burgers"? Nope—or to a beauty salon promoting its franchising scheme. Even Larry's attempts to draw Holly into the process by asking her opinion fell miserably short. "How does 'hairy in to see us' sound?"

"You're kidding, right?"

But even though there was tension between them, the blowup didn't come until the phone bill did. "$237.18?! You spent $237.18 to talk to your mother? What can any mother say that's worth $237.18?" he demanded.

"She kept talking me out of leaving you," Holly fired back.

There was an electric argument that night, and for the first time they went to bed not speaking to one another. The next morning there was a reconciliation of sorts, but both could feel it. Something unresolved lay between them. And they knew it would never be resolved, for they couldn't possibly be in two places at once. Larry couldn't have his job in Springvale and Holly couldn't have her family in Richmond. They each took a few steps away. The intimacy they'd experienced through their honeymoon had been bruised, but worse, Holly later confided that she felt as if she'd been kicked in the stomach. It was a horrible realization to find out that she didn't mean everything to Larry. In fact, she decided, if he was willing to trade a mere job for her happiness and security, she didn't mean much to him at all.

And that's how distancing begins—when one or both partners succumb to the pressures that tear at marriage and work their terrible magic to spoil God's plan for marital harmony and intimacy.

Severely bruised, Holly moved to protect herself. She established an even tighter relationship with her mother. But that relationship wasn't the one her heart truly wanted. She began to find herself at war with other feelings—loneliness, sorrow, hopelessness, regret, resentment, and exhaustion. At this point they hadn't become that severe, but they all had the potential.

Self-preservation became increasingly important for Holly. And for Larry. Over the years, as Holly began to retreat into an even stronger relationship with their children and her mother, Larry found himself the odd man out, almost imperceptibly at first, but then more pronounced. Taking the path of least resistance, Larry found his sense of worth from his work—his coworkers understood how important the work was. And Holly got hers over the phone and from frequent trips back home. When a partner no longer feels selflessly loved—safe, secure, and/or significant—self-preservation takes over and distancing begins. And unless a conscious effort is made to reconnect, it only gets worse.

Being unappreciated turns to a feeling of being used, then being abused, then being nonexistent. Before long, hearts burn with resentment. William James, a pioneering psychologist on the study of relationships said, "There is really no more fiendish a punishment in all the world than to be a part of the world and to go largely unrecognized as such."[1] In marriage, it goes like this: There is really no more fiendish a punishment in all the world than to be a part of a marriage—where you are promised love—and to go largely unrecognized as such.

Before long one or both partners find curious questions roaming about their minds: *Why do I stay? What's wrong with me? Do I exist? Does my spouse even love me at all? What happened?*

These questions all have their roots in abandonment and rejection, and there truly is nothing more fiendish than being *abandoned*. When you are unrecognized by your spouse, you feel abandoned and hurt. It's a reasonable response to an unreasonable situation, but further destructive patterns take over.

In counseling, I try to gauge the amount of distancing that has taken place. In general, I see two distinct levels.

Level A

Early signs of distancing include staying overly busy, tuning out your partner, glossing over important comments, not sharing about everyday life. This often results in a severing of simple acts of thoughtfulness like a note slipped into a lunch box or flowers sent for no reason.

Before long, to our shame, we ignore, hurt, insult, badger, intimidate, withhold intimacy, and embarrass our partners with surprising frequency. It is rare that we would exhibit such behaviors to a friend, but we find it easy to treat our partners this way. If unchecked, this type of behavior gets worse, not better, and ends up in Level B.

Level B

This level is the most severe and begins the downward spiral I spoke of earlier—the one that ends in deep pain. It begins with a very damaging secret held in the heart of at least one spouse. The secret is: *I am unhappy with this marriage.*

Are you harboring that secret in your heart? Or do you suspect that your partner may be harboring it in his or hers?

The next chapter will help you understand the process you're probably very much a part of.

NINE

THE CYCLE OF DISAFFECTION

When you pass through the waters, I will be with you;
and through the rivers, they shall not overflow you.
When you walk through the fire, you shall not be burned,
nor shall the flame scorch you.

—*Isaiah 43:2*

As we've seen, disaffection often begins with small steps, but it's not a steady walk away from love. Rather, it's a clearly definable pattern that circles back on itself.

This cycle acts like quicksand—the more you struggle to extricate yourself, the deeper you get. That isn't to say there's no way out. It does mean, however, that battling with one another to somehow stop the marital decline only tends to make things worse.

So what then is the cycle of disaffection? And where does it begin?

The Core of the Cycle of Disaffection: The Secret

This cycle begins where Level B of disaffection begins, with a secret locked tightly in one spouse's heart: *I am unhappy in this marriage.* This is one powerful secret that quietly widens a breach between partners. The difficulty, of course, is that it remains a secret. But the partner harboring it has decided that voicing this honest thought will only get him or her in trouble. And worse yet, it might smoke out the fact that the other partner is also unhappy with the marriage—forcing some action. It's hard enough to just cope with the marriage let alone change it. And it may not be worth changing anyway.

The secret then is the core from which the unhappiness with the marriage intensifies through a series of clearly definable steps.

Step #1: Increasing Disaffection
Characterized by Gottman's Four Horses

At this point, the couple tends to be very confused. Needs are going unmet; pain and negative behaviors have taken hold. Chief among them are what have come to be called Gottman's four horses. These are four bad patterns that have been identified and labeled by Dr. John Gottman, a well-known and respected expert on marriage, and a professor at the University of Washington.

After researching marriage for twenty years, Dr. Gottman can predict with 95 percent accuracy which marriages will succeed and which will falter. And it primarily boils down to how couples handle conflict resolution. Dr. Gottman and his team have identified the "four horses" that couples ride to their own disaster. The horses represent dangerous ways of communicating that build on one another until little or no communication can take place.[1]

Criticism

When Larry got the second telephone bill and saw that it had only dropped about ten dollars, he was furious. "Holly," he started in. "I told you we can't afford your spending so much time on the phone with your mother. You're being a mama's girl. Can't you stand on your own? Why do you have to clear everything you do with her? How do you expect to raise your own family if you have to check in with your mother all the time? Cut the apron strings, for crying out loud."

Holly missed her mother terribly. Not talking things over with her mother left her feeling incomplete and very much alone. Was such a relationship wrong? No. Was it excessive? Holly realized an argument could be made that it might be. But being in a strange town where she knew no one and feeling the clear distance opening up between her and Larry, she needed the advice and ear her mother gave her. So Larry's criticism really hurt. She didn't consider herself a mama's girl, but hearing Larry, whom she loved and respected, tell her that she was, made her feel ashamed. Maybe she was abnormal; maybe she was weak. Although in Larry's mind the criticism was just and concerned only the phone bill, Holly saw it as an assault against her womanhood and her ability to be a mother. And it was also delivered with anger, not with love. Holly found herself covered in shame, and she resented Larry even more.

Criticism becomes criticism when it attacks and blames people for *who they are* instead of *what they do;* it generally starts with "you always" or "you never." And as the cycle loops back, the criticism becomes more heated and more personal.[2]

Contempt

As the phone bills mounted and Larry's criticism continued, Holly's attitude toward him worsened and the joy of being married to him began to decay. If Larry came home at night and asked what Holly's mother had to say that day, Holly would roll her eyes and sigh dramatically. "What do you care?" she'd fire back, the contempt in her voice hard to miss. Then she'd storm off to the kitchen to make dinner.

While she cooked, Larry read the paper—mostly the TV listings. Holly used to like the way he'd call out what shows they might enjoy together. "*Everybody Loves Raymond* looks good tonight." Or "*The Two Fat Ladies* is on the cooking channel." In what seemed like the old days, she'd call back about something she'd seen listed that they might enjoy as well. Now she just made a special effort to knock the pans around. *Who wants to watch television with him?* she thought. *I'll sew or something. Two Fat Ladies is probably a slam against my weight, anyway.*

After a while, Holly lost her desire to cook, clean, and "take care" of Larry altogether. Oh, she still did—it was her obligation—but she didn't enjoy it. In the old days she'd spend extra time planning a meal so Larry would love it. But now Hamburger Helper was just fine. In fact, she often picked things he didn't like, just to spite him.

Dr. Gottman describes contempt as "the intention to insult and psychologically abuse your partner."[3] Contempt is a deliberate hurt, and it's wielded like a baseball bat. It's the name calling, the making fun of, the put-downs. The results of physical abuse are apparent on the outside—the bruises, the black eyes—but the wounds from being battered by contempt are every bit as raw; they just exist on the inside.

Once contempt has come to visit your marriage, defensiveness comes into play.

Defensiveness

The natural response to being pummeled by contempt is to defend yourself. After all, contempt is not a message of love and understanding; it's a blow meant to shock, to hurt, to gain advantage and superiority. Defensiveness seems very appropriate. Unfortunately, it only leads a couple to further conflict and misunderstanding.

That certainly was true for Larry and Holly, and it became more evident when Larry's mother passed away. Although he and his mother had never been close, her death stirred up some complex feelings. He didn't miss her as much as lament the fact that he'd never had a good relationship with her. It would have been good for him to be able to share these feelings with Holly. Before they were married, he would have, and she would have listened and supported him. But not now. The instant the news of his mother's death came, Holly's back went up. Although she didn't say it, she found the fact that he would spend even a moment mourning his mother when he resented her even talking to hers seemed the greatest of hypocrisy. Sensing this, Larry's defensives mobilized and he shut his feelings down. Then he got terribly angry because he had to. His anger went unexpressed, at least in words, but it appeared in other ways—a general sullenness, the inability to say anything kind.

Defensiveness causes spouses to build separate forts. When defensiveness takes hold, one or both partners have usually been hurt and are simply trying to ward off future pain. Neither partner wants to take ownership of the problems. In protecting themselves, partners also have a hard time receiving love. At this stage, quality communication is virtually impossible, and stonewalling soon follows.

Stonewalling

Stonewalling is perhaps the saddest of the four horses in the communication breakdown. At least one partner no longer trusts the other and is seriously afraid of being hurt. Because of this fear, the one stonewalling usually presents a cold and unresponsive demeanor to his or her mate—a stone wall, if you will, to deal with.

And that's what Holly began presenting to Larry. Rather than trying to break through the growing hostility to discuss their problem openly, Holly found it easier to see Larry as the source of all conflict in their marriage and to reduce that conflict by simply not participating. Whenever Holly perceived danger, she slipped behind her stone wall of protection.

Stonewalling is dangerous to the continued health of a relationship because it signifies that one or both partners have simply given up or decided to stop working through issues. Now at first, the stone wall might only come up at certain times, when certain issues bubble to the surface. Later, as things grind on, the stone wall grows like the Great Wall of China and surrounds the stonewaller to the point where very little, if any, communication gets in. Interestingly, Gottman estimates about 85 percent of stonewallers are men.[4] But whether the stonewaller is the husband or the wife, that stone wall represents the growing distance between them—and it's an arid distance, a distance that will not close. As stonewalling increasingly becomes the norm, it marks the beginning of serious marital breakdown and takes the heart right out of a spoken, "I love you."

You can easily see how these behaviors only add to the ever-increasing dissatisfaction in a relationship. The more criticism or faultfinding there is, the more contempt each partner will show toward the other, and more defensiveness will emerge. And with more defensiveness, the stone wall encompasses more.

A Word of Caution about the Four Horses

If you see the four horses prancing around your house from time to time—that is, if you've responded to your partner now and again with criticism, contempt, defensiveness, or stonewalling—don't automatically assume that your relationship has hit rock bottom and there's no hope of restoration. Sometimes we get caught up in these patterns of communication. Usually we hear it in ourselves or see a spouse's hurt reaction and begin our sincere apologies. Marriage becomes endangered, however, when the four horses take up residence—when you're feeding those horses daily and they're getting bigger and stronger.

Are the four horses familiar to you? Are they standing guard over your pain? Do they keep your spouse at bay while deep inside you cry for someone to simply love you?

What about your marriage? Do you feel the criticism the moment you step into the house? Do you deal with each other with contempt rather than respect? Do you react defensively, or maybe just step behind your stone wall? If you're nodding your head yes, then perhaps you're caught in the vicious cycle of disaffection.

Step #2: Raising the Bar

Larry and Holly remained very active in the church as their marriage began to experience trouble. Church seemed the last thing they wanted to abandon. In fact, as things deteriorated more at home, the church became more important. Of course, they didn't discuss their problems with anyone there—it just didn't seem appropriate. So they were seen as youthful, energetic, and on fire for the Lord.

Until the Christmas potluck, that is. Toward the middle of the evening, right after the talent show, as everyone was finishing up their meals, Larry got up to help clear away the plates, but he got only about two steps from the table.

"You didn't do it," Holly said, in a voice far above a whisper.

"I didn't do what?" Larry asked, surprised.

"You didn't get me any dessert," she said.

Larry could see other people looking their way, and he motioned her to be still. "I didn't think you wanted any." He stepped back toward her, but she didn't lower her voice.

"Why wouldn't I want any?" Holly asked, her tone angry. "I've always had dessert in the past."

"Then why didn't *you* get some?"

"Because you're my husband, and husbands get their wives dessert. That's what loving husbands do."

"I figured you were old enough to get your own food," Larry said, both embarrassed and angry. *What is she talking about?* he thought. *And how could this be worth nailing me here?*

"I just thought that maybe tonight you'd do something to at least show me you care."

Suddenly she remembered where they were. Both embarrassed and very angry now, Holly and Larry beat a quick retreat to the car, then home, then to their separate corners. When they told me about the incident, Holly said this, "It's been so awful between us. I was just hoping that maybe in some small way he'd show me he loved me, like he did when we were dating. I just want him to prove that he cares. I need something to hold on to. You can't blame me for that, can you?"

Has this ever happened to you? Has your spouse suddenly erupted about relatively nothing? Yet it's obviously something that seems very important to your mate, something that means "love" to him or her. Your mate has raised the bar in the name of love. "All I want is to be loved!" is the heart's cry. Now there isn't anything wrong with wanting to be loved. But follow the cycle.

Raising the bar often sets a love trap for your mate. It creates a hurdle your mate must leap in order to prove his or her love. And often your mate doesn't know the hurdle exists. Holly raised the bar by deciding that if Larry didn't get her dessert, if he didn't wait on her as any "loving husband" would, he didn't love her anymore. Larry had no intention of waiting on Holly. Not only didn t he feel much warmth toward Holly because of the pressures tearing at their relationship, but getting her food also left him open to criticism—about getting her the wrong thing or the wrong amount. So he did nothing. And he got nailed for it.

Raising the bar is a form of desperation used by spouses who are just flat wiped out. One or both partners want assurance that they're still loved so they set the hurdle—in secret. One client gave her husband two weeks to come home from work with flowers, then waited with bated breath. Another substituted the flowers for a sexual advance. Yet another with merely a call from work during the day. As the cycle spirals, the bars become increasingly high, and increasingly not hurdled. Raising the bar is a horribly destructive act, and it's doomed to failure. Which, not so surprisingly, is the next step.

Step #3: Sensing Failure in the Relationship

The instant Larry heard the words *You didn't get me dessert*, he felt guilty. Holly was right. He hadn't brought her what she wanted. Before they were married, he would have. When they went to parties, she'd find the seats and he'd get the food. And he'd always known just what she wanted and how much to get. He'd been uncanny in this ability. It wasn't based in ESP, he just loved her and knew what pleased her. But things had changed. He no longer cared as much about pleasing Holly, about being sensitive to her every need. But he hated failure, and it seemed that all he experienced now was failure in the relationship, which, in turn, increased his feelings of shame and guilt. Then he gets mad and she feels bad.

Holly, too, remembered the days when she would find the seats while Larry got food. They worked together in those days and that's why she set the bar where she'd set it. And Larry had failed. Although she knew her test wasn't as valid as it could be, that didn't matter. Larry didn't love her like he used to. And that hurt. Her sense of failure gave way to increased anger and frustration.

That sense of failure leads right to the next step.

Step #4: Evaluating the Relationship Negatively

The talk Larry and Holly had with their pastor was brief. They just said they were having a bad day and things got a little out of hand. On the way home neither spoke. They were locked in the cellars of their own minds and thinking the same thing: Their relationship—their marriage—was getting worse. And the worse they perceived it, the less each became willing to invest in it. They'd reached a dangerous point. They'd developed the CNN Syndrome—all news is basically bad news. And if they're not careful, both can become consumed by how their mates are failing the marriage: *His insensitivity is driving me away. Her nagging is driving me nuts. He's spending too much time with friends and not enough with me.*

No matter what your mate is doing at this point, that behavior is wrecking your marriage and tearing your relationship. And your *mate's* doing it. In this step you do something that is very destructive to your marriage: You vilify your mate. He or she is no longer just someone you're having trouble getting along with, he or she has become the villain of the piece. There is something almost evil going on—whatever he or she is doing, it's on purpose and without regard for how it's hurting you. Negative thoughts and distortions begin to abound.

So now there's a need for greater self-preservation.

Step #5: Increasing the Need for Self-Preservation

As your partner becomes the villain, the walls that protect you go up faster and become thicker. And just to make sure you're safe, you evaluate every move your spouse makes: *That's strange. Could my partner be getting ready to hurt me again?* Your cry for love is met with rejection. So you live in eternal vigilance. And when that happens, the spontaneity in your marriage drains away. It's silly to be spontaneous with someone who's out to hurt you. Defense takes planning. And, of course, the joy in your marriage suffers even more. So much of the joy in marriage stems from the humor and spontaneity shared by two people who love each other.

Often the assault on joy comes from another direction as well. In distress, we notoriously "default to our strengths."[5] The organized person begins to organize everything. The spontaneous person forgets responsibilities. We begin to hate those little things we used to find endearing in our mates, those opposites of our own personalities that brought us a sense of joy and peace. For instance, a gregarious person who chose a mate with a sense of order and responsibility may have seen those traits as a way of grounding him or her in reality. Now they are seen as controlling, intrusive, and dominating. Or the orderly person with a streak of perfectionism may have liked his or her mate's unpredictability, those splashes of spontaneity. Now they are seen as childish, even foolish—certainly not caring.

This also leads to our needs being increasingly unmet, which leads to increased self-medication and distancing.

Cycling Back

As more of the joy in a marriage dies, the cycle circles back on itself repeatedly, intensifying. "I am unhappy with this marriage" becomes "I hate this marriage," and finally, "I want out of this marriage."

The Response Cycle—A Cycle within a Cycle

As the cycle of disaffection grinds on, the response cycle grinds within it. [6] It goes like this: When a spouse complains, as Holly did at being taken from her family, and her complaint is ignored, that leads the offended partner to sulk. When you complain to a loved one, you expect to be heard and expect the loved one to do something to rectify the situation. Holly expected Larry to somehow help her solve the problem—through special phone rates, or frequent visits home, or at least through consideration and sensitivity. But he did none of those things, and she withdrew inside herself and began to sulk.

Sulking is a way of calling attention to pain without saying anything about it. Since the complaint was ignored, we hope our sadness, our sulking, will show the offending spouse how hurt we are. The hope is that the offending spouse will come to his or her senses and make things better—finally. Of course, Larry didn't. He became more adamant and when he did, his actions had the effect of discounting Holly's feelings; her feelings weren't important enough to get him to do what she wanted. This takes sulking to the next step—accusation.

"You don't want me to be happy. You know my mother and I are close. You just want to control me." Holly didn't believe those things as she said them. At the time, she believed Larry was being terribly inconsiderate, but she knew he didn't actually want her to be unhappy, nor did she think he was trying to control her. She knew he just wanted his own selfish way. So, like her original complaint and her sulking, her accusations demanded a response. Holly hoped Larry would come back with, "Of course I want you to be happy, and I know that being away from your mother is making you unhappy, so we'll—" and here he would provide the solution to her problem. But Larry didn't respond that way or in any other satisfactory way.

And so accusations moved to the next level, threats. "You keep acting like this about my mother and I'll call her in the morning and leave the phone off the hook all day." And, "You want to see me unhappy? I'll show you unhappy. You just wait."

A Final Word

As the cycle of disaffection thickens the wall between marriage partners, the response cycle muddies the communication waters.

The cycle of disaffection can also become extremely threatening and overwhelming—easily spinning out of control. By forcing you to work harder and harder on your marriage just to seemingly stay even, it can quickly suck the life out of you. Excessive moodiness or even deep depression or anxiousness can result.

Next we'll take a look at the gaps unmet needs can create and how filling them unwisely can lead to the destruction of a marriage.

TEN

UNMET NEEDS

*In our fast-paced world men and women
need each other more, not less.*
—*Judith Wallerstein and Sandra Blakeslee*

*D*id you recognize your marriage in the preceding chapter? Of course in every marriage there are isolated occurrences of each of those destructive behaviors, but if your marriage is beginning to be defined by them, particularly if you can see criticism, contempt, defensiveness, and stonewalling consistently at work, your marriage is in trouble. And part of that trouble is caused by another dimension that exists as a result of the process of disaffection, the gaps that arise.

Filling the Gaps

Nature hates a vacuum. For example, wind is created when there's an area of low atmospheric pressure, and the air from a high-pressure system rushes in to fill it. The same sort of thing happens with humans. Distancing creates little vacuums—gaps in a marriage, if you will—formed by unmet needs.

When you become distanced from your spouse, the needs God designed to be met in marriage go unmet. And, since nature and relationships rush to fill vacuums, distancing nudges partners to seek ways to get their needs met, for example, through:

- friends—suddenly you're out with the girls or the guys instead of home every night

- workaholism—your job becomes your spouse and gets all of you but your irritability

- your kids—the kids and their needs become all important, and worse, you expect your needs to be satisfied by them, placing a responsibility on them they were never designed to fulfill

- family—holding on to an unhealthy tie to parents or submerging yourself in a family member's troubles makes you feel needed

- unhealthy spirituality—you may try to woo God to get Him on your side rather than create a healthy relationship with Him

- opposite sex friendships—you find yourself having lunch alone with a coworker of the opposite sex who makes you feel important

- false intimacy—you may bury yourself in pornography or romance novels, where your needs are "met vicariously"

- food or drink—you try to pack the empty places in your life with flavors and a false sense of being full

- perfectionism—in an effort to show yourself as above the turmoil, you become perfect in all you do and, in doing so, alienate and separate yourself from those closest to you

Before long, as your needs are increasingly met by elements outside the marriage, the vicious cycle kicks in, and you spiral farther and farther away from your spouse.

The problem with this dimension to the cycle of disaffection is that these *things* that fill the gap all become important. Too important. So you may not only be distancing yourself from your mate but also feel a strong undercurrent that draws you away from your mate. And when you do begin to reconcile, it may become difficult to give these things up. That takes us to where I didn't want to go before: the *affair*.

Meet Toni and Jake

Toni put Jake through law school by working as a receptionist at a growing software development company—we'll call it Thortek. Putting him through law school was something they'd agreed on when they got married, and they both knew that he'd be studying long hours, so the rigors of those first three years were expected. When graduation came, however, Toni's expectations changed. Jake was through studying, and she expected him home more often. She was starved for his attention and affection. But Jake had taken a job. Junior attorneys can be little more than slaves, and that's what Jake became. There were endless days and evenings of research, of putting together depositions, of being at a partner's beck and call. And, frankly, Toni resented it. But at least they had their weekends. Jake made a point of keeping his weekends as free as he could, and he succeeded to a large extent. And those weekends were their salvation. They took walks and worked together in the garden and now and again took day trips. And at night they fixed dinner together—something special with complicated recipes.

Toni, however, had those long evenings to fill. The employees at Thortek were encouraged to take software classes, and she not only took the classes but also learned how to program. She developed a small program that helped the software engineers at her company communicate better. It wasn't a big deal, but it was innovative and caught the attention of the company's management. She was taken off the reception desk and made part of a development team. Although she was a reasonable programmer her true talent lay in software design. She had a knack for seeing the complexity of people-activity and making sense out of it.

Toni is an attractive woman, and she caught the eye of the VP of sales. He sensed she would be good at going into various customer sites, seeing how they do business, then fitting Thortek's software into the business. Suddenly Toni was wearing Liz Claiborne suits to work, making a big income (with commissions and bonuses it reached six figures), and loving the excitement of her new position.

Jake immediately saw the advantage of Toni's stroke of good fortune and chalked it up to the Lord actually helping *him* out. With as much money as she was making, he could leave the firm and start his own. Her income would give him the breathing room to court new clients, and they could begin living a normal life again.

So he handed in his resignation, found an office, and began making his plan reality. Within a week or two, he had his first clients. "God is truly on our side in this," he told her one evening.

"I think so," she replied. "Oh, Thortek is making a push at Boeing, in Seattle. I'll be there for a few days."

Toni stayed over the weekend so she could attend a customer dinner on Saturday night. When she returned Tuesday, she announced they'd gotten the business. Jake, of course, was happy for her.

"You're going to be home for a while, aren't you?" Jake asked.

"Boeing just bought McDonnell Douglas and I need to go to L.A. for a couple of days."

She was there over another weekend. Although she wasn't gone every weekend, her evenings began to fill up, and Jake found himself responding more and more to her schedule. Since Toni was in sales, she often had clients to entertain. When that happened locally, Jake went along. This he particularly resented, for at these functions, he was "Mr. Toni." Wasn't he the attorney? Wasn't he the man of the family? Wasn't he the one who had struggled through college then three years of law school? Yet here he was "Mr. Toni." It drove him nuts.

But what hurt more than anything was that her career had pretty much taken over her life, and he didn't feel he was a part of it anymore. Selling software had replaced him.

When he explained his feelings to Toni, she promised to get a handle on her busy life. "But you have to remember, I waited on you to come home for years. Now it's your turn."

Actually what Jake remembered was that he'd married a woman who loved cooking, taking care of the house, and planning for children. This new Toni wasn't that woman at all; she had a housekeeper, ordered in gourmet food, and talked about putting off children for at least five more years.

It seemed as though the more Jake tried to persuade her to return to the nest, the more intense her desire for a career became. She actually seemed angry that he kept bringing it up, and more and more often she brought up her sacrifice for him and how it was his turn to make the sacrifice for her. There was just no discussing their problems. And Jake could easily see that he just wasn't needed.

The Silent Killer

Distancing became the silent killer of Toni and Jake's marriage. Since distancing is a deliberate, positive response to protect yourself, the negative effects of distancing go unrealized until things become severely strained. As we've seen, it often begins with small injustices or minor inconsiderate acts and quickly builds. And as the gap grows, so does the need to fill it.

Filling That Gap

She looked helpless sitting in his office—with large soulful eyes that she frequently dabbed with a tissue. Her name was Grace, and she told the story of having been neglected by her husband and catching him in an affair with one of his clients.

Jake's heart instantly went out to her. Neglect was a terrible thing. If anyone knew that to be true, he did. After getting all the necessary information from her, he invited her to lunch. She gratefully accepted, and they found themselves at a small French place. It was a warm summer day, so they ate outside beneath the red and white umbrellas.

She didn't talk much, but she listened well—and he craved a good listener. They parted after lunch, but when he get back to the office he realized that he'd forgotten a whole page of questions he should have asked. He called her. After asking the questions, he realized she shouldn't be alone at this delicate time. He invited her to dinner. Toni was out of town.

Dinner was at an out-of-the-way bistro. After dinner as they enjoyed coffee, she began to talk about her hopes for marriage, about her hopes for children and even grandchildren. It became Jake's turn to listen, which he did rapturously. He felt he had found a soul mate. They said good night reasonably early without plans to see each other again until her divorce proceedings required it. But, of course, she was to call if she needed anything.

At home, Jake began to feel terribly guilty. What was he doing? He loved Toni, had always loved Toni, planned to build the rest of his life with her, and here he was longing to see another woman. Yet this woman seemed to need his strength, his wit, his ability to understand and come to her aid. He so longed for those things. When Toni called that night from somewhere east, he tried to recapture some of those feelings with her. He told her how much he loved and missed her. How much he wanted her back home and looked forward to the weekend. "Maybe we can do something special," he said.

"Can't be Saturday night. The boss wants us over at his place. I think we're going to close this thing today, and we're going to want to celebrate. This is a big one. I think we're about to get our hot tub."

"Okay," Jake said, let down. "Saturday's open."

Not ten minutes after he hung up, the phone rang. Grace spoke with a sweet expectancy in her voice. "You were so nice at dinner. I wanted to thank you." And they talked until one in the morning.

Jake and Grace continued seeing one another over the next two weeks. At first they tried to keep it in the context of her divorce, but after a few days of that, they stopped the charade. They just wanted to be together. Although they kept the relationship platonic, Jake knew that couldn't last forever. Before long their lips would meet, then only God knew after that.

God—the thought of God caused Jake to pull back. But only for a moment. The pull of this relationship was just too strong. And before they knew it, they were on a nearby park bench kissing and talking and kissing some more. In the middle of it all, Jake pulled back. An overwhelming sense that everything just seemed to be getting out of hand swept over him. He knew that life with Toni would never be the same if he continued this.

The next day at the airport, waiting for Toni to return, Jake faced the most difficult decision of his life. He knew that if he and Toni were going to experience the happiness they had once known together, he would have to drop his feelings for Grace and invest all his energy in his marriage.

Sitting there, with people milling all around, he wondered how she would respond. He knew he loved her and was proud of her unexpected success, but ultimately, he longed for his mate to need him and care for him. If she responded by putting her career first as she had recently—well, he didn't know what he would do. But he knew now, at least, that he would have to take the first steps in breaking down the barriers. He just hoped she would do the same.

What about Your Gaps?

What have you filled your gaps with? Be honest. Sometimes we don't like to think that we've failed at our primary need-satisfier, marriage, and are out looking for other things to cram into our lives. Look critically at your life and where you needs are satisfied. As I've said before, a spouse can't satisfy all your needs—there will be some that will either go unmet or be met outside the marriage. But those are things that can legitimately be met outside the marriage. One mate might like gardening—might have a need to feel the soil and watch things grow. Being a gardener is not going to threaten a marriage. At least it shouldn't. But the need for relationship and intimacy, the need for safety and significance, the need to feel loved and important—those things are part of a healthy marriage. If you're getting them from somewhere else, there's a problem. Particularly if you are engaged in an affair. If you are investing large parts of you in something or someone other than your spouse and are receiving large returns, whether sexual or not, you're getting needs met somewhere else. I'm thinking particularly about things happening on the Internet nowadays. Even though people have not laid eyes on one another, they're involved in false intimacies. Step back and get control now.

Important statistics show that nearly 50 percent of marriages struck by a spouse having an affair survive.[1] Even if your marriage has suffered from an affair, either yours or your spouse's, there is hope. It could be you're so angry that reconciliation is not one of your goals, but it can be.

A Final Word

In this chapter we've looked at the gaps that appear in marriages, how they're filled, and what that means to the fabric of a marriage. In the next chapter we'll talk about another cycle that also leaves gaps, but often these gaps go unfilled and leave both partners feeling empty, with a deep, seemingly irreparable sense of loss.

ELEVEN

THE DOWNWARD
SPIRITUAL SPIRAL

For all that is in the world—the lust of the flesh, the lust of the
eyes, and the pride of life—is not of the Father but is of the world.

—*1 John 2:16*

I alluded to the downward spiritual spiral in the previous
chapter when Jake, desirous of a relationship with Grace,
suddenly, almost without thinking, brought God into his
relationship. Instead of heeding what he knew God would want him
to do, he at first pushed God's admonitions aside and continued down
the path he'd chosen for himself.

That's the way of it. We do things we know God would not sanction, yet we become increasingly confident that God understands and
actually approves our course. It's a frightening paradox, and it ends
with someone reaching spiritual rock bottom and stating, and *mean-*
ing, some pretty remarkable things, like: "I believe God just doesn't
want me to stay in this marriage anymore."

Let's look at what takes people to this point.

An Example of the Downward Spiritual Spiral

Carla prided herself on the house she kept. John found this a little strange because the house wasn't all that neat. Although it was reasonably picked up, there were always little compromises—a scatter of magazines alongside the couch, the toothpaste laying squished and without a cap on the bathroom counter. And these things would stay that way for days. But Carla still got upset when he left things laying around. "Don't you ever put anything away?" she asked one Saturday afternoon when he left out a screwdriver.

"Sure I do," he said. Then he intentionally let the screwdriver lay on the kitchen counter. He didn't like the idea of being told he had to put his tools away immediately. They always got put away eventually. Anyway, when there's a riot of magazines near the couch, what's the big deal about a screwdriver on the counter?

John knew Carla worked hard around the house—or at least she said she did—so there was also a part of him that knew he should put the screwdriver back. But it was his house too. He walked away and sat down to watch the Pittsburgh Steelers' game.

This act of independence was a small thing, but John remembered it when he finally came in with Carla for counseling.

The first step in the downward spiritual spiral is the rationalization of sin. Usually it's something small and seemingly insignificant. Yet, it's the first step, which makes it very significant, and what makes it more so is that we rationalize hurting the person we've pledged to love.

As he sat there watching the game, John's conscience began to bother him. He loved Carla, and he'd just thumbed his nose at her. Granted it was just a screwdriver—but still, she'd wanted to keep the house looking reasonably tidy and he'd refused to cooperate.

But the house isn't immaculate. The only reason she wanted me to put that tool away is to exert control. That's all this is about. Control. Well, this is my house, too, and I get to exercise control now and then.

And so he sat watching the game with the idea that all she was doing was trying to control him running in his head like a tape. Then another tape started playing, in the background at first, but it soon became louder. *If she finds out how I feel, she'll come unglued. She'll misinterpret what I'm talking about and really be hurt. I just don't want* to be told what to do in my own house, that's all. She's already jealous every time I'm late from work. All I need is for her to get more insecure.

At half-time John decided he'd put his wife through enough and went into the kitchen to put the screwdriver away. It was gone. "I already did it," Carla said, a hint of sarcasm in her voice. "I didn't want you to hurt your back or anything."

Some very subtle things happened here.

God tells us we're to love our spouses; Paul said men are to love their wives and give of themselves as Jesus gave Himself for the church. Wives are to love their husbands, submitting to them as we submit before the Lord. Satan, the world, and our flesh war with us and try to get us to do the opposite. That war was going on in John over that screwdriver. Now this wasn't the first time John had battled Carla over putting things away. He admits that. But this was the first time he didn't repent of it, say he was sorry, and try to get back in Carla's good graces. And although he had a twinge of conscience, John liked exerting his authority—his manhood, if you will. He felt himself stand a little taller. He was just a little more the master of his domain. In his mind he'd gotten his way.

The Steps in the Downward Spiritual Cycle

The steps in the downward spiritual cycle often go like this:

1. You sin in some way against your spouse. The more often you go through the cycle, the more destructive the transgressions get.

2. You feel guilt and/or shame, but instead of repenting right away and seeking forgiveness, which is God's way out of the predicament, you rationalize.

3. You see some value in what you've done. There's a benefit there for you.

4. You convince yourself it's something God would sanction. Or if

He wouldn't directly approve, as a loving God, He surely wouldn't want you to suffer by not getting the benefit.

5. You fear that your true feelings might become exposed, so you keep what you've done secret.

6. You yield to temptation again. This takes you back to step 1. But this time, it's much easier to yield to temptation because your heart is that much more hardened and you've reaped a benefit that you would like to get again.

And so the cycle continues. The cycle finally ends with your warping and fashioning God's Word to your own ends. Subtly at first, blatantly later.

How the Cycle Spun for John

Although there are only a few steps to the cycle, it's repeated with increasing frequency as time goes on and your relationships with your spouse and the Lord deteriorate. John can remember the second time he cycled through it. About a week after the screwdriver incident, he decided to exert his independence again.

John's Second Time Through

As we've seen, Carla has difficulty with jealousy. Because her beloved father had cheated on her mother, and because he was such a saint in so many other ways—at least in her eyes—she believed her mother when she said that all men eventually cheat on their wives. John, of course, had no intention of cheating on Carla. It was the last thing he wanted to do. But her jealousy was getting to him. Because he knew she worried when he came home late from work or if he had to go out by himself during the weekend, he'd kept those times to a minimum—even to the point of not staying late when others in his position at the factory would have. He was beginning to believe that his job performance was suffering. He decided he wouldn't placate Carla anymore.

It was a bold decision, and the moment he made it he felt his conscience activate again. But only for a moment. *Carla has to learn that I'm trustworthy,* he said to himself, and at the first opportunity, he began her "training" program. The object of her first lesson was his secretary—and a perfect lesson she would be. She was about his age, twenty-eight, single, and a very good worker. He decided to reward her with an invitation to dinner. Just the two of them.

"Sure," she said. "Just the two of us? I'm not sure it would be a good idea for us to go out without your wife."

"It'll be fine. Anyway," he began the lie, "the only night I have free is tomorrow, and my wife's busy."

"Well, if you think it'll be okay. It would be nice. I have worked hard. It'll be nice to get the recognition."

"And I'll write a letter for your personnel file as well."

As it turned out, the next night was Carla's night to attend a quilting class at church although she would have decided not to go had she realized a dinner out with her husband was an alternative. John wanted that to be part of the lesson. After all, he wasn't jealous when she went out. Why should she be when he did?

And so he had dinner with his secretary. It was a pleasant couple of hours, and he was home by the time Carla got home. Telling her was a calculated event, just like the rest of the lesson. "Oh, I almost forgot," he said as they were getting ready for bed, "I took my secretary to dinner tonight. For all the extra work she's been doing. We went to Antonio's. Great lasagna at Antonio's."

"Your secretary? She's only been with you for six months."

"But she's worked very hard. I thought she deserved it." And he went about brushing his teeth and getting ready for bed. He almost laughed to himself when he finally snuggled up to her and found her emotionally as cold as ice.

At two o'clock he woke to find the television on, the ghostly gray glow the only light in the room. Carla sat stiffly in bed as if she were watching it. "How come you're still awake?" he asked.

"When did this thing with your secretary start?" she asked, the anger behind the words charging through them like electricity.

"What thing?" he asked, working at sounding innocent.

How This Time through Ended Up

This second time through the cycle, John's conscience was only a minor stumbling block. The perceived end result—the hope that he would eventually get Carla off his back—was, by far, more important to him. A few days afterward, his guilt did erupt, but, again, only for a little while. *You're supposed to love her. You know she has this problem. It's no big thing. You just reassure her, let her know what you're doing so she understands, and allow her to check up on you periodically. None of this puts you out at all.* But that tape only ran a few times and then shut down. Another became a lot louder. *She's only trying to control you with all this jealousy. The last thing you need is to be controlled.* He liked that tape a lot better. *Besides,* he thought, *surely God wants me to toughen her up. Surely He wants me to teach her a lesson. Surely He doesn't want me to have to put up with that kind of stuff. I'm loving her by doing this.*

John's Spiritual Life Began to Suffer

John and Carla's attendance at church became sporadic. He just didn't get as much out of the sermons as he once had. "Why don't we just take a rain check this Sunday?" he began saying more often. What he didn't realize was that his spiritual life was beginning to suffer. John had spent a few minutes every morning reading his Bible and praying since he was sixteen. But now that he was finding meaning in the Word of God that just wasn't there, he began reading his Bible only a couple of times a week, and then not at all. He became uncomfortable in the Word. Of course he didn't recognize it as such; he actually felt he knew the Word pretty well and that his relationship with the Father through Jesus was in pretty good shape. In fact, he felt he had a special relationship with Him, like the favorite son who's allowed to get away with a little more than his siblings. He was beginning to feel above the Word, as if it applied to everyone else, but not to him—God loved him just too much to worry about a few minor infractions. So he started living his life with a princely arrogance instead of a godly humility. In biblical terms, John's heart was getting hard. For it to soften again, he would have to repent and begin to selflessly love his wife again. And he wasn't ready to do that.

John's Last Time through the Cycle

As time went on, John cycled through the downward spiral hundreds of times, and each time he tried to wrest more and more control from Carla. To Carla's way of thinking he was just trying to torture her. But that torture was tempered by the fact that he was also working at being a better husband, by his definition. Even though he made no effort to accommodate her fears or help her to find reasonable solutions to them, he prided himself on doing nice things for her. Every morning he made her coffee to go with her newspaper in bed; he took her out for expensive dinners; they went on nice vacations; and birthdays and Christmas always found him buying expensive presents for her. So, when asked if he was working for the betterment of their marriage, he always answered with a resounding yes. But he was also frequently late, and he frequently shook his relationships with other women in Carla's face. Every time she showed any weakness, he told her that she needed help. He was the perfect husband, so any problems they were having were her problems. He also worked the "screwdriver issue"—control around the house—as often as he could. He never lifted a finger to clean up anything. When challenged, he'd just say, "I work twelve hours a day. Cleaning up is your contribution."

If asked about his spiritual life, he'd say it was great. And he'd be telling what he perceived as the truth. By now he was feeling pretty special before the Lord. He was the favored son; he and God were very tight and because of that, he was able to do just about anything and everything he wanted. God would take care of him.

And so the straw that broke Carla's emotional back finally came.

By now John had progressed to second-level management at the plant and had managers working for him. And one of those men, someone Carla only knew as Watkins, had a reputation as a womanizer. He'd actually been sued for sexual harassment, a charge that had made the papers. The suit went nowhere because the woman's courage faltered, but the scuttlebutt was that he'd done everything she'd accused him of and probably more. When Carla confronted John about him, John laughed it off. "When you have as many women around as we have—well, guys will be guys."

"Will you be?" she asked pointedly.

"No. Other guys will be."

Persistent wounding produces calluses. That's why after the first few weeks of summer, kids can walk barefooted over hot asphalt unfazed. Carla had developed emotional calluses. That didn't mean her jealousy had subsided, rather it had become more of a spear to stab John with. Her opportunity to do so came quickly.

John planned to attend a training seminar in Dallas. About two days before he was due to leave, Carla heard John on the phone discussing the trip and found out that Watkins was going too. John with a womanizer in Dallas. Carla blew.

"I can't take this anymore. I really can't. You know how upset I get about these things, and you insist on rubbing my nose in them. Watkins will drag you down with him. Maybe he already has."

Strangely enough, this was a fight John had been itching for; he could hardly wait to let her have it. "You've been doing this ever since we got married. And it's time you got your head fixed. I'm not cheating on you. I won't cheat on you—God knows why I won't, but I won't. You've been a burden to me and my career. I have no idea how I've gotten as far as I have with all this stupid interference."

"What do you mean, 'God knows why I won't'?" she sputtered. "Do you think God wants you to cheat on me?"

"God can't want me to be going through this. He just can't."

And not a half hour later Carla ended up where we met her at the beginning of chapter 1, in the airport, frightened, not sure what she should do next—defeated and sure God had abandoned her.

John, on the other hand, remained calm and self-righteous. And that's the tragedy of the downward spiritual spiral—during the entire journey, the Word of God becomes so warped by a self-interest-based interpretation, that even the most flagrant sins become something God would sanction. When John first came into counseling, he told me, "God can't want me to stay in this marriage. It's against everything He's given me. It hinders the career He's given me, the friends He's given me, the talents He's given me. It's against everything He's given me for fun. Everything. How could He possibly want me to be married to that woman? How? It just doesn't make sense."

And, of course, we come to believe this because to not do so means we have to change: We have to repent; we have to humbly seek forgiveness; we have to begin living selflessly; we have to become vulnerable again and trust the Lord to keep our emotions safe as we recommit ourselves to Him. And we're not ready to do that.

What about You?

All this boils down to one question: *What about you?* If you are tolerating what you shouldn't in your life, the seeds are being sown and taking root. Take real care. There aren't many warning signs. Look seriously at how you behave in your marriage and, as truthfully as you can, ask yourself how far you've drifted from doing what, in your heart of hearts, you know God wants for your marriage. Are you doing things that you know to run contrary to the Word of God but justifying them? Or do you feel in some way outside God's law? It's easy to do. After all, God loves us and promises to never leave or forsake us. And since this includes when we fall into sin, it's easy to believe that whatever we do, we'll remain in God's graces. Are you counting on that right now? Remember, James 1:15b says quite pointedly, when you yield to sin, it leads to death. Separation. Brokenness.

If this is true for you, stop right now. Acknowledge your sin, come clean about it, ask God for mercy, accept His forgiveness, then discipline yourself to godliness. Don't forget 1 John 1:9, "If we confess our sins, He is faithful and just to forgive us our sins and to cleanse us from all unrighteousness." If your sin has hurt anyone, you need to repair that as well. A clean heart like the one God speaks of in Psalms 51:10 is our road to freedom.

A Final Word

Over the last few chapters I've shown you what happens to a relationship when it slides down the cycle of disaffection and the downward spiritual cycle. When couples hit the bottom of both cycles, when their disaffection from one another is total and they've justified their marital decline spiritually, when they've reached relational and spiritual emptiness, they come to a place of chronic emotional pain—a place of all-out war.

Twelve

Polarization— The Red Zone

It is always your next move.
—*Napoleon Hill*

hen distancing goes unchecked and a couple's anguish increases, partners polarize. They enter the red zone, a very troubling marital state. They dig in their heels and become increasingly disillusioned about their marriage—particularly about their inability to resolve their unhappiness. It's not unusual for me to hear phrases like, "I've had it. All I do is give, and all she does is take." Or, "I give till it hurts and all he gives is the hurt right back."

In this chapter I'm going to dispassionately dissect this arena so you can see in clearer terms where you are or where you're going.

Why?

Because unless you can understand what's happened, you can't defeat it or hold it at bay while you work to neutralize it and rebuild.

Polarization

What characterizes polarization? Chiefly, you feel tired of fighting and eventually you just want to abandon the fight. Any hope you had for the relationship has dissolved to hopelessness, even helplessness. What makes matters worse is that you probably got to this state in your marriage by battling hard to overcome a broken heart, maybe even a deep depression. Perhaps you're still battling. And all you have to show for your effort is more hurt and more anger, a marriage where love has been replaced by demeaning and devaluing one another—openly.

Your only hope seems to be to erect walls—very thick and strong walls that will withstand and deflect the blows that threaten you. To that end, you begin to disengage from one another. You create an island of isolation. Safely on your island, behind your thick walls, you let a "who cares" attitude take hold—"Who cares who hears or knows?" You no longer have any desire to work on the marriage. It seems like such a waste of time and emotional energy. You need all that energy to protect yourself.

If any of this is true for your marriage, you are probably well on your way to becoming polarized from your spouse.

Vast tides of hurt, anger, and burning resentment swirl in this troubling marital state. Emotional backs are stiffened and heels dug in. Talk, if there is any, becomes extremely demoralizing.

Such a couple's pain is visible. By now family and friends can see the marriage is in serious trouble. Even outsiders recognize it. Frankly, everyone believes the relationship is so severely damaged that it's on life-support and the only thing left is to pull the plug.

No Structure

In a healthy marriage relationship, there's an agreed-upon structure. The partners wake up at a given time and get ready to face the day in a reasonably structured way. They go through the day and evening in the same way. They have rules, boundaries, and roles that they generally follow. And if there's rebellion or variation from the structure, there are prescribed ways of handling it. They avoid chaos, and when it occurs, they dampen it quickly to restore order. Although it sounds a little boring, it creates an environment where two people are free to grow and nurture each other. Paradoxically, the structure even offers opportunity for spontaneity and surprises.

But when you've entered the red zone of polarization, structure and order disintegrate and chaos rules. One day, things are nice, as they should be; the next, the atmosphere is hateful, charged with negative forces. Husbands and wives come home from work when they feel like it, and when they do get home, who knows what they'll find? If the wife stays home with the kids, she may plan dinner without consulting her husband about what time he'll be home or even *if* he'll be home. And she may not particularly care. In fact, she may not want him to come home. Morning is just as chaotic. Family members get up and get their day going with little or no concern for anyone else. If their schedules happen to bump against one another, they make superficial contact. There is very little nurturing.

Weekends are just as disengaged. Partners are not so much ships passing in the night as they are bumper cars who now and again try to occupy the same space at the same time, but if they do it's more of an accident than a planned encounter. Now it's not an indifferent encounter—like bumper cars they have a lot of energy and heat when they come together.

No Direction—No Purpose

When you think of stability, what do you see? I picture two people working for their family's continued success: each partner with a clearly defined, well-thought-out job; each working toward the same goals; each aware of any approaching danger and armed to dispatch the dangers that might be lurking out there.

The polarized relationship has no stability. There is no well-defined direction, and neither partner is working for the good of the relationship. Goals? What are those? And if there's danger afoot, one partner might actually wish that danger on the other. Planning activities for the family becomes impossible. In fact, planning is made doubly difficult by the knowledge that the family might explode apart at any moment. Which, of course, makes a polarized relationship incredibly difficult for children. Above just about anything, children need stability. When they have none, the scars of stress and fear of abandonment form quickly.

No Safety

Remember when you and your spouse were dating? Remember what would happen if you were threatened in any way? Your mate's back would go up, and it didn't matter how formidable the foe, your partner would go in there swinging. Or if you were ill, your mate would wait on you hand and foot. Or if you were in trouble, your mate would do anything to help you out of it.

In a polarized relationship, you're on your own. Instead of working with your partner, you feel threatened. Instead of embracing you, your spouse might embarrass you or put you down. Instead of enjoying your differences, you get hateful comments. That sense of feeling safe and accepted is a thing of the past. Not only is there no one to depend on, but there's no one to even lean on, and there's certainly no one to watch your back.

No Honor

As God tells us in 1 Peter 3:7, in a healthy relationship both partners honor each other—each places importance, great respect, and high worth on the other.[1] Partners honor each other's thoughts, ideas, talents, inclinations, and values. Of course there may be times when they don't agree, and may even battle hard about some things, but when all is said and done, they respect and honor each other. Compromise has nothing to do with power but everything to do with firm belief and desire to move forward and meet goals.

In a polarized relationship, there is little honor. Mostly it's been replaced by contempt. Her ideas are silly; his talents are of little use. At parties he's scatterbrained; she's a bore. When it comes to the kids, one's too hard on them and the other's too easy. When it comes to money, one doesn't make enough and the other spends too much. When it comes to making love, one's never satisfied and the other's always got a headache. Compromise is only an issue of power, and resolution is an issue of weakness and unyielding contempt.

Deep Anger and Resentment

You can feel it. The anger is palpable. The resentment hums like electricity. If the anger were somehow to actually get loose, its strength and focus might destroy them both.

Now and then in healthy relationships anger erupts—either justified or unjustified. But in healthy relationships, the anger is dealt with. If someone sins in anger, eventually that person apologizes, explains, maybe even sheds a few tears. The two then come together again in love because they loved each other in the first place.

Not so in a polarized relationship. This anger runs deep and the reasons for it are visceral. These partners *want* to hurt each other. This anger is only going to get worse. Foreseeing the inevitable result of such behavior, God tells us not to return "evil for evil or reviling for reviling, but on the contrary blessing, knowing that you were called to this, that you may inherit a blessing" (1 Pet. 3:9).

The Destruction of a Relationship

But God's warning has gone unheeded and the partners have gone to war—a total battle of wills. And like any war, victory comes with a defeat—in this case the destruction of the relationship.

Neither partner at this point, in spite of all the anger, hurt, and emotional abandonment, will choose to leave the relationship. That would mean an unacceptable defeat, or perhaps an unfair division of property, or the surrendering of the kids. For whatever reason, instead of cutting and running, they stay to fight it out.

And what a fight it is; it seems to take its own course. Through angry frontal assaults and sneaky midnight raids, through battles of attrition and destructive sieges, through any method that seems to be effective. For instance, if they might end up sharing a quiet breakfast, one will remember an early commitment. If one makes a peacemaking overture, the other might cut it off angrily. And there are the battles in the name of keeping themselves safe from harm, keeping the walls strong and unapproachable. And why not? Getting hurt again is too much to risk. So they keep each other off balance by not giving all.

One way to do this is to keep the level of turmoil high. To this end, negative self-fulfilling prophesies abound. For example, one partner may complain that the other is always angry, then push all the anger buttons. A lack of give and take and a lack of investment in the relationship causes frustration to stay high, hearts to burn with discontentment, and partners to react negatively out of pain.

The constant battles result in a lack of safety, stability, and respect. As everybody is caught up in the relationship's demise, along with all the anger there's also at least one of the following:

- self-isolation (insulating self)
- attack (passing out blame and putting up shields for the hostility)
- self-medication
- perfectionism

Self-Isolation

At least one partner insulates him- or herself from any emotional contact by closing off all opportunities for the other to cause pain. These isolated individuals never count on their partners, never make plans that include them, never expect a particular behavior or expect their spouses to satisfy their physical, emotional, or spiritual needs. They also never open themselves up emotionally. You'll rarely see isolated partners sharing a memory or taking a walk down a country lane "just for old times sake." They keep their distance.

Attack

If one or both partners are on the attack, they're continually try-ing to keep others off balance and on the run. Granted they want to inflict some damage—their rage requires it—but mostly they want to keep from getting hurt. And a strong offense is the best way to do that. These attacks can be verbal or physical. Or the attack could come as blame.

There are a thousand ways one partner can hold the other partner down. You know how to push your partner's buttons, don't you? You know where your mate's neuroses are hidden, and you know how to unlock those closets to let them out. In seconds you can stir up a whole host of emotions—anger, frustration, fear. And you know where to direct them. If you're in attack mode you won't be bashful about using every weapon you've got because you know your partner's not bashful. Please be assured that I am not attributing blame for abuse on the victim. Regardless of the level of tension in a relation-ship, an abuser is an abuser. Period. Responsibility and accountability start and stop there.

Self-Medication

The tension is high; you need to calm down, take care of yourself, protect yourself emotionally. Wouldn't a big hot fudge sundae taste good right now? Or maybe a bag of cookies would help bring those nerves down to manageable size. One or both partners may begin to self-medicate—to put things in their bodies that take them to what seems like a nicer place. It could be food, alcohol, or other substances, including drugs. Over the years you've found what works for you. Maybe as a child, when things got a little stressful, something that tasted good helped. Or in college, before a big test or an even bigger date, a few beers got you through. Now, as the high-tension wires crackle, you go back to familiar territory. Well, if you are self-medicating, stop. See the pattern and realize it only complicates your life. Get help. Do what-ever it takes. Healthy relationships begin with healthy people.

Perfectionism

Perfectionism is a form of isolation and control—you surround yourself with absolute order, no-fault insurance. As an example, let's look at your coffee table. If it is perfectly clean and everything on it is in its proper place, you've controlled the coffee table—it's yours now. You know there's nothing on the coffee table that can hurt you. And, if your partner's in the mood to criticize, there's nothing about that coffee table to find fault with. And best of all, if your partner should mess it up—well, let the games begin. Perfectionism has all these benefits, and it tends to drive everyone away—which may be an unintentional goal. Inside you may blame yourself for what's happening in your marriage. And what better punishment than to be in prison? Perfectionism has that effect. You're not only a prisoner of your drive to have everything around you in perfect order, but you also end up driving away those people who might still be on your side—your children, parents, friends.

The Power Struggle

But there's more. While there is probably isolation, attack, self-medication, and/or perfectionism present in your marriage during this terrible time of polarization, there's another dynamic that is *always* present—the power struggle. It provides the reason for and the energy to fight the war, and achieving power is the spoils of this war.

If your marriage is in trouble, you probably see it. Things are no longer just what they are but territory to be won. The power struggle is fought everywhere and over everything. One of my client couples fought all afternoon and into the night about the order family photographs should hang as they progressed up a staircase. Finally, when neither was able to convince the other, they began throwing the pictures at the wall, shattering the glass all over the carpeted stairway as they did. Their battle had nothing to do with pictures. It had everything to do with territory and victory.

Nowhere is the power struggle more evident than in the bedroom. Sex is such an intimate part of marriage; to control that particular battleground is to control a major part of the marriage, and the needs of the other partner. The war may have these elements to it: One partner may deprive the other. Or one may limit contact. And there's the worst possibility, where one partner brings the other to the point of satisfaction, then leaves him or her unfulfilled. Believe me, that only has to happen once before the drawbridge goes up and the *no trespassing* sign is hung out.

A Final Word

Polarization has an ultimate place to go—the war has an inevitable outcome. We'll cover that in the next chapter.

THIRTEEN

ISLANDS OF ME

Make not your thoughts prisons.
—*William Shakespeare*

*P*icture an island in the South Pacific. Beautiful, isn't it? White sands, blue water skirting and nuzzling the beaches, palm trees rustling in the ocean breezes. The interior is green and sparkling with waterfalls, little lakes, and lagoons—lush with shade, warmth, and tropical fruits. There's an abundant self-sufficiency there that, armed with a good hammock, can make us feel safe and happy.

Now, let's say another island not far off decides it wants to attack our little island; it wants to take it over and harm and enslave us. Suddenly we're forced from our hammocks to build fortifications. We put up fortress walls with gun emplacements. Piers for supplies (which we still need) are fortified and access is tightly controlled. Since our lazy life has been replaced by the need to survive, beauty gives way to dark and strident purpose. At all costs, our island must be defended.

And that's what the final stop on the road to absolute polarization becomes—what we become—islands of me. We do everything to close off our vulnerabilities and become as self-sufficient as possible. We dig in our heals, close down our spirits, turn ourselves inward, and often seethe behind those walls in seeming righteous anger. And we protect ourselves at all cost. But because we may not be schooled in protecting ourselves and because we're not particularly good at fighting, when our borders are threatened we lash out like cats—quickly, indiscriminately, and with claws bared.

Wow. Imagine living it—or maybe you are. My clients have assured me it's every bit like that, even worse. For on the island of me, fear rules the days—fear that our borders will be compromised or that supplies will run out. Fear that we'll never be able to leave the island and find love again. And hopelessness rules the night—the hopelessness of ever finding love again, of ever living a happy day again, of ever being content again.

Sorrow, Emptiness, and Expectation

When you reside on an island of me, all the characteristics of polarization become intensified. Any illusion of a safe relationship has dissolved, stability has gone the way of safety, and all the subtlety has gone out of working toward the relationship's defeat—it's become the obvious order of the day. And you begin to wear anger and resentment right on the chin, daring anyone to take a poke at them.

And what's more, any trace of love has been swept away, bringing sorrow, emptiness, and expectation—and the knowledge that those expectations will never be met. What a horrible place to live. Life there is a never-ending string of painful experiences, many of which are also traps of your own design and construction.

Let's go through a few so that even if you decide not to go forward in trying to recreate your marriage, you'll at least be able to recognize and unravel these particular behavior patterns.

Reactions Based in Pain

On the island of me, pain is bitter. We face rejection, abandonment, and the terror of being emotionally battered by the very person who has promised to love us. Frankly, it's hard to think of a worse pain. And when we see ourselves threatened again, we react out of that pain. We don't stop reacting until the threat's gone away.

The way to stop this cycle is to deal with the pain at its source. If you are in that terrible pain of separation, cleave yourself to the One who loves you, and makes no pretense of anything else. I love what Dr. Charles Stanley says about God's faithfulness: "The wonderful thing about God is that He is never at a distance. He is always beside you. Because faithfulness is part of His nature, He cannot be unfaithful and still be God. Even when you are faithless, He is still faithful."[1] Bring your pain to Jesus, lay it at the foot of the cross, and look to Him for love and warmth instead of to those who have thus far failed you. God will never fail you. Know in your heart of hearts that you are His child. I suggest you memorize all of Romans 8, particularly verse 32: "He who did not spare His own Son, but delivered Him up for us all, how shall He not with Him also freely give us all things?" Your pain is natural. You've been terribly hurt, and you need time to heal. But instead of lashing out in your pain, respond as one above pain. Respond as a child of God.

And, as you're healing, give yourself some time and space. For no one is really threatening you. In Romans 8:28, God tells us, "And we know all things work together for good to those who love God, to those who are the called according to His purpose." So stand tall, take the blow if it comes, and respond as God's child in a gentle strength—in love. Soon the pain will become manageable. It may never completely go away, but it will certainly fade into the background and allow you to live your life in greater harmony. Nothing can separate you from the love of God.

A Distorted View of the Other Island

"He's not the man I married. I want the old Jimmy back. This one's a monster." Could it be that after all you've been through, some of the behavior is an indication of a person in serious pain? Or maybe it's your lens. Do you have a distorted view of your spouse?

Stick a pencil in a glass of water and look at the pencil. Although it appears to have become bent and shortened, it has not. You're viewing that other island, your spouse, as if you've pushed his or her head into a bucket of water—something you might even like to do right now. But remember, your spouse is not evil—he or she is a sinner saved by grace. If your partner has not been saved, keep in mind that you're not the only one who's been hurt. You're looking at another island, at someone defending borders and lashing out from pain just like you. But your partner may respond to kindness with kindness (if you can offer kindness consistently). Your spouse might even be willing to meet you halfway on some issues if you don't seem out for revenge. Remember the Golden Rule? Now that doesn't mean you should show weakness. I don't think anyone respects weakness. But politeness and kindness are not weakness.

Emotional (No Win) Games

Keeping a partner off balance is often the way of this war, and nothing works better than emotional games. They can be intricate, defy logic, and be incredibly effective in allowing us to blameshift. We'll look at three all-too-common games here.

The Demand-Reject-Complain Model

Before Carla and John came to see me, John was in the habit of complaining bitterly that he never had an ironed white shirt: "What do you do all day that you can't take five minutes out to iron one of my shirts? You want me to work in bare skin and a tie?" Frankly, Carla wanted to throw every white shirt he owned into the furnace rather than iron even one. But she gave in and one Saturday morning went into the back bedroom, eager to get the ironing over with so she could get to her garden. She grabbed her iron and got started. Within seconds, John was in that back bedroom. "You're not going to burn my shirt, are you? I can just see you trying to get back at me by scorching it. Come on, you can get that wrinkle out."

It was all Carla could do to keep herself from ironing John's cheeks—at both ends. Swallowing her boiling rage, she stood the iron on its end and unplugged it for safety, then left the room.

The following Monday morning John complained again that he never had a wearable white shirt and wondered aloud about why she couldn't take the time to iron one.

This is a game of self-fulfilling prophesy. Demand something. When it comes reject it. Then complain that you never get what you want. You can easily see how this can keep your partner off balance and wondering.

"*React to Me and* You're *Nuts*"

Building on Carla's insecurities, John often waved his relation-ships with women in front of her and then, when her back went up, called her crazy. Holly, Larry's wife, had a way of playing this game as well. She loved gazebos, and Larry had built her one in their backyard in an effort to ease her homesickness. But instead of helping, the glis-tening white gazebo sometimes brought her to tears. Of course, she was careful to keep those tears from Larry. But she couldn't keep from daydreaming. If he came home from work early, something he often did on Fridays, he would find her out in the gazebo, almost zombielike, staring off. He'd approach her quietly and speak softly, afraid of startling her. "You're daydreaming," he'd say.

"I'm not daydreaming. I saw everything you did. Heard every sound you made. You're nuts."

The next game is by far the most destructive. It occurs over the long term and drives the two of you even farther apart.

Monster Time

In the darkest times for Carla and John, just before they began counseling, Carla became nasty. Anything John said, no matter how innocuous, elicited a terribly nasty retort.

"You want eggs for breakfast?" she'd growl, banging the frying pan around. "I'll give you eggs," she'd continue under her breath. "I'll shove 'em up your nose—that's how you'll get your eggs." Then she'd scream at him. "How do you like that?" Or when the subject of his white shirts came up yet again, she ran two of them over with her car. He kept them to show me—two tire tracks right up the back. Then, no matter how she acted and John reacted—and believe me, he reacted—the results of her actions were his fault.

"But you ruined two of my shirts."

"And you didn't drive me to it? That's all you ever do, drive me to something then blame me for it. Well, it's all your fault. Every stinking little bit of it."

Monster time is horribly destructive. One partner turns into a monster, makes life miserable for the other, then blames the other for everything. It not only keeps a partner off balance, but it also spreads negatives all over the marriage.

And the "Winner" Is

As a result of these emotional games, the tormented partner is left to bounce off the walls, unable to regulate or make sense of his or her mate's behavior because everything looks like chaos. Both partners' behavior ends up becoming wild and random. No one wins. One minute the relationship appears to be going in one direction, the next moment it shifts to the opposite. And the anger, resentment (anger with a history), and pain just go on and on. You never know if you're going to be loved or hurt. Inevitably, this causes emotions to shut down and hearts to break.

And while all that destructive activity goes on, speculation as to what happened to the marriage runs wild. "Could it be that she doesn't even know me anymore? Or could it be that I just don't know her anymore?" A comment I frequently hear is, "He just isn't the person I married!" Could it be that the door to your heart is closed, and your partner isn't allowed to love you anymore? If he or she treated you well and told you every minute how much he or she loves you, would it matter? You've heard it all before, and it didn't mean anything then. Surely it means nothing now.

By becoming entangled in these self-fulfilling prophesies, you get caught in a vicious circle that pulls to the surface of the relationship the very behavior you hate. I'm not trying to justify an evil response. I just want to help you see the negative patterns that often enslave a relationship.

It's also time to ask yourself a very pointed question. "What attitudes and beliefs am I holding that may be harmful to my marriage?" Evaluate your own behaviors honestly. And remember, before you throw in the towel in desperation and anger, realize that both distancing and polarization are reasonable responses to unreasonable situations. Maybe you have reacted in the only ways you knew how. And maybe your spouse reacted out of that same sense of reasonableness. Stop and ask yourself, "Is my partner's unkind behavior due to *hate* or it is really coming from some deep-seated *pain*?" Of course, it could be both. But whatever the cause, could it also be that if you gave your partner the opportunity to heal, your partner might be able to embrace the marriage again?

If you both have that opportunity to heal, you may be able to put your new understanding of the cycle of disaffection to work. In doing so, you can learn new positive responses that will take you and your spouse along a different, more fulfilling marital path.

A Final Word

We're going to visit these islands again later and work to build them into very different and positive places, but for now, realize these islands of me are simply prisons. They are the last refuge of the failing marriage; they are proof positive (or negative) that you have failed at love. If you've reached them, if you have become a resident of a terribly dark isle, then you have a choice to make.

Will you choose to *give up* (divorce), *give in* (stay in the marriage in name only), or *give all* (stay in the marriage and fight to make it something beautiful)? In the next chapter, we'll at last begin to reclaim love.

Part Two

Reclaim/
Release

FOURTEEN

COMING OUT
OF THE PAIN

Where there is great love, there are always miracles.
—Willa Carter

*I*n the midst of my struggles in life, I try to remind myself of Proverbs 19:21: "There are many plans in a man's heart, nevertheless the Lord's counsel—that will stand." Strength, hope, and direction always start with God. In Him, I am confident you will prevail.

Change is fundamentally personal. If you've been blinded by pain, maybe unintentionally caught up in the process of disaffection, start with Psalm 139:23–24: "Search me, O God, and know my heart; try me, and know my anxieties; and see if there is any wicked way I me, and lead me in the way everlasting."

Carla and John sat in my office. Both looked tired, battle weary. They slumped on the sofa, eyes not only careful not to look at each other but also pleading with me to perform some kind of miracle in their lives. John, probably wanting to appear in control, spoke first. "Okay. You win. We're willing to work on this thing."

"Yes," echoed Carla with the same sound of doubt. "Willing."

I smiled with incredulity. "*I win?—This thing?*"

"Sure. That's what you want to hear, isn't it?" John sounded very hard.

Carla remained silent, her eyes somewhere distant.

"First, I'm not having a contest with you guys. Choosing your marriage is about you. Not me. You see that, don't you?"

They both nodded shallow, detached nods.

"Before we start, though, I want to make sure you're really ready." I hesitated, then asked, "Are you able to see how you two got here, how you've gotten caught up and spiraled down the cycle of disaffection? And how you each lost at love?"

Carla nodded hesitantly. "I did some things I'm not very proud of. Other things I couldn't help but do."

John also nodded. "I haven't been the husband I should. But it wasn't all my fault."

"I never said it was," Carla snapped.

"Okay, you two. You both have to take some of the responsibility, and I think you're doing that. You fought the pressures assaulting your relationship and, at least for now, they're winning—but only for the moment. The time's come to stop the chaos and take a hard look at going forward and trying to rebuild. From the sound of it, you guys are ready to do that, right?"

"Relief, Tim—we just need a break. We're tired," John said.

A Word to You

Coming out of the pain starts with being able to see at least some of what's happened to your marriage and how you cycled down to this level of disaffection—how you've lost at love. It starts with you each taking some of the responsibility for your journey while also realizing that the forces working to subvert your love are considerable. You must also realize that you need to stop the chaos and the pain by stepping back (not out) and resting a bit. And while resting, you give yourselves the opportunity to restore your strength so that you can begin the journey to life again.

Carla and John

I said, "Scripture says, 'What God has joined together, let not man separate' [Matt. 19:6]. Building a strong marriage is really a *spiritual task*. The two of you are together for a purpose—to influence each other for God. He wants to work through you to encourage growth in Christ in you both. As you consider your relationship, you have to approach it with His strength. For He understands your pain and knows your fears. He also knows your faithfulness and your love for Him. I believe your marriage is part of His divine plan."

"Then His plan's in trouble," John quipped.

"And maybe that's the real point here. Do you want to be responsible for getting in the way? No. What does His plan include? That before Him, the two of you will grow in love and faith and that you will influence your children to love God—assuming one day the Lord blesses you with children."

"I could never have children with him now," Carla said, her voice small and defeated.

"And right now you shouldn't," I said. "But one day maybe you'll feel differently. And your marriage will be a significant part of the foundation your children's faith will rest on. Your marriage is a witness at your jobs, to your friends. You're Christians and people look to you guys to show the way to strong marriage—strong love."

"I have a sister who's watching us," Carla said. "We've invited her to church a few times, and she's really watching us closely."

"God's plan is mirrored in your marriage. What I'd like right now is for the two of you to be willing to take the next six weeks to look closely at your marriage as if it's the most important thing in your lives—which I believe it is—and see where God leads."

John grunted. I could see there was still a strong part of him that felt committing to the marriage was committing to being subjugated. He glanced at Carla, then back at me. "Could I talk to you alone?"

"Why?" Carla snapped. "You want to cut a special deal? No matter what you say, Dr. Clinton's not going to go easy on you."

I nodded. "She's right. But you don't want to cut a deal, do you?"

John shook his head. "Just for a minute."

Carla sighed and agreed, then got to her feet and left the room.

"Okay," I said, "what?"

"What am I doing this for? Why don't I just leave? We've tried before to heal this baby. No marriage can be as bad as ours. Why don't I just cut my losses and find another wife somewhere?"

"Two reasons," I said. "The first one is that in up to ninety percent of second marriages, we see the same patterns and problems that plagued the first marriage. So you might as well at least examine and try to correct what you can in this one."

"What's the second reason?"

"All relationships take work. In a sin-cursed world with sinful people, every relationship will face pressures and develop the bad patterns we talked about. Examining how you lost at love is one of the most important gifts you can give yourself and Carla right now."

John only nodded, but he got up, opened the door, and called Carla back in. "Okay," he said to her as she seated herself. "I want to look at this closely. I'll try." Taking a deep breath, he continued, "I commit to you and to Carla that for the next couple of weeks I will try to make my marriage the most important thing in my life."

"Did you understand what John said, Carla?"

She nodded. Then said, "And I commit to you, John, that I will make our marriage the most important thing in my life—like I haven't been doing that already." That last bit was launched at John like an arrow.

A Word to You

Before I talk to John and Carla about that little zinger, let me talk to you. I'm not asking for much, simply that you'll allow yourself to open slightly and let some life and love get through for your spouse. In opening yourself up, you are giving yourself the gift of knowing that even now, when you are hurting the most, you are willing to invest enough of your emotion to see God's leading and be sensitive to what lessons on life and love you can learn.

Allow me also to give you a word of encouragement. God never wastes a wound. Each one can be used for our eventual and ultimate good. For instance, in 2 Corinthians 12:9, Paul's affliction was used to show him that God's grace is sufficient—so that Paul's faith might be strengthened. God's grace is sufficient for you, also. For it's not by your power that you'll overcome the pressures bent on destroying your marriage; it's by God's. "I can do all things through Christ who strengthens me" God tells us in Philippians 4:13. He is not only our present help but also our refuge (Ps. 46:1). As the journey that follows unfolds, assure yourself that God can be everything to you—your strength, your assurance, your shield, and your refuge. Facing the journey with mounting good cheer can be a real and attainable goal.

But, of course, the journey can be more difficult for some. Particularly for those who feel they're on the road alone.

If You're Alone in Your Commitment

It's actually rare that two people are in the same emotional place at the same time. Usually one partner is more committed to the process than the other, and sometimes I counsel people who are completely alone in their hope for their marriage. My instructions to them are the same as to those where both partners are involved. The only difference is that if you are alone, you need to let your partner know what you're doing and why. Let your spouse know you're trying to do things differently because you love him or her and want your marriage to work. Also invite your partner to participate. This should not only help dispassionately bring him or her along but also introduce your spouse to the cycle of disaffection and allow your spouse to see, as you now do, how you lost at love—and how you are working *for* love.

The partner working alone will also begin to set healthy emotional boundaries. As you tell your spouse what you are doing, you will also share what you see as healthy and acceptable responses. For example, "Hon, I was wrong in calling you names. I'm sorry. That was hurtful, disrespectful, and very unloving. I'm not going to do that anymore. And I would consider it an act of love and respect for me if you didn't call me names, either. If you're angry, tell me so, and we'll work it out. But no more name calling."

You owe it to yourself to keep going. Often one partner working on a resistant spouse is more like erosion than progress. It's a slow process, but be consistent, be loving, be honorable and respectable, and, when appropriate, invite your partner along on the journey.

Releasing

"Now," I said to Carla and John. "There's something else we're going to do here today. But be warned, this is going to be just as scary, if not more so, as your commitment."

John groaned.

Carla shot him a dagger look.

"People sometime coerce, manipulate, and go through all manner of gyrations to keep a partner loving them. I want your union, your marriage, to be paradoxical. You are not only reclaiming each other as partners in a holy marriage vow—your commitment to one another— but you are also releasing each other to love again. There will be no coercion, manipulation, or pressure to love you. And there will be no more walking on eggshells around each other. Love will come as it comes—when it comes."

John and Carla looked at me strangely for a moment, but then they recited to each other the words I'd given them. Instead of a zinger this time Carla ended with a heartfelt, "And I hope it's soon."

Obstacles to Coming Out of the Pain

Now, what if you and/or your spouse has made the commitment, but one or both of you is suffering from a deep, clinical depression? When it comes to the island of me stage of marriage, depression is pretty common. Or what if one or both of you has been abusing alcohol or drugs (prescription or otherwise)? What if there are other issues that may have been brought on by the stress of your faltering marriage?

If any of these situations exist, get help to work through them before or as you begin this process. Even if you're worried that your spouse may not wait around, take care of these issues first. Most partners, seeing their spouses take a positive step like dealing with depression or anger or a drinking problem, will recognize that as a commitment to the marriage. Most will give their partners enough time to get themselves together.

The Third Party

If there is a third party in either partner's life, that third person must go. This doesn't mean the third party waits on the sidelines, preparing to jump into the ring at the end of the marriage's final round. It means the third party is history—no contact, no remembrances, no pictures, no old notes to read. It must be as if the third party no longer exists, never existed before, and never will exist again. With no negative history to overcome and what appears to be a bright, limitless future ahead, a third party sits in the driver's seat. A spouse doesn't stand a chance against such a person. God's design for marriage is exclusive—one man, one woman. Outside help can be instrumental in providing encouragement, a safe place to deal with the issues, and accountability for all parties.

Nothing causes greater stress to the rebuilding process than a third party. But the offended partner must realize: The third party is also a symptom of the problems in the marriage—it is the offending partner's attempt to have needs met that were not being met in the marriage. This doesn't excuse such behavior. An affair is never excusable. It may be hard to let go, but as your relationship becomes more of what it once was, that emotional hole left by the exiting third party will become increasingly small and, finally, will disappear altogether. This may also be true for other sins where the roots are planted deep in unmet needs.

Stop the Pain

The Truce

Call a truce—a cessation of hostilities. Give it all a rest.

I'm not suggesting you give up any territory. No agreements, either in writing or implied, will change. None of the issues that have brought you here have been resolved or lost. All lines in the sand remain where they're drawn. If this is war and you're in your trenches, remain in them. You don't have to jump into each other's arms; just stop lobbing shells at each other.

Stop hurting each other. There's been enough of that, hasn't there?

Remember what Carla said at the end of her commitment statement to John? She jabbed him with a zinger: "Like I haven't been doing that already." That was an attempt on her part to take the upper hand, to proclaim herself innocent, to say that she'd been working all along at this marriage and he hadn't been. It was a negative sting, a jab at John to keep him off balance and force him into defending himself rather than focusing on Carla's behavior. I admonished Carla for that. Zingers do not accomplish anything positive.

Instead, we want positives to accomplish positives.

Research into human behavior shows that it takes five to twenty positives to overcome one negative, and one negative can undo twenty positives.[1] But you didn't need a research study to tell you that. Experience taught you that long ago. Even with dear friends, a single negative remark can put the entire relationship on hold. It's even truer with your spouse. Remember when life was all positive—one compliment or great situation after another? And then one caustic or demeaning comment seemed to make everything unravel. How long did you or your spouse have to work at being "good" before the negative was overcome? A long time. And, of course, it was never really overcome. It was just put away to be pulled out later to bludgeon you —or for you to use as a bludgeon. The issue isn't whether you will fight, but how you fight.

In James 3:8 we're told that hurting another is the natural order of things. "But no man can tame the tongue. It is an unruly evil, full of deadly poison." By hurting someone, you give definition to your dark side, but it's demeaning. It's also demeaning for the one being hurt. That person is being told that he or she is not worthy of esteem, not worthy of being cared about and given something positive—a compliment, a kind word, a gift.

The last thing you or your spouse need right now is more negativity. It's infested your home like termites—eating away at the studs that hold up the walls. It's time to exterminate the negatives.

From now on either be polite or be positive.

Specifically *do* and *don't do* the following:

- *Do* Respect Your Partner: This might be very hard to do right now. Having been hurt as you probably have, *respect* might be a difficult word to reclaim for your vocabulary, particularly when applied to your spouse. But try. You and your spouse may view things very differently. But by learning about those differences and what motivates them, and by exercising patience and understanding, you can come together and find workable solutions to your problems. How do you gain that respect? By behaving respectfully to one another, and by behaving in ways worthy of respect (see 1 Peter 3:7–10). If you make that your rule of the day, respect may come more quickly than either of you can imagine.

- *Don't* Use Words to Hurt: Give up the old patterns of using wild accusations, vulgarity, name calling, raised voices, and threats to make yourself heard. These destructive behaviors accomplish nothing and leave both partners feeling angry and manipulated. Screaming only means that somewhere along the way you've lost control and have failed to get your message across effectively. If you suddenly feel like exploding, stop, realize that you still have some work to do to make your point, and quietly restate your argument. Remember it's the *soft answer* that turns away wrath (Prov. 15:1).

- *Don't* Force Settlements: Insisting that a dispute be settled "immediately," no matter how poor the setting might be—mealtime, bedtime, in public—can be disastrous. A postponement allows tempers to cool and gives both partners time to look over the situation more realistically and less emotionally.

- *Don't* Attack Your Partner's Soft Spot: You know your spouse's buttons—you probably know them better than your spouse does. Stay away from them. Intentional wounding cuts deeply and heals slowly. Stick to the issue.

- *Don't* Shut Down: Not only does the "silent treatment" end effective communication, but it also defeats any possibility of compromise and allows misunderstandings to fester. If you need a break—take one! But come back quickly.

- *Don't* Involve Others: No matter how heated the argument, no matter how important it is that you win, don't drag the children into it—or other relatives, or friends, or the cab driver, or the meter reader. If you need an ally, call on the Lord; and if you need someone to mediate, call on an objective professional counselor or pastor. A kid's world will only be rattled by being dragged into a fight, and loved ones will naturally take sides. In either case the result is just a longer casualty list. And neither of you want that. Believe me.

A Scary Thought

It's scary to think about giving up negatives—the barbs, the intimidation, the yelling and screaming. It's not only been the only way to be heard, but it's also been your method of defense. So, naturally you're frightened. The idea creates a terrible vulnerability. In actuality, standing firm without barbed wire defending your perimeter is a much stronger position to hold.

The day Carla and John committed themselves to their marriage, nothing appeared to have changed. John left my office and went back to work while Carla went home. But that evening when John called and said he was going to be late, instead of feeling her heart go tight in her chest, Carla found a much calmer sensation there. "That's okay, John. I'm fixing that roasted garlic chicken you like, and I'll keep your portion warm for you. Would you prefer Rice-a-Roni or noodles? I could bake a potato, too, if you'd like."

John couldn't believe his ears. Instead of a prickly, demanding voice on the other end of the line, he found pleasantness. He thought about how nice it would be to enjoy dinner with Carla. But he did have another hour's work. "Could you hold off dinner till about seven? I think I could make it by seven."

Carla nearly cried; the words sounded so beautiful. "Is Rice-a-Roni okay? I won't put it on until you get here. That'll give you a chance to enjoy your paper before dinner."

"Sure. Sounds good."

And they hung up.

They had stepped back from the brink. Neither had given up any ground. Each was the master of the same domain. Each had the same responsibilities, the same doubts about the marriage, and the same worries about getting hurt. But they were polite, were reasonably concerned about the other—the same sort of concern you would give to a brother or sister, or even a casual visitor in your home—and tried to accommodate the other where possible.

The Big "O"—Obstacles

As you can imagine, there are obstacles that can rear up that cause couples to hesitate in establishing the truce. Most center around a fear of failure and, ultimately, a fear of being hurt again.

"Before I commit to anything, I want to see a flicker of love from my partner" is the most common statement of hesitation. You want some assurance that if you make the commitment, your partner will love you enough to not turn the commitment against you. But there is no assurance. Even if you could see a flicker of love, it could go out tomorrow. The only safety is to strengthen yourself in the Love of Jesus, to realize that He is the only one whose love never flickers or fails.

By committing to make your marriage the most important thing in your life for the next few weeks and to be polite and positive with your mate, you're risking very little. If betrayed, you can always begin the war again. Of course, once you feel the relief this kind of strength gives you, you may never see the need to rejoin the war.

Another obstacle concerns the cost of love; opening yourself up to being hurt again may seem too great a risk. The fear of being hurt is normal. Some 2,000 years ago, our Savior weighed the price His Father had placed on His love for His people. "Father, if it is Your will, take this cup away from Me; nevertheless not My will, but Yours, be done" (Luke 22:42). Jesus, although prepared to go to the cross and to suffer separation from His Father to save His people from their sins, for a moment poignantly asked God the Father if He might reconsider. If you're concerned about the cost of loving your spouse, consider the cost Jesus paid for loving you.

I also hear, "Making this step is foreign to me," or similar words. I think people who say this just don't want to take the chance that things might only get worse. They'll admit that all this talk of truce and rebuilding sounds good but think, in the end, it won't amount to much. Then they'll have just spent more time on the road getting to safety or the divorce court. But God fashions life; chance never enters into it. He's called you to do the right thing, and loving your spouse and committing yourself to a vital and God-honoring marriage is definitely the right thing.

And finally, I often hear this terribly fatalistic phrase: "I can't love again." It's a terribly forlorn statement. Love is so basic to us—we were born in the garden out of God's love and to believe that love is an emotion of the past is like waking to an eternal winter. What's worse is those who take it a step farther and believe love is at the root of all the evil that's befallen them, that it's actually a blessing to live the rest of their lives loveless. But love is not the culprit; not loving in God's model is.

A Final Word

You've done many important things in response to this chapter. You've called a truce in your marriage. You've recommitted to your marriage for at least four to six weeks. You've released your spouse from being coerced or manipulated into loving you. And you've prepared yourself to take the next step.

And what is that next step? It's beginning the task of connecting those islands of me.

FIFTEEN

PREPARING TO CROSS OVER TROUBLED WATERS

The Lord is near to those who have a broken heart, and saves such as have a contrite spirit. Many are the afflictions of the righteous, but the Lord delivers him out of them all.

—*Psalm 34:17–18*

Y ou've called a truce—you will stop intentionally hurting one another, and you will treat each other politely. You're releasing your spouse to love you when he or she is ready and working to reclaim love. And, in the process, you're drawing strength from the Lord and looking to Him for your comfort and love.

But there are still land mines out there, ways you can hurt each other unintentionally by simply being who you are and doing what comes naturally. We want to minimize those kinds of hurts before we work on ways of connecting your islands of me.

Unrealistic Expectations

As you enter this delicate phase of your relationship—a sort of work-but-wait-and-see-phase—you might have some new unrealistic expectations. And in the gap between expectation and reality is a whole lot of disappointment. For instance, a husband may be watching for that faint glimmer of returning love in his wife. He may be so anxious to see it that he may mistake a caring attitude for that glimmer and be terribly disappointed when he discovers that "passion" was merely politeness. It's important right now to have few expectations. Remember that you both have many conflicting emotions swirling around inside. Expect each other to be human and to fail occasionally. Expect only that you are both going to try hard to make something very tenuous, but very important, work. And since this is meticulous work, neither allow your expectations to soar too high, nor allow them to fall too low.

One way to moderate expectations is to periodically, perhaps weekly, check with your partner. Ask your partner where he or she is in the relationship, how he or she is dealing with things. Then believe what your partner tells you and leave it at that. That way you'll always stay within the confines of reality.

For that's what reclaiming love is. It's releasing you from the emotional bondage that took you through chapters 1 through 13. It's allowing yourself to be free of the pain, allowing yourself to tear down the walls. It's throwing open love's door and standing there as you really are. So when love blooms, it's blooming in the truest, richest soil, which you cultivated yourself.

Staying in the calm of reality has another effect, it allows you to *respond* rather than *react*.

Respond Instead of React

When we're in threatening situations, we often "respond" by reacting. We perceive a threat and let our instincts take over. There's little time to do anything else. We could be dead if we stop to think about things. If we find ourselves in threatening situations often, if for instance, we're police or firefighters, we've trained our instincts to react in constructive ways. The problem is that when a marriage is falling apart, there is little or no time to train those instincts. When something threatens our emotional well-being, we react in some way to protect ourselves.

Over time, reacting like this makes things worse. But we can't really see that. All we see is that we're increasingly being hurt, which means there's a greater and greater threat, which means we have to protect ourselves by reacting more and more strongly.

But now there's a truce. Your spouse has said that for the next six weeks he or she will not hurt you intentionally. Now you know your spouse might slip now and then, just as you might. But you've both committed to apologizing as quickly and as sincerely as possible. So, in a real sense, the threat is gone.

That means, instead of reacting to situations, you have time to respond. What's the difference? Reaction is like the mallet hitting the knee, causing the leg to jerk instinctively. Response implies thought. Remember Carla's response in the last chapter when John called to say he was going to be late? Although her tendency to be jealous and lash out was still fully energized, she stopped to think and allowed a cooler head to rule over a chaotic heart. She ascribed a positive motive to John—he couldn't help it—and tried to make things as easy for him as she could. She responded.

What about You?

We all have buttons that our spouses are experts at pushing to send us up the walls. What are yours? This isn't an idle question. It's a good idea to think about them. What sets you off? Write them down. Then think about your reactions when those buttons are pushed. Do you hit the roof? Shut down? Seethe? Sulk? Maybe your reactions differ depending on where you are or how you feel at the time. But however you feel, there's a reaction. So what happens between you and your spouse when you react? Do you fight? Or do you end up huddled on separate emotional ice floes? Before, of course, the fight was to put your spouse away, to keep him or her at a distance so you couldn't be hurt. But assuming the truce between you is alive and well, that reason no longer exists. Now if the button is pushed, it's either an accident or there was no viable alternative. Hitting the roof is no longer acceptable. What response is, though? And what response will get you the desired response back? Think about that. And plan for it.

Improve Communication

Improving communications will also help your relationship. Prior to making the commitment to work on your marriage and calling the truce, it may have been difficult for you to talk at all. Anything you said to each other bubbled out of anger and mistrust. Words were meant more to hurt than to convey meaning. Issues remained unresolved or become resolved only through painful battling. With the truce and your commitment to treat each other politely, at least the stinging barbs should stop, but communication might still be strained. You may not trust one another yet.

So how do you improve verbal communications in an environment like this? I suggest the following:

Talk frequently about neutral things. There are many things going on in your life that can give your partner a better, more personal look at you. Things that happened at work or with friends, things you read in the newspaper or in Scripture. Talk about how you think or feel about them. Then elicit a response from your partner.

These nonthreatening exchanges allow you to begin building common ground again. It also allows you to find out things about your spouse you may not know.

Talk honestly about your emotions without pointing fingers. Emotions are one of the first things to get bottled up when marriages begin to go bad. Putting your feelings out there makes you vulnerable, and when your spouse becomes less trustworthy with your feelings, you quickly learn to hold them back. But emotions are very useful.

Bring them out, but not in order to control things. Rather, talk about them as your possessions, as your responsibilities.

Talking about your feelings gives your partner the opportunity to talk as well. It also gives you the opportunity to find out that you're not all that different, after all.

Communicate clearly. Speak clearly, in full sentences, with words and phrases your partner understands. If you leave a note, leave it where your spouse will find it, and write it so the meaning is clear. Some of my clients have used the way they communicate during this truce period to covertly continue the war. Perhaps a message will be purposefully vague. "Get bread on the way home." But what kind of bread? "You know I like Hillbrook's wheat. Why'd you get this stuff?" And so a spouse who's done something good for the family is left feeling inadequate. None of that. If you want something specific, name it. And if you don't, take what you get graciously.

Engage in judicious editing. As you speak, engage in judicious editing.[1] Think about what you're saying and edit out anything that might push your partner's buttons or, because of your history, might be misunderstood.

Nonverbal Communications

Of great importance at this point are the nonverbal communications—the body language, the hidden messages that are sent by the cock of a head, the roll of an eye, the tightness of muscles. From an early age, some believe from the womb, our drive to survive and flourish forces us to discern these messages. And nonverbal communications are often far truer than words.

An equally important form of communication involves deeds. What you do rings louder and with greater clarity than what you say. The examples are legion.

"Sure I love you honey. And, really, I miss you terribly when I'm away. Oh, by the way, Butch and I are playing golf tomorrow then spending the afternoon at the nineteenth hole watching the football game. Usually there's a few racks of billiards after that, so don't expect me until late." How much does this guy really miss his wife? How much do you think his wife believes he misses her?

So, how do we improve communications? Of course the question now has a much broader and more profound answer than you may have given before. Yet the answer is surprisingly simple: *As issues arise, tell the truth. Tell it politely, caringly, even emphatically, but tell it.*

As best you can, make your actions and your words match up. And if you get into a place where you feel you have to misrepresent yourself—to say you're happy when you're not, to say you like something when you don't—deal with that issue right away. During this time of truce, you're allowed to be who you are. If you feel pressure to be someone else, the truce is beginning to break down. Reestablish it. And the best way to do that is to speak your truth in love.

As a final preparation step, I'm going to suggest you do something that's symbolic of what your love once was and what it can be again— something you can look at when you're struggling to remind you of what you're struggling for.

Erect a Memorial

Maybe you haven't thought recently about what your wedding ring symbolizes. It is a wonderful symbol of what marriage should be. The gold withstands fire to become pure, and the unbroken circle is a reminder of how our love should always remain. You exchanged rings with your spouse before witnesses—family, friends, those representing the state, and usually those representing God. And the love those rings symbolize is strong, certainly strong enough to take these first brave steps toward the path of healing.

Erect a memorial that will stand as a tribute to your marriage as it undergoes transformation. You will one day be able to look back and see how far you have traveled. John Trent, in his book *Life Mapping,* calls these "Memorial Markers."[2] But John would be the first to admit that he didn't think them up. God did and there are numerous biblical accounts of such memorials, many still seen today. Every rainbow we see signifies God's promise that the earth will never again be deluged by a flood.

We also have the bread and drink of communion services—the memorial to the great and supreme sacrifice that God made for us through His Son Jesus Christ.

What about your memorial?

It can be something simple—a flower pressed into the page of your Bible, a picture of you and your spouse, or a small memento that holds special meaning to your marriage or your recommitment to your marriage. Each time you think about or look at your memorial, it will serve as a reminder of the commitment you've made.

Of course, you may still be wondering if all the hurt and anger you've recently experienced will ever go away, or if the future will be any better than the past. These concerns are even more reason to erect a memorial. For God is the author of change, and He can help you fashion something good, right, and redeeming from any circumstance.

A memorial serves to remind the brokenhearted that God longs to bind up the shattered and grieving and brings about real and dynamic change.

But regardless of the outcome, your memorial is proof that you reached inside and found the courage and strength to be an instrument of God's redeeming spirit as you allow Him to work in and through you to accomplish His glory. It becomes the purest symbol of your love as it was and as it will be again. And that's the love that Paul proclaims to us in 1 Corinthians 13: "Love is patient, love is kind. It does not envy, it does not boast, it is not proud. It is not rude, it is not self-seeking, it is not easily angered, it keeps no record of wrongs. Love does not delight in evil but rejoices with the truth. It always protects, always trusts, always hopes, always perseveres" (vv. 4–7 NIV).

I hope that your memorial will be something special to you, something of deep and lasting meaning, something over which you'll shed many healing tears.

Where to Now?

We've made quite a few preparations, but in the next chapter we're going to make the most important one of all—truly seeing your marriage as a spiritual task.

SIXTEEN

CALLED TO A
SPIRITUAL TASK

*We must imitate Christ's life and His ways if we are to be truly
enlightened and set free from the darkness of our hearts. Let it be the
most important thing we do, then, to reflect on the life of Jesus Christ.*
—*Thomas à Kempis*

Above just about every spiritual thing, except your love
for the Lord Himself, is the spiritual impact of your
marriage for the kingdom. Not only does it hone you
into much stronger spiritual beings, but your marriage is also a
tremendous spiritual witness. Remember how you feel when you're
sitting in church and it's announced that Mr. and Mrs. So-and-so are
celebrating their fiftieth wedding anniversary?

And what does your heart feel like when you hear about a couple
in the church separating, then divorcing? You begin to see Satan's
footprints all over that marriage. And you see people who succumbed
to temptations, perhaps even unrepentant people whose hearts have
become hard and unresponsive to God's leading. Sometimes you
think, "Isn't it good that not everyone knows they're Christians?"

So your marriage is important not only to you but also to many
others, Christians and non-Christians alike, some you may not even
know, who hear about your situation and are affected by it.

Making Your Marriage a Spiritual Task

Engage in a Spiritual Love

The world's definition of love, and there's really nothing wrong with it as far as it goes, is a horizontal relationship. It's a shared bond between a man and a woman eager to come together and make themselves one. But a spiritual relationship includes a third—God. Rather than a horizontal relationship, marriage becomes a triad. It can be seen as three circles at the tips of a triangle, with arrows flowing between them all. A spiritual love is one where God is not only a part but also the dominant part.¹ But how do we put that into practice?

Frankly it's a matter of focus and attitude. The simplest way is to acknowledge and live the truth—God brought you together for His purposes, He is with you every step of the way, and His word must act as a "lamp to [your] feet" (Ps. 119:105).

For His Purposes

It's hard to come to grips with the fact that the God of the universe, the Creator of atoms and electrons and the Mississippi River and Niagara Falls has somehow factored us into His plans. He has not only factored us in but has also made us an integral part of His plan, perhaps even a focal point occasionally.

Of course, there are those who believe that God is a hands-off God. That He merely wound up the universe and is not letting it wind down. And there are those who believe God just gets involved when things get so far out of whack that He feels compelled to do something. But that's not what God's Word says. Ephesians 1:11 puts it this way, "In Him also we have obtained an inheritance, being predestined according to the purpose of Him who works all things according to the counsel of His will." The operative words here are *all things*. God is a planning God. He's about bringing His people to Himself, and He has a plan to do that. We are all part of that plan. God desires to work through us to impact others for His sake.

And we see it unfolding all around us.

I see it when I counsel young-marrieds on how to strengthen their marriages and hopefully to bring stronger Christian children into the world. I see it when those with failing marriages see and are inspired by the strength of others' and use the methods they've employed to keep them strong. Your marriage is every bit as important to God's plan, perhaps more so.

"I wasn't sure how to react to this," John said, after I'd broached this subject with him and Carla. "I'm not a theologian. In fact, there are times I think I'm not much of a Christian at all. But then I thought of the whole situation this way: Our marriage is important to someone who gave His life for our eternal happiness. And because of that, I want to give back to Him the best marriage I can."

How then do you make your marriage one that reflects God's plan in His kingdom? The first thing you do is create as strong a marriage as you can, and we're in the process of doing that. The second thing is to respond in a godly way to the situations your marriage encounters. The best way to do that is to realize that He's always there.

God Is Always with You

The Bible is filled with verses that stress that God is with His people all the time, a thought that has always been quite convicting, challenging, and comforting to me. The most definitive verse is: "I will never leave you nor forsake you" (Heb. 13:5). God, through His Spirit, is with you. And because He is right there, seek to know Him, be mindful of Him, and behave as if you'd want Him to be proud of what you are doing. You always have an audience of one. Consider the fact that every word you say, He hears. Every thought you have, He knows. Everything you do, He sees. Nothing under heaven is hidden from Him to whom you will give account.

Something happens when you begin to realize this and let it make a difference in your life. Your speech becomes more edifying. Your fights become fairer and less frequent. Your negotiations become less demanding and more giving. Your focus becomes more on your spouse and less on yourself. Sacrificing becomes normal and pleasurable. Lovemaking becomes more giving, more tender, more passionate. Rather than being self-conscious about what you say and do, you become more Christlike. Instead of becoming nervous about what God might think, you become more relaxed, knowing that He loves you and He rewards those who diligently seek Him. When you both know and act like He's there, humor comes more easily, a sense of rightness settles in on most situations, and a courage comes to your everyday walk.

Love comes far more easily.

So, know that He's there with you. Know that He loves you and wants the best for you and is powerful enough to give it to you. Know that He's also powerful and loving enough to keep you from what you cannot bear. When you bring Him into your decision making, you can relax a little more. Perhaps even be a little bolder. But above all, be a little more loving and godly. And how do you become more godly in your decision making?

•

Let God's Word Be a Lamp to Your Feet

In biblical times, when travelers walked at night, they carried oil lamps with light bright enough to illuminate the path just ahead. Of course, they couldn't see the road yards ahead, so they had to keep their eyes right where their feet would fall next. They traveled one step at a time. And that's how we go through life, isn't it? One step at a time. We can't see even seconds ahead. All we see is the present and what God's given us to deal with in that moment. And as a member of a family, those things we deal with concern our families and what impacts them.

Learn the Word and Apply It to Your Life by Faith

Ministers go to seminary for years to learn the Scriptures then spend the rest of their lives learning more and trying to apply those lessons to their lives. So blithely telling you to learn the Word smacks of telling you to do something that no one's been able to completely do. But, in actuality, the issue is to simply learn the Word as best you can and practice other spiritual disciplines, applying what you do know to your life—by faith. And as a result, you tap into God's resources; you have His power to live in a new way. For most couples, learning and applying Ephesians 5:21–33 is an excellent start.

> . . . submitting to one another in the fear of God.
>
> Wives, submit to your own husbands, as to the Lord. For the husband is head of the wife, as also Christ is head of the church; and He is the Savior of the body. Therefore, just as the church is subject to Christ, so let the wives be to their own husbands in everything.
>
> Husbands, love your wives, just as Christ also loved the church and gave Himself for her, that He might sanctify and cleanse her with the washing of water by the word, that He might present her to Himself a glorious church, not having spot or wrinkle or any such thing, but that she should be holy and without blemish. So husbands ought to love their own wives as their own bodies; he who loves his wife loves himself. For no one ever hated his own flesh, but nourishes and cherishes it, just as the Lord does the church. For we are members of His body, of His flesh and of His bones. "For this reason a man shall leave his father and mother and be joined to his wife, and the two shall become one flesh." This is a great mystery, but I speak concerning Christ and the church. Nevertheless let each one of you in particular so love his own wife as himself, and let the wife see that she respects her husband.

It's all in there—submitting to each other spiritually and lovingly, the chain of command, the responsibility of the husband to the relationship, and the responsibility of the wife. But how do we, as married couples, apply all that to our lives?

By faith.

Carla and John

As I was growing up, my dad, a country preacher, spent many Saturday afternoons keeping his vehicles running. That effort of his brought me many lessons—thrift, the value of stewardship, and the value of testing. One day he was repairing a cracked manifold on an old Jeep. I was young and was fascinated when he used a welder to repair the crack. After waiting a moment to let the weld set, he shocked me by taking a hammer and striking the manifold. "Why did you do that?" I gasped. "It might have broken again."

"I was just testing it," he answered. "It's better for it to break here when I can fix it again that out on the road someplace."

God tests our resolve and our faith sometimes too. Carla and John had been abiding by their truce for about a month when their first test came. Like all couples coming out of pain, they had ups and downs, but on the whole, the journey had been positive. Then John came home with a tentative expression. "The company wants to send me to school in Chicago. Management school. Two pretty intense weeks. If I do well, I'll be put on a list—a short list, actually—to be made third-level management. The next stop after that is vice president. It's a big career opportunity."

Carla swallowed hard. "Okay, then you should go."

"I have to tell you. One other person from our group is going. Charlene Demures."

Carla felt her heart catch. They'd agreed that there would be no traveling with any women, even in a group, during the six-week truce, and she suddenly felt betrayed. But she also knew that John hadn't planned this. And he was right. It was a huge career opportunity. Over the years she'd become aware of how his company worked. The managers were very methodical and very straight with their employees. If they said there was a possibility for a vice president's position, they were telling John the truth.

Of course, maybe *he* wasn't telling the truth. Maybe he was waving the VP thing out there to make the trip sound more important. Maybe he really just wanted to get away with Ms. Demures.

"I have to think about this," Carla finally said. "Is there anything else you want me to know to help your case?"

"No."

"I don't mean to doubt you, John. But you know our agreement."

"I do," he said, his eyes telling her that he understood and empathized with her decision.

Carla spent much of that evening thinking about John's class—and Ephesians 5. John was her husband. She was supposed to submit to his authority in the marriage. But he had not asked her to submit. He'd left her in charge of weighing the pros and cons—the big pro, of course, was the potential boost to his career. But she also knew that even though she'd been working hard to control her jealousy, his spending two weeks away—with Ms. Demures—would be very difficult for her. She grappled with respecting her husband. What did the word *respect* mean? Was there some sort of action associated with it, or was it just a feeling? And did respect have anything to do with her decision?

She fell asleep next to John about 11:00 thinking about everything, then woke up about 2:30, stewing. Around 4:00 she went into the kitchen to make herself chamomile tea and think some more. Near 5:00 she'd decided to let him go. After all, he was her husband, and he'd committed to her. She had to start trusting in him again—she had to test their relationship. And it might as well be now. She decided that the respect she was to give to him was somehow wrapped up in that trust. You can't respect what you don't trust, is how she thought it. So, as she wearily prepared his morning coffee, she also prepared to tell him he could go.

Before she could take him the coffee, though, he showed up at the kitchen door.

"I can't do this to you," he said. "I'm going to ask to go to the next class. I've been thinking all night about the admonition to love your wife—to give myself up for you—and I can't ask you to go through this now. Maybe in a while, when you're feeling more secure. If I'm good, the company will keep me in mind."

"Really? I was about to tell you to go."

"I knew you would. But let's take time to rebuild first. Things seem to be going pretty well, and I don't want to do anything to jeopardize that. No promotion's worth that."

So—by faith a wife submits to her husband, leaving herself vulnerable to be taken advantage of. By faith a man gives himself up for his wife, leaving himself vulnerable to be taken advantage of. By faith each submitted spiritually to the other as an equal before the Lord. By faith in whom? In the Lord. For God says that He's the rewarder of those who diligently seek Him. Following Him may lead you through some valleys but never to defeat.

A Final Word

As you make your marriage a spiritual task, you and your spouse will see several things happening. First, each of you will reflect Jesus' sacrificial love. And you will, by example, help bring Jesus out in your spouse. John told his boss that he preferred to wait on the class, explaining, "Carla and I both made some errors in our marriage, but we're committed to making it work. I think it's best for us if I hold off on that class for a while."

"You know what you're saying?" his boss replied.

"Sure. If God wants me to be a VP around here, I'll have another opportunity. And if He doesn't, this opportunity wouldn't matter anyway."

John's marriage became a spiritual force at work.

Your battle will also require bold love, forgiveness, confession, repentance, confrontation, suffering, humiliation, and more. To win the day will take great strength, as only God can give. Seeing your marriage as belonging to God will help you to gain victory on the battlefield against the forces at work trying to defeat it.

Also, by applying the Word to your life, you'll find yourself walking closer to God, being blessed more abundantly. And the closer you walk to God, the closer you'll walk with each other.

In the next chapter we'll continue working for your marriage and reformulating your love as we address forgiving each other and achieving empathy.

SEVENTEEN

THE POWER
OF LOVE

The great acts of love are done by those who are habitu-
ally performing small acts of kindness.

—*Anonymous*

The first step on any journey, particularly one as important as this, is to define your destination—Where are you going? How will you know when you get there?

On this journey, you'll know you've arrived when you share in "love" again, when you're consciously, naturally, unconditionally loving again.

It could be that, during this period of truce, you're not sure you ever will get there. But in all probability, you still *want* to get there. In fact, every client I've ever worked with has had a desire for love. Isn't that why we raise the bar in the cycle of disaffection? In a recent survey, 90 percent of respondents said that what makes a good marriage is love.[1] The problem is that few people really know what love is. Let's explore it a bit, starting by defining the elements of godly, biblically-based love.

The Elements of Love

In order to understand godly love and determine if we are living up to the model for love God has revealed to us in Scripture, let's look at its elements. The first concerns our reason for loving.[2]

We Can Love because God First Loved Us

In 1 John 4:8b we learn that "God is love." And He loves the pinnacle of His creation, His people, as demonstrated in Christ (John 3:16; Rom. 8:32; Phil. 2; 1 John 4:10). That means He loves you and me (1 John 4:15–17a). Therefore, "let us love one another, for love is of God; and everyone who loves is born of God, and knows God" (1 John 4:7). We can love because God has given us His Spirit to fill our hearts. In His love, let the fruit of the Spirit rule (Gal. 5:22–23). It is only in His love that we can find safety, security, and true significance. Hence, as we grow in our relationship with God, our ability to reach out and truly love our mates grows along with it. How strong is your relationship with God?

Godly Love Is Unconditional

God's love for us began when we were yet sinners (Rom. 5:8), before we even knew Him. Then He drew us to him (John 6:44), and when we accept Christ, we become His. Nowhere in the process does He ask anything from us. He loves us unconditionally. And there's nothing in all creation that can snatch us from His love (Rom. 8:37–39). That's the way, then, that we are to love our husbands and wives (Eph. 5:28). Our love is never to be based on what we might get in return. We're just to love, to do those things that make our spouses feel good and make their lives as fulfilled as we can. We need to show our mates Jesus' love flowing through us.

Godly Love Involves Action

"Let us not love in word or in tongue, but in deed and in truth" (1 John 3:18; see also John 14:21, 21:15–17). Godly love is backed up by action—sandwiches and sodas for his buddies during a football game, roses planted just where she wants them, helping out around the house and with the kids. Love flows out of us and, because we care about our mates' well-being, we look for and do things that will make their lives better.

Godly Love Involves Sacrifice

Many believe that the best marriages are the "50-50 marriages," those based on give and take. If you don't get something in return for everything you give, if at the end of the day the scales are not somehow balanced evenly, then you have cause for complaint. But that's not God's ideal. God's marriages are 100-100. Ephesians 5:25 leaves no room to doubt this: "Husbands love your wives, just as Christ also loved the church and gave Himself for her." How much did Jesus reserve for Himself? Nothing. He gave it all. And giving it all involves the obvious sacrifice.

Of course, the immediate implication here is that husbands must be willing to sacrifice their lives for their wives. There's probably not one of us who has not contemplated being called upon to give up our lives for our wives—pushing them out of the way of a speeding truck only to be caught in its path ourselves. And the admonition is there for wives as well. We understand this kind of sacrifice. It's heroic. Above and beyond. But God focuses on our daily walk, a continuing sacrifice on behalf of our mates, giving 100 percent of ourselves without regard for how much we might get back.

That means you may sometimes find yourself holding the bag. You'll have given your 100 percent share when your mate has not. What then?

Godly Love Involves Forgiveness

The Father in heaven has forgiven you, one of His people, for every sin you've ever committed or will commit against Him—those times you took His name in vain, or failed to worship Him, or thought ill of someone, or put yourself first, or any of the uncountable number of times you rebelled against Him. Through the blood of Jesus Christ, He's forgiven you and cast your sins into the sea of forgiveness. That's love with a capital *L*. And that's the kind of love we're to have for our mates. All spouses fall short sometimes and when they do, we're to be right there forgiving them. Keep in mind that you fall short too. You don't give 100 percent all the time. You get angry now and then, or say the wrong thing, or become forgetful, or abandon your mate emotionally.

Why is forgiveness essential to love? Because it tears down the walls. Each time you forgive and turn an incident over to the Lord to deal with, a wall, or at least a good section of a wall, comes tumbling down. You and your spouse become closer, and love becomes far easier. So forgive as God the Father forgives you in Christ.

As you begin to practice forgiveness, you will come to see your spouse as just a human being trying as you are to do the best job he or she can.

Godly Love Includes Complete Acceptance

God sees us through the sacrifice that Jesus made on the cross. Because of the work of Christ, He sees us as "not having spot or wrinkle or any such thing" (Eph. 5:27). He accepts us completely, without reservation. Even though we are not stainless, even though we are wrinkled in a thousand ways, God the Father accepts us in Christ as His own heirs (Gal. 4:4–7).

This is how we are to accept our mates. Sure our mates have faults. In fact, we know those faults better than anyone. But we're to accept our mates completely, faults, flaws and all, just as we want to be accepted—unconditionally.

How many people get married and try to change their spouses— make them more sensitive, more responsible, or more responsive? We're all sensitive to being loved conditionally. We're all in tune with that horrible feeling of being loved only when we fit the "acceptable mold," when we do those things or be those things that make us *lovable*. And we all run from it. "Love me as I am or not at all!" is our cry. And a legitimate cry it is!

Just as God the Father loves us so we are to love our mates.

Godly Love Is Committed

In the second chapter of Genesis, God stresses commitment in love. In Genesis 2:24 He tells us that we're to leave our fathers and mothers and "be joined to" our mates, to become one flesh—in every way. Let's examine this idea of love lasting "till death do us part." It's a tough concept for a lot of us to swallow. After all, didn't that wonderfully compelling feeling we felt at the beginning of our relationship fade? Wasn't that love, and didn't it start like a hot bonfire and over time dwindle to just a few orange embers? Or maybe it died altogether. How can you be committed to something that's so fleeting?

That wasn't love; that was emotion. Love is the *commitment*. Love is seeing your mate through the valleys—the times when the rest of the world has turned away. Love is seeing your mate through the mountains—when he or she might be on a high for reasons other than you and you're in essence forgotten until he or she begins to come back down. Love is seeing your mate through physical and emotional sicknesses when the only thing keeping you going is the knowledge that you've given your word to be there. And, as that kind of commitment becomes more important in the relationship, the highs are replaced by something deeper and far more beautiful—a wonderful sense of belonging, of rightness, of comfort, of knowing that you are worthy of love and able to give love.

Godly Love Results in Praise

It builds us up, makes us feel valuable, shows us that we are appreciated and that our efforts have not only succeeded but have also been effective enough to elicit a positive response. As you love, as you want the best for your spouse, you'll naturally want to praise him or her.

Love gives itself a voice in praise.

Now when you say "I love you," you're saying an awful lot, aren't you? You're saying that your love flows from God, that it's unconditional and sacrificial, and that you're committed to your mate. They're wonderfully rich words to say, aren't they? Of course, you may not be there yet, and that's okay. You're in the process of rebuilding.

How will you know when you get there? You'll probably recognize when it starts flowing from you. You'll feel that well-defined joy in loving your mate again. But how will you know when love starts flowing your way again? You'd think we'd know that instinctively, but often we don't. People may have trouble understanding the vocabulary of love their partners use.

The Vocabulary of Love

Holly and Larry sat in my office. It had been nearly six months since Holly's note on the microwave announced her departure. The fact that they were sitting before me was a major victory for Larry. Holly had immediately gone to live with her mother and, until about a week before, had made good on her vow to speak to Larry only when she had to. By passing messages through her mother, she barely had to at all.

Her mother believed in marriage and had wanted her to move back. "Every couple has problems," she'd said when Holly showed up. "You have to work through them." But that message changed when Holly told her mother what Larry had said: "You're just a mama's girl. Can't you ever break away from that woman?"

"*That woman?*" Holly's mother had huffed. "He said *that woman?*— Stay as long as you like!"

Holly figured that would be the rest of her life. And it well might have been. For her mother made a point of always answering the phone. And she wielded the phrase *that woman* like a baseball bat every time Larry called. "That woman's not here right now," she would say and slam down the receiver. But about a week before Holly and Larry came to my office, Holly answered the phone herself.

"Holly, you don't know what it means to hear your voice," Larry began.

"What do you want?" Holly's tone was icy.

"I know you're angry. I can't blame you for being upset. I've been so wrong and I love you so much. Please just talk to me, that's all I ask. Just talk to me."

"About what?" Although still standoffish, her tone warmed a little.

He sensed the thaw. "About anything. Tell me how you're doing. Tell me what you're feeling. I'm just sick about everything. I really love you, and I've been so foolish. Being away from you has been horrible. More than I can bear. Please just tell me about you."

They talked for about fifteen minutes and although Holly's side of the conversation was marked by quick, cool answers, toward the fifteen-minute mark the thaw became more pronounced. But the time came when she had to go. "I have to get the kids up from their nap and begin getting dinner and cleaning up the house before Dad comes home. I'm sharing the chores with Mom."

"Tell your mother I'm sorry too. I've been terribly unfair to her."

And so they sat in my office. Holly is smallish women, but there was nothing about her that appeared weak. She looked perfectly capable of taking care of herself no matter how big the adversary. That's good, because Larry is a tall, thickly built guy who probably did well on a football team's defensive line. But today he wasn't thinking about defense. He was just very happy. Holly sat beside him again, something he'd thought would never happen. Of course, his happiness might have been a bit premature. She looked very hard.

"I'm glad you're here," I said. "Thanks for joining us."

Holly spoke first and said something that was quite surprising. The way she said it was even more surprising; she didn't smile or soften in any way. "I think he still loves me," she said. "Maybe he really loves me for the first time."

Larry couldn't believe his ears, and his jaw dropped. "For the first time? But I've always loved you. Haven't I said so?"

"But you meant it only a week ago," Holly said, her eyes only half on him. "You meant it only then."

"How did you know?" I asked.

"Because he cared about what I was thinking and feeling, and it mattered to him what I said. Now we'll see if that keeps up. He never talked about himself at all unless I asked. And he kept calling. He didn't give up."

The vocabulary of love. We all have one: What we do and say to show our love, what we see and hear that we interpret as love.

What's your love vocabulary?

It's important to know how each gives and receives love. If you don't, how will either of you know when you're showing you love?

Your Vocabulary of Love

To discover your vocabulary of love, you and your spouse need to answer some questions.

What do you do to show love? One of my female clients was asked this and she answered, "I do his icky laundry, don't I? Tell me that's not showing love." Her husband didn't like the answer. He wanted something like, "I make him his favorite dinner." Or, "I'm there for him anytime he needs me." But he got "icky laundry." Was it a good answer? Sure it was. It would be nice if there were other ways mentioned as well, but as we've learned, showing love is often *sacrificial.* It's doing something for your spouse that you wouldn't do unless you loved him or her. But, in fairness to both of you, showing love can also be something you initiate that you both enjoy. "After she's had a hard day, I like to bring dinner home." Or, "I clean the house and put the newspaper right by his chair so when he gets home he doesn't have to search for it." Or, "Every morning I get her coffee and the newspaper, bring it up to her in bed."

It could be any number of things. List ten ways that you show love—be specific. And tell the truth.

What does your spouse do to show you love? Try to list ten ways your spouse shows love to you—messages you see and hear. Be specific. By the way, your spouse may have been shouting loudly that he or she loves you, and you may not have heard. Or your spouse may have been voicing a concern that you may not have heard.

For example, when Larry heard what Holly said about what his phone calls had meant to her, he was both elated and confused. "But I'd been telling you I loved you all along. I kept up the house. We went out on dates. I told you I loved you all the time."

"Those were things you did because you wanted to do them. We went out on dates because you like movies. You like plays. You like that piano and jazz place. You kept the house up because of that neurotic thing about your dad." She turned to me. "His dad always said that it was a man's job to make a home for his family. Taught him everything there was to know about nailing and plumbing but nothing about electricity. He can hardly change a light bulb, but he can sure keep a toilet running." Then back to him. "It was nice you could do all those things. Don't get me wrong. But saying I love you through them. . ."

"But that's how my dad said he loved us. We always had a warm, comfortable, functioning home to live in. He was just scared of electricity—lightning—you know. But that's what I was saying. You know I'm more of an office kind of guy. I really don't like crawling under the house or on the roof, or putting up shelves. That's really not my thing. But I wanted you to have a nice home. And then I got on that 'mother' thing. And that was stupid. Early on, I was just being insensitive about your mom and your family. I was just wrong. A job's just a job. I can get a job anywhere. I'm sure God would have made sure we were all right no matter where we were."

I made a quick note and when my head came up I saw Holly's hand reach over to grab Larry's. "I never looked at it that way before. I just figured your dad—well, I just never looked at it that way before."

So, how does your spouse show you love? These are questions you should answer together. In fact, you can make a little game out of it. You might be surprised. But for now don't compare notes. Keep going.

How would you like your spouse to show love to you? Be specific—most couples tend not to be. Most would like to set some ground rules and allow a partner to be creative. That's okay. But be appreciative even if you don't like the way your spouse chooses. When your spouse is trying, give him or her the benefit of any doubts you might have. If you'd prefer more specific expressions, share them with your spouse—don't make him or her guess.

There are advantages and disadvantages to encouraging your spouse to be creative. But in any case, you want your spouse to want to use your language of love—you want him or her to look and listen for ways to tell you that you are loved. And the way to do that is to know and be able to speak your spouse's language of love. Realize that the vocabulary may change from time to time, so look and listen. And as you speak your spouse's language, you'll see your language being spoken.

An excellent work, *The Five Languages of Love* by Gary Chapman, succinctly breaks expressions of love into the following categories:[3]

1. Words of love and encouragement

2. Physical touch and closeness

3. Acts of service

4. Quality time

5. Gifts

Learn them and act on them. Becoming sensitive to one another's styles and needs opens your hearts.

What keeps you from getting the love God wants for you? God loves you. Even in times of trouble, He's with you. And often He shows His love through other people—those who are there when you're sick or unhappy, those who go out of their way for you when you need help or do an occasional kindness when kindness means so much.

Perhaps there are some things about you that make it difficult for people to show you love. Maybe you get angry a little too quickly. Or maybe you're judgmental or abrasive. Maybe as part of your protection mechanisms, you create a persona that's not approachable.

These sorts of things aren't fun to identify, so you may have trouble coming up with any. But it's worth the try. If you are able to deal with the behaviors that keep you from getting all the love God desires for you, then you'll get far more love—and that's never a bad thing. Remember, love doesn't fail—people do.

There's another set of people, though, who manage to keep love at a distance more duplicitously. These people cry, "Love me, please"—then reject or thwart any attempts directed at them. Next they complain about not being loved at all. Be wary of this love-spoiling pattern. It often stems from a fear of rejection.

How do you identify those elements of your emotional make-up that keep you from being loved? First, search and know the Scriptures to prepare yourself. Then ask your spouse and friends: "What keeps people from loving me?" The answers may hurt. But face the reality of what's being said, then work to do something about it. Bottom line, it's not enough to say you love. Be sure your love message—your heart—is being communicated clearly; be sure that it's understood, seen, felt, and shared.

The Love Account

As your spouse penetrates your heart with love and as you perceive yourself increasingly loved, something curious usually happens—you want to give love in return.

We learned earlier that love is to be unconditional and willful. Here we're learning the principle that love is also powerful—showing love can foster love. First John 4:19 helps us understand this: "We love Him because He first loved us." As we perceive how much He truly loves us, we are compelled to love Him in return. When we do, "His love [is] perfected in us" (1 John 4:12b). Think with me about a love account—an account that reflects the balance of the love that has flowed between the two of you.

Right now the balance of your love account may be near zero. You and your partner have gone through some pretty difficult times when there have probably been very few, if any, love transactions. You may have decided you're not loved at all. Hopefully, that will change soon. Just watch. As you and your spouse do loving things for each other, your accounts will have something to draw from.[4]

It's tough to give when your account is empty. Of course, in this early stage of rebuilding, you may also experience some negative transactions, but hopefully their numbers will diminish and soon the loving transactions will flow with greater frequency. The faster they do, the more quickly they'll take over, and soon you'll be faced with the biggest questions of all.

The Big Questions

How can I love you again? Loving someone means making yourself vulnerable. It involves risk and opening your heart, but it's more than that: It's *giving* your heart to someone. And what did that someone do the last time he or she had your heart? Mishandled it! *Love again? Are you nuts?!* I had a client who cried for an entire session over the prospect of having to love completely again.

I believe the answer to loving your spouse again starts with a decision; then it's a function of the transactions flowing in and out of your love accounts. If the vast majority are positive—if each speaks to the love your spouse has for you and vice versa, love will reign again. If a negative transaction slips in there now and again, keep in mind the 5–20 to 1 rule. One negative will erase as many as twenty positives. So it doesn't take many of those negative transactions—a harsh voice, an angry response, untrustworthy behavior—to empty the bank again and place any hope of future expressions of love at risk.

And pray for love—not only your own but also your spouse's. Real love. Resilient and lasting love. A love with all the elements we discussed earlier. Particularly the unconditional, committed love we all long for. Pray hard and humbly. God desires your marriage to work. So pray for Him to work in your hearts and minds to plant and nurture a re-blooming of your love for each other. I can't imagine you'd be ignored.

How can I trust you with my heart again? Although a companion question to the first big question, this is not exactly the same. Although the purest love includes trust, it would appear that love can exist independently for a time. You must build trust.

Much of the pain you're suffering from now stems from betrayal. You expected that you and your spouse would always be there for each other. That expectation was not met. When the marriage, for whatever reason, became less than your ideal—and perhaps only marginally less—the distance came and grew. You felt the dagger in your heart.

Trust is primarily an intellectual activity that involves being trustworthy and trusting. One act of betrayal can destroy trust forever. So how can you trust a spouse who may have betrayed your love many times? It simply takes time and effort—sometimes a lot of time and effort. It may seem forever out of reach. Ultimately, trust is built out of love, which speaks of fidelity. Only love can cover a multitude of sins. A caution while you're working on trust. Just as you wouldn't trust a thief with your wallet, you'll probably not trust your spouse with your heart for a while. But that's okay. During this time of truce, you will learn to build your future relationship in such a way as to help you regain and keep trust. For now let's just say that during the truce you'll each insist that the other behave in a trustworthy manner. If that doesn't happen, you'll undoubtedly rethink your commitment. So be careful with delicate hearts. Be trusting and trustworthy.

The answer to this question is not about a specific point in time or a specific set of circumstances. Rather it is a process of reestablishing trustworthiness and defining it loosely enough to allow normal human beings to achieve it. Assuming you love one another, you each want to be trusted by the other. A breach of trust is a horrible event, so if you are both sincere about reclaiming your marriage, neither will want to fail again.

With the Questions Answered . . .

Now that you've begun to understand your joint language of love and started the transaction flow to and from your love accounts, what's next? The level of intimacy in your marriage will never rise above the level of fear and anger in it. In the next chapter, we will attack both and start to construct your "safe zone."

EIGHTEEN

THE SAFE ZONE

Be still, and know that I am God; I will be exalted
among the nations, I will be exalted in the earth!
—*Psalm 46:10*

$\mathcal{I}$t's a hostile world out there. But when you have a healthy marriage, you have a secure harbor—a safe zone—where all that hostility rarely visits. In the safe zone there's acceptance, an understanding ear, a gentle word, and a warm hand. Just thinking about it when you're on the outside can bring peace.

But it hasn't been that way for you lately, has it? The hostility of the world outside has actually looked preferable to your home. Your safe harbor is no safer than a snake pit, and not quite as inviting. Safety is defined as "from your partner" not "with your partner."

If your marriage is to succeed, you need to change that. You need to re-create a safe zone for your marriage.

Create a Safe Zone

Practice Soft Love

Soft love is physical and emotional tenderness, gentleness, sweetness, encouragement. It involves sympathy and empathy. John Gottman says it involves "sharing interest in the other person, and what the other person is saying, being affectionate in obvious and subtle ways, showing you care through acts of thoughtfulness, being generously empathetic, being accepting, joking and laughing and sharing your joy."[1]

Although you can see the obvious advantages of practicing soft love with your spouse, it has another, not so obvious, advantage. Soft love brings safety to a marriage.

After Holly and Larry had been coming to counseling for about a month and we'd identified the issues that seemed to be standing in their way, we got down to dealing with some of the core issues.

"I felt so inadequate for you," Holly told Larry. "You were this great explorer, heading off four hundred miles from home to make a new start. And I was tied to my mom's apron strings. I both hated you for it and was jealous of your courage."

Larry looked at the floor. "I wasn't brave. I was scared to death. My mom and I never got along, and my dad had his career and didn't much care what I did as long as I was a success at it. All I wanted to do was get away from them. But when I got there, I was scared. I couldn't let you know because then you'd think I was weak."

"You were scared?" I could actually see Holly's heart go out to Larry. She took his hand and began massaging it. There was a simple tenderness in the act. When next we met, I asked them how things had been going. Larry smiled sheepishly, "Fine," he said. Soft love.

Tenderness, gentleness, sweetness, touching, embracing, cuddling—these soft expressions of love begin to create the safe zone.

Recognize Complementary Strengths

You and your spouse are probably good at complementary things. Carla and John came to realize that even though he was a manager at a manufacturing plant and was used to creating yearly budgets, he was no good with the family finances. Carla, on the other hand, could put a family budget together in an instant, then make it work. John turned out to have impeccable taste when picking out Carla's clothes—something he never did before their marital difficulties—but he couldn't fix a thing around the house. Even the simplest repair stumped him. Carla though, had a knack for fixing things. Anything with more than two moving parts fascinated her.

"In the past," Carla said during one counseling session, "I used to deride John for his lack of fix-it ability. My dad was good at fixing things, and he and I often worked together. I used to make John feel like less of a man because he couldn't fix things. But now I realize that there are things he does far better than I do and together we've got most things covered. In fact, it's better than both of us having the same strengths—we might actually get into arguments if we did. This way we both focus on what we do best. It works really well."

The next key to creating a safe environment is to celebrate your abilities and your differences. God can help you to be stronger and more effective as a couple than you were separately. And if there are things you both do well, consider doing them together, building an even more fulfilling relationship through them.

But no matter how complementary your strengths might be, there will always be disputes. To keep those disputes from undoing what you've worked so hard to achieve so far, use these solid, time-tested ways of dealing with them.

Ground Rules for Solving Problems and Disputes

The prevailing wisdom says that marriages flourish if the partners see eye to eye on most issues—thereby minimizing the battles and the likelihood of war. Dr. John Gottman's groundbreaking research showed just the opposite. The couples who were most likely to stay together were those who had differences and experienced those differences early in marriage. These couples fought, and at times fought hard, for what they believed and wanted. But their battles never got negative—they had constructive instead of destructive ways of resolving their differences.[2]

Based on his twenty years of research, Dr. Howard Markman estimates that if couples used positive methods of conflict resolution, 50 percent of marriages that now end in divorce could be saved.[3] An excellent method follows.

Accept Each Other

In any relationship, problems and disputes come with the territory, and you naturally want to minimize the impact they have. The first step is to concentrate on solving the problems that actually have workable solutions. Sounds reasonable, doesn't it? Some couples, however, generate a lot of heat and ill will by trying to solve problems that, for the time being, have no workable solutions, those that center around personality traits, likes and dislikes, behavioral tendencies, or a hundred other issues that essentially make you and your partner who you are.

Stop Criticizing

Criticizing your mate for creating a problem does nothing but cause your mate to react—usually destructively. When a problem comes, face it, accept it, and work to solve it. Even if your partner's consistent behavior seems to warrant criticizing, don't. For instance, if your partner gets speeding tickets and forces your car insurance rates higher than you can afford, it's still best not to criticize. The offending spouse will know there's a problem, and if allowed to come to that conclusion and change the behavior on his or her own, you will both be better off for it.

Double-Check and Paraphrase

As you go through the problem-solving process, frequently double-check and paraphrase what has been said to make sure you understand each other. This will not only help decrease misunderstandings, but it will also help reduce mind reading and jumping to conclusions. This technique may be a little awkward at first, but as you and your partner solve more and more problems, you'll come to appreciate it and will begin to do it without thinking.

In a heated discussion, which happens periodically in the early stages of reclaiming a marriage, a more formally defined method of communication might be helpful. Scott Stanley and his associates devised such a method, the Speaker-Listener Technique.[4] It can be used with two or more people, which means you can include the kids to solve family disputes.

The Speaker-Listener Technique

The speaker has the floor. To make sure the speaker has the opportunity to fully express an idea, he or she is given the floor and is not interrupted. The "floor" can be an actual object that designates the speaker. After he or she has spoken, the listeners will paraphrase or practice other techniques that help to make sure they understand.

The floor is shared. No one person gets to monopolize the floor. Each may say a number of things but then must hand the floor to another person. The speaker then becomes a listener.

Do not attempt to solve problems. This element of the problem-solving technique is to make sure that all ideas get their fair hearing. Actually coming to a solution will happen later. For now, just present information and/or ideas and try to understand the others'.

As you can imagine, there are specific rules for both the speaker and the listeners.

Rules for the Speaker

Speak for yourself. These are your ideas and information you know, not ideas you've read minds to collect or information that is only rumor or innuendo.

Talk in small, digestible chunks. Organize what you're going to say into small, understandable packets. Don't ramble. Don't intertwine several notions and then chase the strands. You want your ideas to have impact, so state them clearly and understandably.

Stop and let the listeners paraphrase. After each packet of information, stop and make sure the listeners have an opportunity to restate your thoughts. When the paraphrase comes back, acknowledge whether it's right or wrong. If it's wrong, state your point again even more clearly; don't stop until your idea has been received correctly.

Rules for Listeners

Paraphrase what you hear. Restate what you've heard, telling the speaker what you think he or she means. "I won't be home for dinner," might mean to you, "My cooking isn't good enough for you and you're going to stop for a burger on the way home." Such a response gives your spouse the opportunity to say, "No. I love your cooking. I just have a staff meeting that's going to last until about 8:00." That, of course, is a flippant example, but you get the idea.

Don't rebut; hear the speaker's message. You'll have a chance during your time as speaker to present a differing opinion. Right now, just make sure you understand the speaker. If you jump in and disagree, you could be disagreeing with something he or she didn't really say and causing tension unnecessarily.

By using this method, particularly when things get heated, you'll be better prepared to go on to the next step in problem solving, or conflict resolution.

Don't Make Your Spouse a Monster

Just before bed one night some friends we know got into a little tiff. It was nothing major, but it caused them to have to kiss and make up before turning off the lights. The next morning the husband got up early and went off to work. Since their argument the night before had caused them to stay up later than normal, the husband decided to let his wife sleep in and he didn't wake her to say goodbye. The wife woke angry; she thought his leaving without saying goodbye had been a snub, a continuation of their fight the night before. She called her husband at work angry and hurt. When he explained, she didn't believe him.

The solution to this kind of problem is to simply not ascribe bad intentions to anything your spouse says or does. Give your spouse the benefit of the doubt and go on. If you do ascribe bad intentions, your spouse will end up having to defend his or her motives—and motives are unproveable. Such arguments just tear you down and make things more stressful.

Define the Problem

Resolving any dispute begins with defining the problem. What is this dispute really about? Sometimes it's not easy: Your child has gotten in trouble at school. You both work. Who's going to see the teacher? The problem with some issues is that they can have undercurrents of a power struggle, revenge, or other hidden agendas. One spouse might use such a problem to win some "turf." Defining each problem as it comes up gets these hidden agendas either out of the way or out in the open where the two of you can deal with them.

How, then, do you define a problem? Get at the root cause. If one of you has to go see little Johnny's teacher during the day and you both work, the problem of who goes boils down to the cost if you go versus the cost if your spouse goes. You both might suffer some diffi- culty, but the one to go is the one whose going will hurt you least as a couple. When the problem is stated in that way, the solution becomes reasonably easy. You need to discuss the loss that you each would experience as objectively as possible. Then decide based on some objective measure—money lost, good will at work lost, or the ability to juggle a schedule.

Sometimes that measure includes an emotional toll. Talk about these issues, particularly the softer ones—love, loneliness, tenderness, abandonment, personal pride. Two clients had grown up poor. They married, worked hard, and were finally able to afford a nice home in a nice neighborhood and a new car. Still counting their pennies, they got auto insurance with a $500 deductible. Well, someone hit their parked car one night and didn't leave a note. The passenger-side rear end was crushed and, although the car was still drivable, the estimate to fix the car was nearly two thousand dollars. Of course, they were only liable for $500 of it, but $500 to these folks, as it probably is to all of us, was a lot of money. The husband thought they should wait and fix the car after they had saved up the money, something that would probably take a long time. The wife wanted it fixed now. "All my life I've wanted the respect that goes with having a nice car. Not a Rolls or anything, but just a nice car. I think we should get it fixed now and cut bare bones on expenses." Since both had experienced the feelings the wife expressed, it gave them a common ground on which to build a solution.

Finally, stick to just one problem. Often during the truce period, couples have pent-up issues they want resolved. These old issues can bubble up and grab the focus. When they do, suddenly the couple becomes so embroiled in the past that current, pressing problems go unresolved. If a past issue rears its head, out of respect for the person who brought it up, write the problem down so you can deal with it another time, then get back to the problem at hand.

Collect Data

If the couple with the crunched car got it fixed immediately, where would the $500 come from? Could they squeeze their expenses that much? With calculator, pencil, and paper in hand, they went to work. They looked at all their bills and their due dates. They looked at all their discretionary expenses to see if anything could be cut.

The couple with the teacher's appointment went through schedules and discussed the impact of moving appointments around.

During this phase, be as thorough as you can. Make sure you have all the relevant data, and if there's information you need to get, decide who will get it and when so that you can get back to solving the problem as quickly as possible.

When both partners agree that all relevant data has been accumulated, go on to the next phase.

Look at Alternative Solutions

Some might call this brainstorming; I prefer to call it going through the alternatives. Like brainstorming, though, there are no bad alternatives at first. Every suggestion is a worthy one until it's evaluated. Start by presenting possible solutions and writing them down in full sentences—that way there will be no confusion later as to what was meant. Practice your double-checking and paraphrasing techniques to make sure you really understand each other. When this phase ends, you should have a list of possibilities to begin to evaluate against the data.

Evaluate the Alternatives

You're coming closer to the bottom line—the solution. And as you evaluate all the alternatives, some hidden agendas may pop up— data that you or your spouse knew about but were reluctant to share. In the case of the teacher's appointment, one partner may be having trouble at work that he or she's kept secret. In the case of the damaged car, one partner might owe some money the other might not know about. It's important that both partners come clean about everything. Hidden agendas do nothing but drive wedges between you and subvert the process of building trust. If there are issues that need to come into the open, get them out there.

Hopefully there are none of those, and the process of evaluation will go smoothly. That process isn't all that hard: Together go through each alternative and match it against the constraints posed by the data you have. As you do, be free to bring up any pros and cons or subjective feelings, anything, really, that would affect the final choice.

Get to Yes

The final step is to select an alternative. This selection should be as emotion- and "arbitrariness"-free as possible—and certainly free of any bullying. Choose the course that is best for the marriage and for each of you. As it turned out, the couple with the dent found that if they waited two weeks, they could make do and cut back enough to fix the car. Although the wife didn't like driving a dented car for two weeks, she decided that two weeks was a lot better than a month or forever. So she said okay. The husband didn't like the idea of going without their Friday night dates and cutting back on groceries, but he knew how important getting the car fixed was to his wife. So he said okay.

The couple with the teacher's appointment discovered that neither could make the meeting without creating problems at work. But they both could make it if the time was changed to two hours later. They called the teacher, who was willing to make the change. Both parents went.

Use Feedback Mechanisms

After you make a decision, revisit it at appropriate intervals to make sure your decision is really working. The couple with the dent came back to the issue once a week to make sure their spending estimates were on track and that there weren't any unexpected expenses that would throw their decision off. The couple with the teacher's appointment came together about a week later to see if they had estimated the impact correctly. As it turned out, the changed appointment had caused one of them more of a problem than expected, and there was some animosity about it. But, by talking it out, they came to understand what the costs would be if this happened again. Some of those costs they passed on to their child for having caused the problem in the first place; he got an extra week's detention to learn the consequences of his actions.

Learn to Respect Again

At the center of a love relationship is respect, holding each other in high regard. That doesn't mean you will always completely agree with your partner. Quite the contrary. You might heatedly disagree on any number of issues, but we'd like to add to your new problem-solving skills a respect for the thoughtfulness of each other's arguments, the passion with which they're presented, the uprightness of the argument's underpinnings.

The centerpiece of a polarized relationship is a lack of respect—for each other and often for yourself. In the heat of battle you've come to see what you think is the core of your mate, and you may not like what you've seen: the meanness, the willingness to be unjust, or any number of negative characteristics. You may not see the goodness you used to see in your spouse. And you have lost respect for him or her.

So, how do you rekindle respect?

Begin by looking at your spouse as a human being. A person with strengths and weaknesses, likes and dislikes, who is dealing with the fears and doubts we all deal with. A person God views through Jesus as holy and blameless, as "without blemish" (Eph. 5:27). As Oswald Chambers says, a person you should see as perfect in Christ.[5]

Next, begin to *treat* your spouse with respect. This may be difficult because, in all likelihood, your spouse has not treated you very respectfully. Focus on what you can construct. When your spouse has an idea, listen to it and evaluate it on its merits. Never ridicule or ignore. What your spouse has to say is important. Don't exclude your partner from any decision that will affect your family. In fact, work to bring your spouse into the process. Even if he or she resists.

Soon after John and Carla recommitted to working on their marriage, John did something very wise. Knowing that he had treated Carla with a great deal of contempt by deliberately pushing her jealousy button—a very disrespectful act—he came home one day from work and sat at the kitchen table while Carla worked on dinner. "I've got a problem at work. Can you help me with it?" he asked.

"Me?" she answered, surprised. "I don't know anything about what you do at work."

"You know more than you think you do. I've got two women on staff who just don't get along. They're both good workers, but this feud between them is starting to affect not only their work but everybody else's too. Got any ideas?"

"Why?"

"You're a smart woman, and I trust your judgment. HR says I can't fire them. And I don't want to."

Carla stopped working on dinner, turned, and looked at John with thoughtful eyes. "You've talked to them?"

"Twice. Nothing. It's like lecturing to a couple of icebergs."

"Then you have to make it important for them to listen."

"How?"

"Do they get along with the other people on the line?"

"Sure. It's like a family. That's the problem. Everybody's choosing sides."

"Then make them responsible for the group's success. My sister and I used to fight all the time. We couldn't work together on a project to save our souls. Then my dad—who never said anything unless he meant it—put us in charge of getting ready for our vacation. If we didn't work together, we wouldn't get to go. So we found a way to work together. We definitely wanted to go on vacation. If everyone's success depends on your two employees working together successfully, they'll figure out a way."

John thought about her suggestion and nodded. "I'll give it a try."

From that moment on, he and Carla became a team. As with any couple coming out of a painfully polarized situation, they had more bumps and bruises along the way, but they began to communicate better.

Another vital element in fostering respect for each other is to take down the high bar of perfectionism. Your partner does not have to be perfect to deserve your respect. Nor do you have to be perfect to be respected. We must always work the sin out of our lives and daily try to live closer and closer to Jesus' example. That said, give your spouse some slack—give big points for trying and big points for confessing and repenting. There are few things in life worth fighting over. Forgive each other, even when it might be difficult. Be tolerant, loving, and accepting.

Next, laugh *with* your spouse. Joke around. See the humor in things. Proverbs 15:13 tells us, "A merry heart makes a cheerful countenance." It's hard to laugh with someone you don't respect; mutual humor, healthy humor, is based on a comfortable respect. If your spouse says something funny, enjoy it. And don't be afraid to make a joke. When you were dating, the moments that brought you the closest were probably filled with laughter.

Ease the Grip of Fear

There's so much of the future you can find to fear. Divorce is a frightening prospect. Being tied to someone you don't love for the rest of your life can be even more frightening. Being held in contempt by someone who's supposed to love you can be terrifying. And finally, perhaps most frightening of all, wondering if your spouse will let you down again and leave you abandoned with more excruciating pain can be almost unbearable.

These are all realistic fears.

But embracing them does you no good. They keep the joy and good feelings you might be rekindling in your relationship at bay. For the more precious your relationship becomes, the greater the loss will be if it goes sour again. Therefore, you create a vested interest, because of your fears, to push those good times away.

Let loose of your fear. This is easier said than done, but there is a way to do so. Start by being realistic about the worst-case scenario. No matter what happens in the future, you'll have your health, you'll still be alive, you'll still have your friends, and you'll still be one of God's children. Consciously replace your fear with faith.

Jesus has promised never to leave you nor forsake you. He's called Himself the author and finisher of your faith. He is your fortress against fear. Although perfect faith, and therefore perfect fearlessness, is a goal we'll reach only in heaven, the more we loosen our grip on fear, the more we free ourselves to love.

So, pray for and work at your faith. Throw fear away. "For God has not given us a spirit of fear, but of power and of love and of a sound mind" (2 Tim. 1:7).

Confess the Past

The key to confessing—which makes true confession possible—is to take responsibility for the sins of your past. As you begin to respect your spouse again, as the truce matures and your love accounts begin to fill, you'll also begin to see very clearly the times when you treated your spouse disrespectfully or with contempt; times when you ignored your spouse or, worse, abused him or her; times when you sinned. When these occur to you, confess them to your spouse. Then ask for forgiveness from God and your mate. Not only does such confession and forgiveness bring a spiritual cleansing and a renewed investment in the relationship, but your partner will see that you understand. That understanding goes a long way toward eliminating the wedges between you.

Submit, but Not Like Before

Ephesians 5:21 and 22 both have the word *submit* in them. "Submitting to one another in the fear of God" (v. 21). "Wives, submit to your own husbands, as to the Lord" (v. 22). The first commands us to see each other as spiritual equals before the Lord. We're to respect each other as God's children and realize we are working together in God's army. Within a deteriorating marriage, submitting to one another became an impossible task. You may have yourself begrudgingly submitting to someone you didn't respect.

But like so many things, with the coming of the truce and recommitment, this spiritual task will change with God's direction. As love and respect grows, you will recapture the meaning of verse 21 in your lives. You'll again see yourselves as in God's design, working together for the kingdom. This will likely come slowly, but as it does, take note of it. The same should be true of the command in verse 22. As respect grows, as a sense of rightness takes root, as serving one another in love increases, a proper, loving submission will increasingly become the order of the day.

Set Healthy Boundaries

You and your spouse are individuals. Even though God has brought you together and has made you one, you're still separate people. As you lost at love and began to polarize, you became even more separated. To make an orderly process of attempting to come back together, you need to set boundaries that will be respected. Again that word—*respect*. And let's add another—*honor*. As Dr. Henry Cloud and Dr. John Townsend put it in *Boundaries,* "A boundary is anything that helps to differentiate you from someone else or shows where you begin and end."[6] Relational boundaries set up rules and roles that allow for harmony and help to foster respect and honor.

War against Negative Thoughts

Negative thoughts shut out the light in a relationship, an impact that Carla and John experienced. John had used Carla's suggestion concerning the warring women at work, and it had had the desired result. Although the women hadn't become fast friends, they had begun to work together. For all practical purposes, their war was over. John came home eager to tell Carla the news.

Carla, however, wasn't in the mood for good news—frankly she wasn't in the mood for any news at all. The washing machine had gone on the fritz early that morning, and it had taken baby-sitting the thing all day just to get a couple loads done. During the ordeal, Carla had found herself comparing John's fix-it abilities with those of her father's again—and John consistently came up short. So when he came home, she was less than enthusiastic in her greeting. And John felt a return of the old animosities. *She's moody again. I was only a few minutes late too. Geez, it's starting again.*

He went into the living room and buried himself in the newspaper. Carla had seen his happy expression and immediately resented him. *He's probably been sitting in his air-conditioned office all day not thinking about me at all while I've been trying to get his underwear clean. And he'll be no help fixing the machine either.*

Negative thoughts. It's putting the worst possible face on an event and allowing the negative thought to become the accepted truth by making it the rule of your heart. God frowns on this and tells us so in Romans 12:1–2, 1 Corinthians 10:5b, and particularly in Philippians 4:8: "Finally, brethren, whatever things are true, whatever things are noble, whatever things are just, whatever things are pure, whatever things are lovely, whatever things are of good report, if there is any virtue and if there is anything praiseworthy—meditate on these things."

Fortunately, John looked up from his newspaper and, rather coolly at first, told Carla his news. She realized how she'd shut him down and apologized. After she told him about her day, he understood and they ended up having a few nice moments making up.

But often the opposite is true. Negative thoughts remain the truth, and the more they do, the more they occur. Soon the relationship becomes a tangled web of them. The best way to avoid that tangled web is to not allow negative thoughts to go unchecked.

Noted psychiatrist Aaron Beck has identified and studied a pattern of thinking that assails the truth of a situation. Some common thinking distortions couples engage in include:

- *Arbitrary inference.* This overlaps the negative thoughts and attributes a negative motive to someone's behavior in the absence of evidence.

- *Selective abstraction.* Information is taken out of context. Certain details are highlighted while others are ignored. "John must be lazy. He didn't take out the garbage again today." But John didn't take out the garbage because he was sick in bed.

- *Over-generalization.* An isolated incident becomes defined as the norm. A wife is reading a book when her husband speaks to her. She hears his voice but not what he's said because her mind is on her reading. "What did you say?" she asks. He replies, "You never listen to me. It's like talking to a wall."

- *Magnification and minimization.* Things are blown way out of proportion. A usually conscientious husband fails to record a check he wrote. The wife explodes and accuses him of financial negligence then begins to fret that they're about to go bankrupt.

- *Personalization.* External events are attributed to one's self when insufficient evidence exists to render the conclusion. For example, a man says he'll grab dinner out because he has to work late. The wife assumes he hates her cooking.

- *Dichotomous thinking:* Experiences are codified as either all or nothing, a complete success or complete failure.

- *Labeling and mislabeling.* Past mistakes are allowed to define self-worth, in spite of growth.

- *Tunnel vision.* Sometimes partners see only what they want to see or what fits their current state of mind. One day a man might feel generous and suggest his wife splurge on herself. The next day he might feel more frugal, and accuse her of being a spendthrift.

- *Biased thinking.* This thinking assumes a devious negative motive to a spouse's actions without evidence.

Monitor your thinking and determine whether you're falling into any of these patterns. If you are, stop and search for the truth of the situation.

Work on Trust

We've discussed the importance of trust, but not how to build it. Building trust is a process that begins with small things. For John it was a willingness to call if he was going to be late and a promise to not push Carla's jealousy buttons. Over the weeks of their initial truce, he followed the rules religiously. Carla was to be supportive of John's work and to try to make his home a warm and inviting place, which she did. As the weeks melted away, Carla's trust of John grew—as did his trust of her. Even though both worked at earning the other's trust, neither performed perfectly. There were a couple of times during the six-week period when John failed to call. But he'd been in meetings and had lost track of time. Carla believed him without hesitation.

A component of trust is knowing that your spouse wants your trust and is willing to work, and even sacrifice, for it. That willingness allows each the space to fail now and again.

So as the truce progresses, work on trust. Remember, it's about being trustworthy as well as trusting. You'll find little else more important.

Carla and John's trust grew to the point where at the end of their six-week truce, they renewed their commitment for another six weeks. And another after that.

Sex

During the time of polarization, sex may have become your only means of expression. It may also have become a battle ground, a power struggle, or a hundred other things—none of them what a gracious, loving God created sex for. Sex is an expression of your love; in a healthy marriage it's a time of wondrous acceptance, accessibility, and fun. As your truce unfolds, work to bring sex back to its rightful place in your marriage. Go slowly at first, tenderly taking care with each other's feelings and expectations. And, as your lovemaking evolves, allow it to become what each of you desires. Help each other to achieve the unfathomable beauty of the physical expression of love.

A Final Word

The safe zone is completed in theory. What's left now is to make it a reality. Begin by actually putting into practice what this chapter is suggesting. It might take a bit of time, and you might have a few false starts. Expect that. But false starts or not, don't neglect the safe zone's construction. The rest of your journey depends on it.

PART THREE

Reconcile

NINETEEN

TURN YOUR
LOVE AROUND

*Married life offers no panacea—if it is going to reach its potential,
it will require an all-out investment by both husband and wife.*

—James C. Dobson

p to this point I've asked you to reframe your marital journey and begin to work through your anger, your hurt, and the injustice you've suffered over the years—to stack it behind a truce bathed in godly directives with the assurance that the truce would at least challenge you to stop hurting each other and begin rebuilding your love account. That's important because it gives you breathing room and provides freedom to refashion your love and your relationship. But now the time has come for you to take a very big step, to literally turn your love around. Up to now your love has been growing—if it has been growing—primarily because of your desire to achieve what God desires.

Now it's time for your love to grow because of who you and your spouse have become. And to pave the way for that to happen, you and partner must *forgive* each other, if you haven't already, for the sins that you have perpetrated against each other. Next begin to *empathize* with each other, to understand who you are today, what made you that way, and what forces guide what you do.

The Road to Forgiveness

Holly and Larry got a sitter for the weekend and made their way to a lake about fifty miles from their home. It was beautiful, particularly this time of year. The fall trees blazed with reds, oranges, and a haunting peach, and crackly leaves deeply carpeted the paths. There were several cabins at the north end of the lake, and they rented one not far from the boat dock. Neither Holly nor Larry cared about the boats, though. They were up there for other reasons. We'd discussed that it was time for them to truly forgive each other, and they wanted a quiet, private place where they could work on doing just that.

I'd given them a list of things to do; the first was to just talk about what they had done to each other. I told them that this was going to be difficult because it provided an opportunity to be accusatory and to open up some old wounds. But it's important for a couple to be able to talk about these things, no matter how uncomfortable. And it was uncomfortable for Larry, for he considered himself very much at fault for driving Holly away.

Talk about the Hurts

"I know you feel responsible," Holly said. They'd made themselves some coffee and settled in before the fire to talk. "But I'm not sure you should shoulder all the blame."

"I shouldn't?" Larry's interest was peaked. He'd not heard her talk like this before.

"That first time you criticized me for calling mom too much, my back went up and I was determined to call her even more. I was going to show you who was boss."

"When I saw that second bill, I didn't know what to do. My manhood was questioned. My role as a husband was questioned. We couldn't afford the payment—there were so many moving bills—so I was worried about that. Plus I didn't want to make you mad, but I knew I had to say something again. And I got so defensive."

"I really was a mama's girl. I can remember calling her up to find out how to make Hamburger Helper. I knew she did some things a little different—she threw peas into it or something. All I really had to do was read the box. But I felt so lost being away."

"And I felt so lost too," Larry said. "And then when you reacted like you did, I felt alone. I didn't have a mother to talk to."

"Wow, it never crossed my mind that you might feel that way."

Larry nodded, "I kept my defenses up so you wouldn't see it."

"But I should have," Holly said. "I really should have."

By talking about the issues and feelings that came up as a result of your interactions, by being understanding and attributing no ill will to each other, the two of you can get everything out on the table—all the hurts, the injustices, the misunderstandings, everything that drove wedges between you. By talking about your past and understanding its impact, you can give it a proper burial.

Ask for Forgiveness

Holly went silent for a moment and took a long drink of coffee. She was stalling. She knew that the next thing on the list was to ask for forgiveness, but something inside her didn't want to. Instead of burying this feeling, she did something quite brave. "I don't want to ask you for forgiveness," she said. "I know I'm supposed to. But I don't want to."

"Why not?" Larry asked, clearly confused. "I can hardly wait to ask you for it. Man, all I want to hear is that you forgive me."

"I don't know. Maybe we'd better talk about it."

"Okay," Larry said. He sat quietly, waiting to hear Holly's thoughts.

"Tim always says," she began tentatively, "when you're tempted to say, 'I don't know,' to go with whatever's bubbling to the surface. Well," she stopped, taking a moment to collect her words, "I think I still want revenge."

"Revenge," Larry repeated, taking in the full meaning of the word.

"You know, it really hurt when you called me a mama's girl. I know we've batted that phrase around a lot, but it really hurt. It said you didn't respect me, that I was somehow seriously flawed, weak. And I didn't like it at all. In fact it made me angry. I guess it still does."

"So you're not ready to forgive me," Larry said. "But that's okay. I'll forgive—"

"No," she interrupted. "If you forgive me, then I have to forgive you and at this moment I don't think I ever want to forgive you."

Larry whispered, "Come on."

But then the steam went out of her. "And you know why? Because you were right, and I knew you were," she said. "I felt really weak. I *was* a mama's girl. And all you were doing was pointing it out. That's what made me angry." She stared at her coffee for a moment. "Can you ever forgive me for being such a—well, such a difficult person to live with?"

"In a heartbeat," Larry said. He looked like he wanted to kiss her, but he didn't. Instead he asked, "And can you ever forgive me for demeaning you like that? For not understanding what you were going through?"

What Is Forgiveness?

But instead of coming quickly back with a syrupy, "I forgive you too," Holly's mouth opened then snapped shut. She began reading a hand-written note: "*Forgiveness* is the act of letting go of the anger and offense and turning all desire for retribution and revenge over to the Lord. It's being prepared to reconcile if you can and, *if wisdom permits*, to reestablish all necessary ties with the person being forgiven.[1] Forgiveness is about canceling a debt, and it's something I do. Reconciling is our responsibility—it takes two."

"What's wrong?" Larry asked, confused.

Holly looked up. "How could you not understand?" She blurted out incredulously. "You dragged me away from home. I was only twenty-two. Granted I wasn't a baby anymore, but I wasn't a mature woman. Sometimes even though I have two kids, I wonder if I'm a mature woman now. How could you not understand?"

"You're still angry."

"You bet I'm angry. It's like the whole world revolved around you, and I was just someone to get dragged along. I'm getting madder and madder as I think about it."

She got to her feet and splashed the dregs of her coffee into the sink. "I don't want to talk about this anymore. I need to cool off." She grabbed her puffy ski jacket and went outside.

Larry could do nothing. After a moment, he went to the kitchen window and peered out. But she'd disappeared.

A moment later he saw her at the tiller of an aluminum catch, the ten-horsepower motor whining as she took it toward the center of the lake. The lake was only a couple acres across, so she wasn't all that far out. When she got there, she killed the engine and just sat.

Larry wasn't sure what to do; the woman he loved had quite effectively cut off all communications with him. He poured himself another cup of coffee and sat on the couch, waiting for her next move.

About five minutes later, Larry heard thunder right overhead. Within seconds, an icy rain began to fall. And moments after the first barrage of drops pummeled the lake, Larry heard the outboard's insistent whine. On his feet again, Larry watched as Holly, deeply buried in the hood of her jacket, headed back to the dock.

Bursting through the cabin door a few minutes later, she threw her wet jacket over a chair and ran to the fireplace. As she began thawing, she said, "I couldn't believe it. I've never seen rain come up that fast. Have you ever seen rain come up that fast?"

"I'm glad it wasn't snow."

"Yeah," she shivered. "Right."

"You didn't have much time to think."

"Yes I did," she said. "And I had time to pray. You know God, through Jesus, forgave me a whole bunch of stuff before you even came along. And He was quick to remind me of that out there."

"The rain?"

"No, before the rain," she said. "The rain came because I was still hesitating, like my grievances with you were bigger than His with me. Well, I'm still angry. But, then, you have every right to be angry with me, too, and you're not. I'll deal with my anger somehow. But I just have to forgive you." She moved toward him and put warmer arms around him. "We've come too far and have much too far left to go for me to not forgive you."

Forgiveness is not something that just happens. In fact, the *opposite* of forgiveness is what just happens. Forgiveness is something you have to work at, and sometimes it's not easy at all. Let's just go over all the steps involved.

Step 1: Air your grievances and listen to your partner's grievances. Do this in a nonaccusatory manner with continuous reference to the emotions that come up. Listen actively.

Step 2: Ask each other for forgiveness for specific things. This forces you each to take responsibility for what you did.

Step 3: Discuss and deal with any obstacles to forgiveness, such as a continued desire for revenge or a continued streak of anger.

Step 4: Use God's forgiveness of you through Jesus' sacrifice on the cross as a model and reason for your forgiveness. See Ephesians 4:32.

Step 5: Forgive. *Forgiveness* is the act of letting go of the anger and offense and turning all desire for retribution and revenge over to the Lord. It's being prepared to reconcile if you can and, *if wisdom permits,* to reestablish all necessary ties with the person being forgiven.

Step 6: Continue to pray, and if the anger and hurt return, which they undoubtedly will, work your way through the steps again.

Forgiveness is the act of wiping the slate clean. In Psalms 103:12, God tells us, "As far as the east is from the west, so far has He removed our transgressions from us." Later on He tells us He casts our sins into the depths of the sea. But we're human. There's not one of us who can easily forget the hurts or bruises of a spouse's transgressions. As step 6 says, those hurts will probably come again, so strongly, in fact, that we'll have to go through some of the steps of forgiving again. While our slates may never be spotless, they will be reasonably clean, certainly clean enough to write on it again.

Empathy: The Heart of Consistent Love

We saw empathy at work in John in a previous chapter when he decided not to take the class. Some of you may have thought he had given in to the weakest part of Carla and in doing so failed to give her the opportunity to grow and he shut himself off from a business opportunity. But in reality, John put himself in Carla's shoes. That's what empathy is—and it's the mark of true Christian love. It's the act of understanding the person you love and trying on a situation before you present it to another. It hopefully will result in making a decision that is bathed in someone else's perspective.

So, how do we empathize?

First, and foremost, learn as much as you can about your partner. I don't mean just the chronology of places and events, but how those places and events shaped him or her and how they are influencing things now.

John knew there would come a time—maybe in a few months, maybe in a few years, when he would go to the class and perhaps even attend the class with a woman. But the best time for Carla to endure that would be later, after they'd had a little more time to build the necessary trust and work though some of her issues with jealousy. How did he come to that conclusion? By becoming Carla for a while. He allowed himself to be molded by the pain of her experiences. That night, lying in bed, realizing that his wife was downstairs struggling, he took himself back to the moment so many years before when Carla came home and found her mother and father locked in icy silence. How devastating must that have been for a young girl filled with all the insecurities of just growing up?

Lying there in bed he mapped that onto feelings he'd had growing up, experiences he'd never told anyone about. Now, so many years later, he relived his insecurities so he could better understand Carla's. John shuddered. Every time he'd put Carla into a situation where her jealousy was exposed, he had forced her to relive that childhood moment, forced her to hear her mother's words again, forced her to see her father's face again, knowing he was an adulterer.

Suddenly, the thought of forcing her to go through it, for whatever the benefit, was something he just couldn't do.

So, in a nutshell, that's what empathy is. Let's review the steps that get you there.

Step 1: Commit yourself to selflessly loving your spouse. It's only through this commitment that you have the energy and interest to empathize.

Step 2: Learn those elements of your spouse's life that had significant impact. During this step you build the emotional mold into which you step when you empathize.

Step 3: Learn how those elements affect your spouse's emotional and physical reactions to situations—particularly situations you author. This allows you to step into the mold you created in step 2 and understand the true impact your behavior, and the behavior of the world, has on her.

Step 4: When appropriate, and it's appropriate quite often, empathize with your spouse. This step brings your love up to the level of Christ's love for us. This is "giving yourself" for your spouse.

The Effect of Empathy

The first effect of empathy is immediate. It shows your spouse more clearly than words that you love him or her. You are not only willing to pay lip service to love, but you are also willing to give place to your spouse's needs and issues.

Empathy will also produce strength and courage in your partner. When John pushed his career into the background to keep Carla from having to go through a bout of jealousy, she saw how much her jealousy cost not only John but also their partnership. She soon asked me for special help to deal with it. As with any counseling, what matters most is that an individual sees a problem and becomes invested in the solution. It took Carla about six months of solid work to begin to trust men as a sex, which allowed her trust in John to grow that much faster.

Forgiving and empathizing are not minor achievements. In fact, they're ongoing processes. Hurt can revisit you and require you to renew your forgiveness. Empathy is also an ongoing process that grows as your knowledge of your spouse grows. You may want to reread this chapter periodically, for there are no more important building blocks to a strong, healthy, godly marriage than forgiveness and empathy.

TWENTY

CHOOSE TO
LOVE AGAIN

Hope deferred makes the heart sick, but
when the desire comes, it is a tree of life.
—*Proverbs 13:12*

We don't usually think of love as a choice; it's often seen more as spontaneous combustion. It certainly doesn't seem like a choice in high school or college. "Love" is that moment when your eyes meet across a classroom, or you're taking tickets at the game in the gym and suddenly he's standing in front of you. In that instant your heart's his, and you can't rest until you've met, talked, held hands. Love is the sudden connection of a thousand threads—where you seem to have everything in common, and what you don't doesn't matter.

There's no way to predict it, guard against it, or force it to occur. It just happens. In fact, if we could choose the magic of love, wouldn't we be choosing love all the time?

But you've been hurt. And not just any old hurt, but a real hurt, a blow to the heart. On your island of me, the drawbridge went up.

Letting down that drawbridge again is a choice. In this chapter we will discuss the choices you might make to begin to love again. You may not be ready to act on them yet. You may want to go slowly. Banishing hurt and gaining the comfort necessary to love again may take time. As you read this chapter, think of the small steps you might be willing to take.

Choose to Care about (and Help) Your Spouse

When you're huddled and isolated on your island of me, if someone asks you how your partner is doing and you're in the mood to be absolutely truthful, you'll probably say, "I don't care." Your mate could be having trouble with just about anyone or anything, and you might respond, "Well, it serves him right." Or, "What did she expect, being the way she is?" A large part of severing emotional ties with someone is to just stop caring.

Choosing to love again is choosing to start caring again—choosing to get invested and give appropriate comfort. Holly began doing that with Larry. Early on in their marriage, as Larry became more critical of her relationship with her mother, Holly had just stopped caring about him. Oh, if he were in an auto accident or violently mugged, she figured she might manage some sympathy, but the first tie that went in their relationship was her caring about Larry. However, when he became more sympathetic to her plight and signed up with a long-distance company that offered a reduced rate, she became more sensitive to him. Unexpectedly, Larry found himself sitting at the dinner table answering sincere questions about his day. "So, tell me about the advertising campaigns you're working on."

"I have two right now."

"They both coming easy for you?" she asked.

"One of them is pretty standard," he answered, sensing he was venturing into some new territory. "The guy wants us to basically copy a campaign he saw in San Francisco. The other one's giving me fits, though."

"Really? It must be difficult to be under the gun and still have to be creative."

She'd hit his dilemma on the head. Larry instantly became animated. "It's all but impossible. The boss has been standing over my shoulder, second-guessing every idea I have."

"That's got to be frustrating. Is there anything I can do?"

And that's the next, logical step in caring and sympathizing—helping where you can. For Larry, Holly's simple act of caring was enough. It made him feel less like he was fighting alone.

Caring is an investment. It takes you outside yourself and places you in your partner's arena.

Caring also makes you vulnerable; that's why caring in a difficult relationship can feel risky. You're putting your feelings for your spouse out there and giving your spouse the opportunity to reject them. Larry could have said, "The ad campaigns are my job. You just take care of the kids. I'll let you know if I need you." Of course, if he had, Holly would have probably decided caring could wait.

Another possible drawback is that caring, and offering to help, can get you embroiled in something you're not prepared for. You may be asked to type thirty pages of a report due in the morning and feel that your spouse has taken advantage of you. Again, though, you'd probably only get taken advantage of once. Your guard would be way up the next time. So even though there are risks involved, they are risks of the heart, of exposing yourself to feel hurt again. Only you can judge when you're ready to take that risk. Remember, no investment, no return. And with a little investment, the return can be great. After all, isn't love the greatest thing? Caring about your spouse can give him or her enough faith in the relationship to begin caring about you again. Accept Paul's challenge in Philippians 2:3–4 to regard others as more important than yourself.

C. S. Lewis describes the effect of selfish isolation on the heart this way:

Love anything, and your heart will certainly be wrung, possibly be broken. If you want to make sure of keeping it intact, you must give your heart to no one, not even to an animal. Wrap it carefully around with hobbies and little luxuries; avoid all entanglements; lock it up safe in the casket or coffin of your selfishness. But in that casket—safe, dark, motionless, airless—it will change. It will not be broken; it will become unbreakable, impenetrable, irredeemable. The alternative to tragedy, or at least to the risk of tragedy, is damnation. The only place outside heaven where you can be perfectly safe from all the dangers and perturbations of love is hell.[1]

Choose to Forgive and Empathize

Choosing to love again includes putting into action what we talked about in the last chapter. Choosing to love again says that you will wipe the slate as clean as the eraser will let you. And it means that you will begin to love selflessly, putting yourself into your spouse's situation to begin to understand the impact your decisions have on your partner. And when you do forgive, do so as Matthew 18:21–35 directs—from the heart. Forgiving and empathizing, as with caring, helps your partner become comfortable enough to do the same for you.

Choose to Have a Life in Harmony with Your Mate's

Carla faced a decision about harmony one day. John was on his way to becoming a vice president, and while she and I were discussing her tendency toward jealousy, she stopped mid-session and just began to talk: "Sometimes I wonder if John's goals are my goals. Here I have this problem with jealousy, and I know it's a problem. But should I be putting myself into a situation where my problem will always be aggravated? There are three plants: here, Chicago, and Atlanta. I constantly hear about John's bosses being called to meetings at the various plants. John's going to be traveling at least a week a month. Is that what I want for myself? Not only will I be without my husband for a week or so a month, but I'll also be dealing with my insecurity alone. Do I really want to put myself through that? If I say no, I could just walk away now, before I invest any more of myself in this marriage. If I say yes, then I need to be prepared for the inevitable."

Carla was asking herself, "Should I risk loving deeply again?" The conversation she had with herself may be as real to you as it was to her. Loving your spouse means bringing your lives into harmony. For some that's no big deal. But for others, life may be a bit unusual. Perhaps it involves a lot of traveling, or entertaining, or late nights at the computer, or any number of other things that might be inconvenient. If you choose to reach out to your spouse again, you need to consider what your life will be like.

This doesn't mean you have to be in lockstep. It doesn't mean that your spouse's life *becomes* your life, but it does mean that neither of your lives should be too disruptive of the other's and that you recommit with full knowledge of what you're committing to.

Neither does it mean that you should become inflexible. The vow is, ". . . for better or worse, in sickness and in health." As things change and the unexpected occurs, you'll have to adjust. But choosing to love again does mean that you and your spouse have a commitment to choose new directions together. Distance destroys the oneness of God's design, and we no longer want any distance between you.

Define and Accept the Purpose for Your Marriage

In chapter 16 we looked at the spiritual purpose of your marriage. That was to point out that your marriage is important; it is of God's design and has a godly purpose. It's important not only that you realize this but also that you put into place a spiritual vision for your marriage. Consider incorporating the answers to the following questions into your vision.

- What ministries might you engage in together?

- How will you handle devotions, prayer, and other spiritual disciplines as a couple?

- How will you tithe?

- How will you bring up your children in the fear and admonition of the Lord?

- How will you work as a couple to be a godly witness?

It's a good idea to discuss these things seriously. During this time of readjustment and recommitment to your marriage, your journey to agreement will be as important as the agreement itself.

As you consider the vision, the purpose, for your marriage, an excellent working definition might be: To develop a mutually satisfying, love-based relationship in Christ.

Other questions to ponder include:

- What kind of environment do you want your children to know? As believers, you plan to bring them up in spiritual harmony with the Bible, but there are many ways to accomplish that. How are you going to teach and discipline your children? How are you going to instill the work ethic and Christian values? Create a vision and purpose for your family as a raiser of children.

- Does your marriage have a community purpose? Granted, we're all called to spread the gospel, but what form will that take? Do you both have political leanings? Are there ways you're both interested in helping around the community that would increase your visibility as a witness?

- What about your neighborhood? Perhaps you might want to get involved in a Neighborhood Watch program. Or, if you have younger children, perhaps a child watch group of parents could use your efforts. These things not only make your neighborhood a safer place to live, but they also give you the opportunity to meet other people and build a broader social circle both for fun and for ministry.

Discussing these issues and acting on them will help you build your presence in the community.

Practice Unconditional Love

Considering 1 Corinthians 13, Dan Allender in his work, *Bold Love,* said: "Talent without love is deafening; spiritual discernment and power without love is debasing; and sacrifice of possession or body without love is defrauding."[2]

What is unconditional love? First, it's the realization that the only thing that matters in life is that we love as God heralds love in 1 Corinthians 13.

Simply stated, it's loving your spouse as one of God's children, no matter what he or she does. It's putting your mate's needs above your own, no matter what the circumstance. Unconditional love is an act of the will. It's what you do, not what you feel. But the rewards of unconditional love are enormous. Dan Allender also says, "Love is a sacrifice for the undeserving that opens the door to restoration of relationship with the Father, with others, and with ourselves."[3] Loving this way may sound like a tall order during this phase of your relationship, when you're both trying to build trust again. The fact is that if your spouse behaves in ways that run contrary to your hope for the relationship, you may begin to question the validity of the truce, and boundaries may become very significant. (Study 1 Corinthians 13, 1 John, Ephesians 5:25, and Colossians 3:15.) But remember, we are always called to practice unconditional love.

Begin to Undress Emotionally before Your Spouse

Undressing emotionally sounds sexy, doesn't it? And in a way, it is. At times there's nothing sexier than a vulnerable spouse who reaches out to you. And undressing emotionally certainly makes you vulnerable, but it also gives the two of you the opportunity to achieve, like nothing else, true emotional intimacy. In a very real sense, it is like opening the door to your inner self and asking your mate to come in. Of course, at this point, you may want to open that door slowly. You can start by revealing your heart—your minor fears, small instances of insecurity. As your comfort level grows, you can move on to more substantial issues. It was an important event when Holly admitted that she really was a mama's girl and felt afraid at being so far away from home.

As you reveal more and more of your inner self—those emotions that·make you who you are—and find your spouse reacting lovingly, caringly, and empathetically, you will move closer together.

Set Aside Time for Fun

I can't stress time alone together enough. Even though you're engaged in a truce, even though you've created a safe zone at home, even though you're doing everything you can to decrease the stress in your relationship, by the very fact that you had to call a truce, you know there's still a war raging around you. Strong forces still threaten you. Just having fun together not only lightens that stress, but also builds a bridge between you like nothing else. Having fun together was probably what drew you to each other in the first place. Go to a ball game, or dinner, or out boating, or skiing. You name it—just do it. And during this special time, try to forget your problems, forget the recent past, forget your fears for the future, and just enjoy being with one another; have a little faith in each other. Every chance you get, laugh, particularly at each other's jokes, at each other's silliness. Be funny; give yourselves a lot to laugh about. And do it as a couple.

Taking Steps toward Intimacy

Each choice we've covered in this chapter is a step toward spiritual, emotional, and physical intimacy. The idea is not to be buried in one another, not to lose your identity before the Lord in one another, but to be joined together so closely that Satan will break his hammer before he's able to drive a wedge between you.

And each time you and your spouse become more intense at

practicing these steps, you move closer to oneness. It becomes less likely the threads between you will ever be severed.

Choosing to love again is a risky investment. But like any risky investment, the payoff can be enormous—a revitalized and refashioned love, a stronger marriage. I started this chapter by suggesting that you go cautiously at first. By doing so you'll lessen your risk and make it more likely to later take those bold steps necessary for healthy love. Soon you'll both step through love's open door.

In the next chapter we'll look at what follows these important choices.

TWENTY-ONE

HELP YOUR
LOVE GROW

Hatred stirs up strife, but love covers all sins.
—*Proverbs 10:12*

*I*n my experience as a counselor, I often see a curious thing happen to couples who take the steps toward love and intimacy. Their focus changes from the hurt of the past to the hope of the future. The farther they travel along that road and allow their love to grow, the more intense that forward focus becomes.

Begin to Savor Love—In All Its Flavors—Together

Can you name the flavors of love?

Holly may not be able to name them all, but after paying attention to them, she can name quite a few.

Holly and Larry's marriage became strained soon after their wedding. As a result, in all the time they'd been married, she'd never given herself the chance to explore her love for Larry. In a very real sense, her love took a quick backseat to defending herself. Now their truce is in full swing, and she's beginning to feel something for Larry again. The truce isn't why she loves, but it does make it a lot easier.

One night while they were just sitting together watching television, she simply reached over and touched him—a light stroke over his hand. He looked up and smiled at her then stroked her hand and kept it in his. It was such a sweet little moment, merely one reminding the other that they were together. A little later, Larry got up and made some popcorn. Handing Holly her own small bowl of popcorn, he resumed watching television with her. But the show got boring, and suddenly Holly felt a white puff of popcorn bounce against her nose. She immediately returned fire and was hit by another. Seconds later they were laughing through a playful snowfall of popcorn, and seconds after that they were kissing passionately.

The next morning, still glowing from the night before, Holly rolled over in bed and cuddled against Larry. He caressed her hand with a velvety touch and whispered something she didn't quite understand. But she did understand the warmth of just lying there. Although she knew they had a long way to go before she could trust him completely, at that moment, she felt supremely happy.

About noon, when Larry was probably heading out to lunch with friends, Holly heard a knock at the back door. That was unusual. She stepped quietly through the kitchen, a bit spooked, and parted the backdoor curtains. There stood Larry with a huge grin on his face. He mouthed, "Got a minute?"

She had more than that.

That evening she had a meeting at church and Larry stayed home. Although it was her job to take care of the kitchen, when she got home she found all the dishes done and the floor washed. She also found Larry standing in the middle of it with an erotic glint in his eye. But Holly was tired. "What say we just cuddle on the couch a bit?" she suggested. Although he was disappointed, he recovered quickly, and they sat together, talking softly. Then she placed her head wearily on his chest and went to sleep.

The flavors of love according to Holly are passion, gentleness, velvety, playful, steady, embracing, sacrificial, a simple touch, sad, happy, the stolen moment, petting, erotic, slow, and warm.

How many can you name? Is it a list with an end to it? I don't think so. And what a wonderful hobby to make the list grow. It's something God wants you to do. God encourages this exploration for married couples. So I urge you to realize that while you may have a long way to go before you have a carefree marriage, that doesn't preclude loving each other on the way. Love each other with all the flavors, all the scents, all the subtleties and passions that emotion and imagination can find. Savor and appreciate every one like a precious jewel. And remember that jewels are not only precious but also strong—strive for a love as strong as diamonds.

Let Love Work in Your Lives

In a recent study of 605 people who were asked what makes romantic love and marriage strong, a telling response was given: "Being in love proves to be an important and serious quality in a relationship and its absence cannot be compensated for by mere sympathy, respect and rational arguments."[1]

Married partners often gauge their love by how they feel about each other. The positive feelings that accompany love are God-given, but authentic love involves even more. Love is first and foremost a commitment. Sure it involves a physical, passionate side and an emotional, relational side, but Paul also described the bond between God and us and between a man and a woman as *agape* or "out of the will, other-centered." It is unconditional, sacrificial, and seeks to esteem the other. Loyalty, caring, patience, and kindness are all aspects of the face of love.

But to allow love to work in your lives, you first have to recognize when it's there.

Stand by Your Commitment

Being conscious of your commitment to your spouse may come and go; its presence often depends on circumstance. For instance, if you're out shopping or out raking leaves you might not think about your commitment at all. However, if your spouse is behaving badly, your commitment might be the only thing on your mind. What I'd like to suggest is that you make the commitment to your spouse something you consider often.

Let Your Love Initiate Action

So do things that show your spouse your love. First John reminds us to love in both word and deed (3:18). They may be reckless, unscheduled, random acts of love like getting up and making your spouse breakfast or washing the dishes or initiating a popcorn fight. Or they may be more serious things like praying for and with your spouse. You decide.

Let Your Love Interpret Your Spouse's Actions

John had been working on his department budget all evening. Although Carla sat on the love seat no more than two feet from him for nearly two hours, neither spoke. She watched the regular Tuesday night lineup on television while he poured over a matrix of numbers displayed on his laptop. Carla had known he needed to finish the budget and was glad he felt comfortable enough to do it at home, so she didn't mind being ignored.

After two hours with his computer, John set his laptop aside, and got to his feet. A few minutes later he returned with a cup of Carla's favorite herbal tea. "Just thought you'd like this."

"Oh, thank you. Aren't you having anything?"

"You know, I got into the kitchen and realized nothing sounded good. But I thought you'd like this."

She thanked him, but her brows knitted. "What's going on?"

"What do you mean?"

"Why'd you get me this? Are you getting ready to give me some bad news?"

"Bad news? No. Just thought you'd like a cup of tea. It's your favorite right?"

"John, if you're taking a trip, just tell me. I don't like it when you have hidden agendas."

John's tone became exasperated. "There's no hidden agenda here. There's just a cup of tea."

Carla took a sip but instead of smacking her lips with enjoyment as she usually did, she set the cup on the coffee table and began staring at John as if her stare could will the truth from him.

"Don't do that," John finally said. "I feel like you're working voodoo on me or something."

"I know you. You've got some bad news you're trying to soften me up for."

John merely shook his head and muttered, "See how many cups of tea you get in the future."

Allow your love to interpret your spouse's motives. In other words, allow your spouse to love you too. Tear down your defensive walls and don't attribute bad motives to his or her actions. That doesn't mean you should interpret things foolishly. If your spouse does something to overtly hurt you, don't interpret away your right to be concerned. But certainly, if your spouse does something loving, don't push that love away like Carla did. Assume you are loved and only be convinced to the contrary if there's adequate proof.

Let the River of Love Carry You Along

I like the image of the two of you lounging on a raft or nestled at the center of an inner tube being carried along the current of love. It's spontaneous. It's being swept away. It's allowing yourselves to be caught up in love and letting your hearts take control for a while. Maybe it's a Friday night and the two of you are having a private little barbecue in the backyard. Or it's a Wednesday morning and you're looking forward to another boring day at work, so you just grab your mate and say, "Let's go to Six Flags." And you take a vacation day and go.

It's all because of love, all because you can't imagine anything more fun than just being with your mate, doing something silly, or fun, or out of the ordinary, or a little reckless (but not too reckless). It's just doing—but doing together. And each time you do something, life gets that much sweeter, and love gets that much stronger, and your life together just gets that much better than your life apart would be.

Allow Yourself to Enjoy Loving and Being Loved

Sometimes things are just difficult—your job, the family, the world in general. It just seems life has become an endurance race and the weight you're carrying gets heavier with each lap. At such times, think about the fact that you are loved. God loves you deeply. Your spouse cares for you and is there for you. Certainly he or she does not love perfectly, but perfectly enough. And the next time you see your mate, he or she will be prepared to listen, sympathize, and empathize.

When your spouse comes home and says, "You know, things were just the pits today, but I found a lot of comfort just knowing you were here waiting for me," what do you say? (a.) "In your dreams, bud. Who wants to listen to all that negative stuff anyway?" (b.) "Why would you possibly think that?" (c.) "You know, you might have been thinking about me, but I never gave you a second thought." (d.) "And I was thinking about you, too, and boy, am I glad you're home!"

Make love a reason for joy, a reason for buoyancy, a reason for getting over the rough spots.

Be Flexible

If your spouse comes home and tells you about something horrible that's happened, make love enough. Offer a hug, promise you'll weather the storm together, and just go on. Or maybe your spouse has been lazy and neglected to do something he or she had promised to do around the house. Is it the end of the world? No. Because you love each other, and right now love is enough. Let it go.

Am I saying do this all the time? Of course not. If your spouse habitually violates the commitment you have to one another or habitually crosses important boundaries you've set together, then you must take corrective actions. But sometimes just let the fact that you love your spouse be enough to cover a sin.

Carry out a Program of Personal Change and Growth

As part of the movement toward a higher love, stop all efforts to change each other. It doesn't work, and it causes a lot of animosity. Rather, focus on who you *can* change—yourself and your reactions to what your spouse does.

Remember Matthew 7:3: "Why do you look at the speck in your bother's eye, but do not consider the plank in your own eye?" None of us is perfect, and our imperfections often take a toll on marriage. The best thing you can do to strengthen your marriage is to change those things about yourself that cause friction or discomfort for your spouse. What are they? Search the Scripture. Ask your spouse. I'm sure he or she has the list.

Now this is risky. None of us likes to be told what's wrong with us. We all bristle when we hear it—or perhaps there are several *its*. But that's okay. Put yourself on an improvement regimen. Carla came to me for help in getting her jealousy under control. If you have security issues, or arrogance issues, or fear or carelessness issues, or whatever, take the steps toward change. No one expects that change to occur overnight; it may take years. But slow, steady, solid improvement goes a long way toward strengthening a marriage. Not only does the behavior become less of a problem, but you will have shown yourself willing to put your spouse first—and that may be worth more than the change itself.

Grow also in grace and the fruit of the Spirit—love, joy, peace, longsuffering, kindness, goodness, faithfulness, gentleness, and self-control (Gal. 5:22). Grow in your knowledge of Scripture and how to apply it to your life. Grow in your understanding of how God works in the world, and how He's worked in the past. Grow in discernment; stretch your ability to recognize right from wrong. Grow in your anger toward the works of Satan. Grow in your desire to spread the gospel and to engage in ministry. As you grow you'll sense yourself growing closer to God and to your spouse.

A Final Word

We've covered some very important directives in this chapter, all offered to help your love grow. And from a teaching standpoint, we've come to the end of part three. But there is one more chapter to this section, and in it I will ask a very important question.

TWENTY-TWO

A POINT OF COMMITMENT

Love is a decision.
—Gary Smalley and John Trent

Salespeople, when they push a contract in front of you, say things like, "Why don't you just *okay* this and we'll get you into a new car." Or, "Go ahead and *authorize* this and that new washer and dryer are as good as installed." *Okay. Authorize.* People like to okay things and authorize things, so those are the words salespeople use. They don't say, "Please *sign* this." Or, "Please *commit* to this." Because most people don't like to sign or commit. Signing and committing sound like promises, something permanent. It's a much harder decision to make. And so someone anxious to make a sale, anxious to get your signature on the bottom line, will play word games to make that happen.

There are no word games here. If anything, I want to make these words as meaningful as possible.

You've stopped hurting each other by calling a six-week truce. And to give you a haven from the world, you've created a safe zone, a place where you can be accepted and loved for who you are before

God. This safe zone led to reconciliation, bolstered by forgiveness and empathy. You've examined your ability to love again, and, I hope, your love for your spouse is beginning to grow. You have also begun a regimen of personal change and growth.

Now it's time to *commit* to your marriage—and to another six weeks. During this next leg of the journey we'll examine the physical, spiritual, and emotional techniques that will help you foster and maintain a truly intimate relationship.

PART
FOUR

Refashion

TWENTY-THREE

I'LL GO ON LOVING YOU

And this I pray, that your love may abound still more and more in knowledge and all discernment, that you may approve the things that are excellent, that you may be sincere and without offense till the day of Christ, being filled with the fruits of righteousness which are by Jesus Christ, to the glory and praise of God.

—Philippians 1:9–11

*I*n the last chapter I asked you to recommit to your marriage. The fact that you're reading this tells me that you did or that you're at least interested in doing so. I'm glad. In this chapter, however, I want you to consider a much longer, more permanent commitment. It's the until-death-do-us-part commitment—not to recreate what has failed but to refashion your love. In a way, it's like redecorating your house. The structure remains the same, but the rooms look fresh, new, pleasing.

So, why if I only asked you to stay for another six weeks am I already scaring you off by talking about committing for much longer? Because certainty brings order out of uncertainty. And because that's what this next six weeks are for—to set the stage for building a relationship that will flourish much longer.

The Grass Isn't Greener Over There

There was an important moment in Holly's relationship with Larry when I asked her to consider whether the grass was greener somewhere else. Up to that point, I sensed some hesitancy on her part to wholly commit herself to the marriage. I'm not sure exactly what it was, but something told me that even when she said, "I commit," not all of her agreed.

So I asked her the question.

She was about to give what was probably a stock answer—"I'm sure Larry's the one"—but for whatever reason she swallowed her words and glanced at Larry. It was a quick glance, but it was loaded with evaluation. In that instant it looked as if she'd sized Larry up both inside and out.

Almost to my surprise, that evaluation brought, "Yes. He's the one. He really is."

For Holly, the grass wasn't greener somewhere else.

You and your spouse have just come through some difficult times. You've seen each other at your worst. And now that you're on your way back, perhaps you're beginning to see each other differently, maybe even at your best again.

There might be someone out there who's a bit more attractive. Maybe there's someone who has even shown you some interest and gets your heart beating a little faster. But God can even restore that in your relationship, and look what you've worked through with your spouse. Look at how well you and your spouse know each other. That's something to build on. There is no such thing as a perfect match. All relationships take work—often hard work.

Mark 10:9 says, "Therefore what God has joined together, let not man separate." If you're God's children, rest assured. God can work through any situation, any couple, to bring glory to Himself and allow you to enjoy the love He desires in your marriage.

Your eyes might wander. And you may think someone or something else will be better, but, as you're finding out right now, that's not God's plan.

I'm Working to Make Things Better Right Here

John flipped a steak on the barbecue and watched the flame sizzle up around it. Without even waiting a minute, he flipped it again. It sizzled again, more yellow. After taking a quick sip of soda, he flipped it again.

"What's going on?" Carla said, slipping up behind him and taking a sip of his drink too.

"I'm restless."

Carla felt her heart catch. "Restless? What's that mean?"

"I was thinking about it at work today."

"Thinking about being restless?" Carla asked, a hint of caution in her voice. Things had been going really well for them the past few weeks. She'd been attending frequent counseling sessions and was beginning to make progress. We both knew the counsel was going to take a while, but we also both had real hope. John had curtailed his traveling, so they now had a lot of nice evenings together. But now John was restless. Her heart caught again.

"I discovered something. I like traveling."

"You like traveling," she repeated quietly.

"You know how sometimes you don't miss something until it's gone? Well, now that I've been home so much, I've discovered I like the occasional trip."

"What do you like about traveling?" Carla asked, her tone measured. She could begin to hear herself wince.

"Getting away." He flipped the steak again. "Nice dinners on the expense account. Getting movies in the room. Hot tubs. After working all day there's nothing nicer than a hot tub. Well, almost nothing." And he smiled at her.

But she didn't smile back. "But we were working everything out. You said you didn't want to jeopardize—"

"Oh—gosh." His expression twisted into shock. "Sure," he said, as if to himself, "sure, you'd think that. Actually I was building up to asking you if you'd like to go along with me."

"Go along?"

"Sure. I was building up how nice those hotels were to make it a little easier for you to say yes. I know traveling hasn't ever been your favorite thing."

"You want me to go along?"

John gave her an understanding, loving smile. "I'm sorry. You know what a bull in a China shop I can be. They want me to go to Chicago in a couple weeks and I hoped you would go with me. We could make a sort of vacation out of it. I need to work during the day, but we could see the sights at night. It'd only be for three days."

"Why, sure, I'd love to go."

John could have tried to solve his problem by working outside the context of their agreement, perhaps by telling Carla that he had to go or he would lose his job. But instead, he worked out a solution within the confines of their agreement and actually made the solution a fun experience for both of them.

What Water There Is Comes from This Well

Larry attended a meeting with a prospective client. When he'd gotten the call, he'd instantly thought he could do a good job for the car dealership. He'd quickly worked up a possible campaign and headed over to the owner's office. The owner was a widow whose husband had left her the dealership. She was determined to make a go of it. She was also beautiful and exciting. And the instant Larry stepped into her office, her eyes began to devour him.

Holly is a wonderful woman. She works hard and loves her husband and family, but when it comes to glamour or the wild kind of sex appeal of Larry's new client, she's in another league. And Larry immediately saw that. He also immediately saw that for whatever reason, this new client was more appreciative of his proposal than seemed normal to him.

A moment later she placed a hand on his leg—and a moment after that, he removed her hand and said that he would ask one of the other people in his office to handle her account. And then he left. On the way back to the office, Larry had a conversation with himself. One side of it wondered why he'd acted so quickly. After all, Holly didn't fill the need he seemed to have to be courted by someone a little wild. The other side of the conversation, however, made the point that that particular need wasn't a need at all. It was a trap—one that would destroy his relationship with God and with Holly.

For Larry, the search was over. His primary needs were going to be met only at home. Isn't it something how temptation will knock at times like these?!

But there was another reason Larry moved quickly to remove himself from temptation. When your search is over and you've committed to your marriage, you want to protect it.

I'll Protect This Marriage Because It's Right before God

Tree farmers put protective enclosures around their saplings. Gardeners place mulch over seeds to protect them as they germinate. We want to protect what we've worked hard for.

In a way, your marriage is like a seedling. It has both a strength and a vulnerability, and right now you need to take steps to protect it. How? By exercising the Golden Rule—*do unto your spouse what you would hope your spouse would do unto you.* Seek out the Scriptures while practicing the presence of God. Remember, you always have an audience of one. When you get into a situation, behave as you would want your spouse to behave. Larry did. If Holly were tempted by someone, he would want her to act the same way.

But protecting your marriage is only partially about reacting to situations. It's also about making sure that you're not placed in tempting situations in the first place. Your marriage is in a sensitive place right now. But marriages are always vulnerable—in fact, they're most at risk when they seem the least vulnerable—when you get back to being comfortable. So now might be the very time to build defenses to keep your marriage whole.

I Belong Here

Take a look at your own marriage. Is the search over for you? I hope you see that it is. And if you do, it's not a stretch to look at your spouse and say, "I belong here. This is where I should be. Nowhere else." Go ahead. Tell your spouse. Go on loving him or her. For you do belong here. Not only isn't there anywhere else more appropriate, but if you believe God is a planning God who works out everything according to His purpose, then you know God can honor you here. He wants you to see that what He's joined can be beautiful. And He wants you to work to develop it and keep it beautiful. In the next chapter we'll take a look at how to do just that.

TWENTY-FOUR

BEGIN TO CELEBRATE

In the day of prosperity be joyful. . . .
—*Ecclesiastes 7:14a*

*T*here is a real cause for celebration right now. Of course, things are not perfect. In fact, you probably have a whole host of scars that need to heal, maybe some anger that must find an outlet, trust that has to be earned and built. But with continued work and love, most will diminish over time.

So celebrate—do whatever you do to mark a wonderful occasion. You've come through a very difficult time and have begun to mend. And at the end of your celebration, commit anew to making your marriage even more beautiful before the Lord.

Don't Look Back

Carla joined John on his trip to Chicago. They spent three nights at a fine hotel downtown and ate at wonderful restaurants. While John was at his seminar, Carla strolled around town shopping, visiting museums, and sightseeing. Those three days were romantic, luxurious, and wonderfully exhausting. When they got home, Carla thanked John for taking her along. "I really enjoyed that. And I did okay in the traveling, didn't I?"

"You did great."

"So when do we go again?" she asked, nibbling at his ear.

John laughed. "Probably a couple of months. And maybe we could plan a real vacation away this year."

The future. It's all new—a great, exciting adventure. Now that might sound a little Pollyannaish, but even the difficult times will be less dark when you face them together with a mature love and realistic expectations. Frankly, except when you wish to learn lessons from it, move beyond the past and keep your eyes on the future.

What to Look For

What specific goals do you have for your marriage? Goals provide a purpose for behavior. As you set them, be realistic. You may want to focus on bite-sized, short-term, easily attainable goals at first. After all, nothing breeds success like success. Keeping that in mind, let's look at a few areas of possibility.

- Spiritual goals (committing to regular devotions and family prayers, reading Scripture together, attending church)

- Entertaining goals (having friends over once a month, inviting neighbors or acquaintances over spontaneously)

- Vacation and long weekend goals (taking a cruise, visiting family, traveling to Europe or around the states)

- Financial goals (saving, investing, planning for retirement or college for the kids)

- Employment goals (balancing money with needs)

There are probably a hundred other goals you can identify together. Not only does talking about and setting them give you an opportunity to share your views on what's important and how much time and energy you're willing to spend, but it also gives you each the opportunity to help direct your marriage. By keeping your eyes focused on what's ahead, determining the best way to get there, and using your combined talents, you'll expend your energies in the right direction— toward the growth of your marriage and yourselves as members of God's family.

Set aside time and energy for this process. Anything worthwhile demands attention and must be augmented with discipline, perseverance, and obedience. We see in Hebrews 3:14 that when we are faithful to the end, we will enjoy the reward. This is especially true regarding meaningful marital growth. (See also 1 Timothy 4:7; 2 Peter 1:5–8; James 3:1–12.)

Another effect of keeping yourselves focused on the road ahead is that you never get overly comfortable or complacent and you keep investing in each other and your marriage.

Becoming Comfortable

There's something very nice about becoming comfortable. Picture yourself on a hammock on a lazy summer afternoon. Comfort is one of those basic needs that we all have and I certainly don't want to label it as bad. But it can lead to some bad choices if you, as half of a married couple, become too addicted to it and allow your marriage to drift into complacency.

So how do you guard against this? First, as we've already suggested, keep working toward your goals and make new goals when old ones are achieved. But even while working together, it is possible to take your relationship for granted. "Sure she knows I love her. I don't have to treat her with all the reverence I used to. I don't have to keep telling her I love her so much."

The second-best defense against complacency is to be able to recognize it and to make the effort to smother it in attention.

Signs of Marital Complacency

The key sign of complacency is that it becomes less important to give your full attention to your spouse. Instead of considering your mate's feelings first, you discount those feelings. If she's angry, she doesn't have any reason to be. If he's anxious, he's overreacting. And whatever the offending issue, it just doesn't mean as much to you as it once did. The instant you find yourself discounting your mate's feelings even one iota, it's time tighten things up. It's time to begin treating your spouse as you would want to be treated in similar circumstances. Even better, lavish affection and attention on your spouse to avoid complacency in the first place.

Another sign that complacency has taken root is when you find yourself taking your spouse's love for granted. You begin doing things that your spouse doesn't like and excuse them by telling yourself that your spouse's love for you will absorb any hurt that results. Of course, love does cover a multitude of sins, and love can be the reason you'd face death for your spouse. But love won't endure being ignored.

Complacency has also found a home if you just stop caring about what your spouse is doing. Your partner's presence just doesn't ignite the flames as it once did—love's fires are burning cooler, less insistently. You feel your relationship begin to drift, but you don't see that as important enough to even raise an eyebrow and you don't care that most of your activities are separate.

If you feel your love being taken for granted, or if you're taking your spouse's love for granted, or if you feel yourself not caring as much as you once did, don't allow complacency to grow. Do something immediately. Love between you and your spouse is the most important asset you have. Make an effort to value your spouse's love. If your find yourself treating your love with contempt, stop. Apologize. And don't devalue it again.

If you find yourself not caring as much, just drifting away, choosing to do separate activities when you used to do things together, it's time to rekindle the fire. Now every couple needs a bit of separation. Even the most devoted spouses need time with friends occasionally or time alone to work on some special project. I'm not talking about that. I'm talking about when you see yourself not caring whether your spouse is sharing time with you. Then take note and throw some more wood on that fire, get the bellows working, and get those coals white-hot again. How? You know the way. A weekend away. A cozy dinner by firelight. A project you both love. Something that draws you together and helps you enjoy each other again—helps you laugh together again.

Another way to keep complacency at bay is to revisit your memorial.

Remember your memorial, that symbol you and your spouse put together as a reminder of your love and your recommitment to one another? When you see complacency slipping in, take a long look at your memorial and remember. Remember the love you once shared and are beginning to share again. Remember the struggle you've made to not only regain what you've lost but also appropriate so much more. Remember the hope you have for this new relationship and the work you've put in to make that hope reality. Complacency has no part here—in fact, complacency is an enemy. And the last thing you need lurking around your relationship is an enemy. Allow your memorial to reawaken your commitment and your resolve to be one.

Invest in Your Spouse

Invest your innermost feelings—your love, your hopes—in your spouse. Or moments of tenderness—secret little presents, moonlight dinners, flowers, warm little whispers. Bring them to your spouse with an open, vulnerable heart. And do it often. Nothing is more romantic than selfless acts of love and tenderness.

Even investing fears and anxieties can bring rewards when your spouse invests hope and support in return.

The investment, the payoff. I know it sounds callous to speak of it this way. But these investments can bring you closer together.

Invest in your spouse's happiness by contributing to his or her dreams for the future. Does your mate have a scholastic or artistic dream? Perhaps he or she wants to finish college, become a painter, or write a novel. Your investment might take the form of lessons, or self-help books, or discussions with those who are already living that dream. If your spouse wants to go to college, an investment might take the form of tuition or volunteering to do extra chores to give your spouse the time to study. Frankly, it doesn't matter what that dream is, if it has a realistic component to it, you can help it happen in material ways. Do you make this investment in order to receive a similar treatment? Perhaps, but the likelihood is that the greatest return will be appreciation as your spouse realizes how deep your love goes and that you have his or her best interests at heart. And maybe one day your spouse will be in a position to help some of your dreams come true. Help your mate become everything God desires for him or her.

And as you both move toward the realization of your dreams, invest in warm memories together. Gather those special moments to draw on when you need a shot of warmth or belonging. Holly and Larry decided to make creating memories a summer project.

They flew into Albany, New York, rented a car, and drove up to Vermont. In Bennington they stopped at the Grandma Moses Museum, then they went to the Norman Rockwell Museum in Arlington where they spent several more hours. Next they made their way up the middle of the state to the Ben and Jerry's Ice Cream factory where they took pictures of each other in front of cow paintings. Then on to Stowe and up through Smuggler's Notch and over to Lake Willoughby where they stopped at a wonderful inn and had coffee and pie while overlooking an incredibly beautiful glacial lake. The memories never stopped, one right after another. They visited a maple farm and saw a syrup cooker and took pictures of each other at the base of a huge maple. They took walks along country streams beside herds of dairy cows who munched contentedly on grass and eyed them with casual disinterest.

And when they returned, they put together an album, which they kept on their coffee table. For years afterward, when times got quiet, or they were at a loss for something to do, they opened the album.

Invest in memories. You don't have to got to Vermont to make them. Just do something together—something a little unique, something you both enjoy—and let the memories happen. And like Holly and Larry, when you want a shot of warmth, bask in the memories' glow. And remember: Often you're not making memories—you are the memories.

Finally, invest in your spouse's spirituality. Invest the time for devotions, for prayers, for learning the Word and more. Invest the time to attend church together and pray that your spouse may grow in the fruits of the Spirit, and that you and your spouse might bring glory to the Lord through your witness. Invest the time to talk about the gospel and about how the Lord's working in your lives. And, above all else, invest your life as a witness to your spouse. Mirror in your life every spiritual thing you hope to see in your spouse's—particularly selfless love.

And as you invest in each other, as you keep looking forward, only looking back for an occasional history lesson, as you make a conscious effort to fight complacency, your celebration of your new life together will become increasingly vibrant and meaningful.

TWENTY-FIVE

INTIMACY—
THE ISLAND OF WE

. . . a oneness with a healthy sense of separateness.
—*Ron Hawkins*

ave you had the thrill of real intimacy yet? Perhaps it came as you lay in the dark watching your love sleep— watching the blankets rise and fall to the rhythmic breathing of slumbering peace. You may have whispered, "Will you ever doubt the way I feel about you in my heart?" Or perhaps it came when the two of you suddenly connected and saw into each other, completely understanding each other in that moment. When you experienced it, was it new, or had you been there before? If it was new, did you recognize it as intimacy? Or did you just think it an incredible moment you'd like to revisit?

Earlier we discussed the opposite of that feeling—polarization. At that point, you'd both taken up residence on your islands of me. Since then, we've worked on building bridges between your islands, bridges I hope you are both frequently using now. But in spite of those bridges—the safe zone you built, the love you've been cultivating— you're probably still living on and maintaining your own islands, only *visiting* each other, prepared at any moment to flee to your separate islands and crank up the drawbridges again.

But that's not what I want for your marriage. I want you to swim in a whole sea of those intimate moments you're beginning to enjoy—so many, in fact, that they run together and you can't distinguish between them. I want them to become your norm—where a break in intimacy will become as noticeable as an earthquake. For if your marriage is made up of such intimate moments, it will have reached higher ground—you will have achieved higher love—and it will be far more rewarding and fulfilling than a marriage where you're merely *visiting* each other's islands of me.

It's time to move in together. It's time to surround your marriage with a deep sea of intimacy. To do that, you need to build and occupy an "island of we"—a place where you can reside as a loving couple away from the turmoil of the rest of the world.

Achieving Intimacy—The Island of We

Intimacy is a oneness. It's the fulfillment of God's plan for marriage—that a husband and wife leave their parents and join together and become one. Yet while you become one emotionally, spiritually, relationally, and physically, you also maintain a healthy separateness. The depth of intimacy is then measured by the level of total connectedness you experience as a couple.

But what does that really mean? How do you achieve such oneness? Is there really any way for two unique people, particularly a male and a female, to become one person? And if they can, and if it is so wonderful, why hasn't *everyone* achieved it by now?

One reason might be that becoming one is like many other things we're asked to strive for here on earth; it's a goal we humans will only experience in heaven. But, even though we might not achieve *perfect* oneness on earth, as we work on it we'll get closer and closer to it. And the closer two people get to achieving oneness, the more beautiful and enduring their relationship will become. So, even though perfection is unattainable, getting close is certainly worth the effort.

How Do You Work Toward Oneness?

The perfect example of biblical oneness is modeled for us in the Godhead: the Father, Son, and Holy Spirit. The trinity is one God yet three distinct persons. If our marriages grow in the appropriate characteristics of the Godhead, they will mirror that loving, divine intimacy. In this chapter we'll look at each of those applicable characteristics and help guide you toward achieving them in your marriage.

Know Each Other

First, the three persons of the Godhead completely know and understand one another. They can predict with absolute assurance the reactions the others will have to a given situation. The Father knew, for instance, that the Son would obey Him and go to the cross for His people. The Son knew that after His death on the cross, the Spirit would obey the Father and come to earth and begin applying Jesus' sacrificial life to the hearts of those who would be His people.

Marriage partners who have achieved a strong level of intimacy know and understand one another, and can predict with a reasonable level of certainty what the other will do in a given situation. Take Carla and John, for instance.

After John was promoted to second-level manager, we realized it would be advantageous for him to entertain his associates, including his boss, in his home. But he knew that Carla didn't like to entertain. The insecurity that fueled her jealousy also caused her to become extremely anxious about hosting dinners. So, when John told her that he'd given it a lot of thought and felt that both of them would benefit from entertaining more often at home, he knew what the news would do to Carla. And he was right.

She instantly became anxious.

But he followed up quickly and calmly with, "How can I make this as easy on you as possible?"

Carla took a deep breath and said, "Just shoot me now."

John managed a laugh. "No. Really. I know that this is hard for you. So what can I do to make it easier?"

Carla took a moment to think. Finally, her voice still apprehensive, she said, "I want entertaining to be fun. And you'll need some time to get together with the other managers and talk business. That means we need lots of food, and the house and the yard need to be thoroughly cleaned—" And she began to list what help she would need to make everything right—a cleaning person, gardeners, someone to help cook and set up. John figured it was a small price to pay.

When the two of you embark on the wonderful task of building your island of we, the first step is to take the time to learn about each other. Of course, you probably think you already know all there is to know about your mate. And you might. But my challenge to you is to learn *more*. I have a male client who was married for sixteen years before he discovered that his wife had always dreamed of seeing the waving wheat fields of Kansas. He found that out by *asking* her if she ever had any unfulfilled dreams.

So talk. Talk about situations, dreams, life, and responses to situations. Share and ask questions of your spouse—all kinds of questions. And when the answers come back, really listen to what's being said and to what's not being said. "I know you had an uncle, but you never talk about him. Why?" Such a question opened a long-locked door that hid sexual abuse in one of my clients.

Remember the chapters on being loving and empathetic? During this questioning; use both skills. As you listen to your spouse, put yourself in his or her shoes. Then respond as you would like your spouse to respond to you. Take copious mental notes, and if anything you hear just doesn't sound right, check it out.

Not only do you want to learn more about your spouse, but you should also illuminate everything you learn about your mate with a positive light—certainly never with ridicule. For instance, John could have looked at Carla's insecurities as a real negative—a career impediment. But he didn't. John saw Carla's insecurities first with understanding, and then as a positive. Carla's insecurities would drive her to be meticulous about every element of the evening—from the food to the music, from the table centerpiece to the room he and his associates would retire to and talk about work. His job, of course, was to help her prepare for the evening so she could be less anxious and better able to enjoy herself. This he did.

Of course, there are no positives to physical abuse, particularly sexual abuse—but you can respond to such news with understanding, love, support, and encouragement. And if it's appropriate, help your spouse unmask the culprit and make sure he or she never abuses another person.

Trust Each Other

The next characteristic of the Godhead that is foundational to intimacy is the trust between the Father, Son, and Holy Spirit. Jesus certainly trusted the Father. If He hadn't, Jesus probably would not have left His heavenly throne to become a mere man to be humiliated and nailed to a cross. And what if the Spirit had decided not to do His job of applying Jesus' sacrifice to the hearts of sinful people? Jesus' suffering would have been for naught.

So how do we build trust? In chapter 18, we discussed this as part of constructing your safe zone. Let's expand on it a bit here. Trust not only grows as you see your spouse being trustworthy with the rules and boundaries you've set together regarding your relationship, but real heart-engaging trust also grows as you find increasing acceptance from your spouse for who you really are.

Therefore, as you explore your partner's makeup and begin to know who he or she really is—and your spouse sees that you still love him or her with all your heart—trust grows. As you experience the joy of holding each other up when you're at your most vulnerable, holding each other with warmth and safety—trust grows.

And when you laugh and joke around together, when you share just plain funny stuff—trust grows. When you begin to see the plans you've made together come to fruition—trust grows. And as trust grows, you each feel more comfortable becoming closer spiritually, emotionally, and physically—and trust grows all the more.

Of course, I've emphasized positive things you can do to *build* trust. But believe me, there are some negative things you can do that will quickly kill the trust you've worked so hard to build. Commit the following list to your heart to draw on in dealing with your spouse (or anyone for that matter).

- Don't lie—be as diplomatic as you need to be, but never lie. It's better to tell the truth and hurt your spouse a little than to lie and risk destroying trust.

- Don't ridicule or put down—when your spouse feels vulnerable, the worst thing you can do is put him or her down.

- Don't do anything that could be construed as contemptuous—a roll of the eyes, a strategic groan, a withering look. If you feel arrogant, keep it to yourself.

- Don't ignore—you only ignore what's of no value to you. Your spouse knows that.

Gain Fulfillment from Each Other

I'm going to leave the analogy of the Godhead for a moment. God in His three persons is self-fulfilling. He needs nothing He can't supply. He wants the praise of His people; He wants our love as a completion for the love He's lavished on us. But He doesn't *need* it.

We, on the other hand, have many needs. As you work to fulfill your needs in the context of your marriage, the intimacy within the marriage grows. Take John's desire to travel. Carla's trust for John grew, and her counseling helped her deal with her jealousy, she didn't mind John taking an occasional trip without her. The problem came—and it really wasn't a problem at all—when John decided that he truly enjoyed Carla's company when he traveled. Before he had been content with the companionship provided by the businesspeople that he met while traveling, but after taking a couple of trips with Carla and experiencing the fun they had together, interacting with his business associates paled in comparison. John's need for companionship was increasingly satisfied only by his marriage and he began to miss Carla when she wasn't there—his phone calls home came more frequently, and their talk became more intimate. Carla's need to be missed and loved became satisfied by those phone calls. Intimacy between them grew.

How do you gain more and more fulfillment from your marriage? Allow your marriage—your spouse—to become a more important part of your life. This doesn't mean you must do everything with your spouse; in a bit, we'll discuss healthy separateness. But the more you do with your spouse and the more your needs are fulfilled within your marriage, the more important your marriage will become to you— and the more intimate you will be with your mate.

Use Your Combined Strengths

It's hard to believe that God would be weaker if there was only one person in the Godhead. God is God—infinite power is infinite power. But there are three persons, and they each have separate functions. For example, as I understand Ephesians 1, the Father plans and holds the power. The Son then takes each plan and creates reality from it. Consider the plan of salvation; Jesus is the person who works the plan out in history. The Holy Spirit then applies the plan. Through the Holy Spirit history unfolds, and the Father's plan is applied to the hearts of His people. We have a sense that the three persons of the Godhead make it more powerful and effective.

In a human marriage, each partner is a finite being with finite and varied abilities. However, when a person pairs with someone who has complementary strengths, they become far more powerful together than either one was separately. For a primary example of combined effectiveness, look at a single-parent versus a two-parent family. One parent trying to raise children can quickly become exhausted trying to be both breadwinner and homemaker. In a two-parent home, the load is shared, and although things may be hectic, life seems far more manageable. There are other examples too. A husband and wife getting ready for a party can split the work. One may get the house ready while the other prepares the food. Or one might start the barbecue while the other works on the hors d'oeuvres. Together they're stronger, more effective. As partners see themselves being more effective, stronger, more resilient, the value of the marriage goes up in both their eyes.

Carla and John did entertain in their home—about three times the first year. The first party went okay. Carla and John were both learning. But the second one turned out very well. Carla felt more relaxed and the help they chose was more competent, but the help wasn't the reason for the party's success. Feeling more relaxed, Carla found the energy to charm not only the wives, but also a few of John's associates, including his boss. She has a natural sense of humor that everyone enjoyed, and as John's boss left, he told John that Carla was a real find and that he appreciated her company. Together John and Carla were far more effective than either one was separately. That kind of appreciation transforms itself into greater intimacy.

Watch for those times when you're more effective as a couple than you are as individuals. And if you don't see all that many, search for the reasons why and make changes. It's important for couples to see how much value they have. And, believe me, there will be value. God brought you together for a reason. If you would have been more effective apart, you would have remained apart. So revel in the power you have as a couple—appreciate that power and turn it into a celebration and another reason to grow closer.

Respect Each Other

Respect grows out of realizing the value of your partner. You can only imagine how much respect one member of the Godhead has for the others. It's impossible to even conceive of one member of the Godhead not respecting a characteristic of one of the others.

And respect is important. It was respect for His heavenly Father that brought Jesus to His knees in the Garden of Gethsemane. "O my Father, if it is possible, let this cup pass from Me; nevertheless, not as I will, but as You will" (Matt. 26:39). Can you feel the respect? Imagine that same request coming from someone with less respect: "I know you set this ridiculous situation up. Now come to your senses and let me off this hook."

When God the Father sent the Holy Spirit to work in the lives of His people, He obviously respected the Holy Spirit's ability to do the job. But you know that. You know what respect is. You can certainly answer the question of whether you respect your parents. Or your employer. Or your spouse. In fact, if you were asked if you respected your spouse a few short months ago, you might have answered resoundingly, "No!" But as with so many things, that was then—this is now. Now love is being re-created, trust is on the rise, as respect should be.

Today you might hesitate if asked about your spouse. There's probably still a part of you that remembers all those characteristics you despised a few months back. Although he or she has hopefully repented of wrongdoing and you've been working on forgiveness, you've seen the anger, the injustice, the intentional hurting that came from your spouse. You might be reluctant to tell your spouse, "I respect you."

In Ephesians 5:33, God tells men to love their wives as they love themselves. And since respect is implied in love, the Lord is telling men to respect their wives. He then goes on to tell wives to respect their husbands. I believe mutual respect is a command.

But the command would be far easier to obey if the past didn't keep coming to mind. So let's deal with it. I'm assuming that you've already gone through the steps of forgiveness that were outlined in chapter 19, so you've forgiven the behaviors. But respect is another matter, isn't it? Respecting your spouse says that you esteem the characteristics of your spouse. And you've seen characteristics that you don't necessarily esteem. So what can you do?

I know it's hard to believe, but respect is a choice. We think of respect as a natural outgrowth of seeing things we like about a person. Therefore, a lack of respect seems a natural outgrowth of seeing things we don't like. That's true enough. But how many times have you met someone, liked what you saw initially, and respected the person for what you saw? Then when you got to know that person a little bit better, you saw other things you just didn't like or couldn't respect. And how many times have your first impressions been negative, only to change as you learned other things, things you not only like but also respect? Your choice is to discover things about your spouse that you can respect. Perhaps, for all his faults, your husband is a hard worker and a good provider, and although you two went through very rocky times, he didn't leave. He stayed to work things out—he's not a quitter. Respect those things about him. Perhaps your wife took a lot of abuse from you but didn't quit either. In fact, when she set proper boundaries and began dealing with you firmly, you saw a strength in her you could respect.

That's how this works. None of us is perfect. We all have weaknesses that others might not respect. But we all also have strengths, talents God has given us, characteristics that often allow us to rise above others—patience, stick-to-itiveness, discernment. Find those things in your spouse and respect your spouse for them.

Over time as you grow more intimate, as you share the island of we, you'll find more and more to respect. Why? Because all those negative things will dissolve into the past—they will be replaced by more positive feelings and realities. But for now, take a long look at your spouse. See the positive traits. Write them down. And esteem your spouse for them. And as your esteem grows, so will your intimacy.

Move Forward as a Team

In a prayer, just before his crucifixion, Jesus offered these words: "Now I am no longer in the world, but these are in the world, and I come to You. Holy Father, keep through Your name those whom You have given Me, that they may be one as We are" (John 17:11).

There's something about calling the Godhead a team that seems sacrilegious, but they sure seem to be. Three persons, each with a job to do and carrying it out effectively with trust and respect—that's a team. Of course, since their goals are executed flawlessly, there's no friction in the Godhead as there often is in an earthly team.

Married couples are also teams. And as partners see themselves working together well as a team, they have victory and gain appreciation for each other's efforts and closeness. One of Larry and Holly's great moments as a team came when their oldest child entered kindergarten. Larry took the day off from work so he and Holly could walk their daughter into her first classroom and help her find her first assigned desk. Afterward, Holly and Larry went for a cup of coffee. "She looked so cute," Holly gushed.

"That dress you made was incredible. She's the best-looking kid there."

Holly beamed. "And she's got your creativity. Did you see the way she chose those paints and made sure they were at her desk? We did good, Larry. We did real good."

"Yeah," Larry smiled Cheshire-like. "We did, didn't we?"

There's nothing more wonderful than the sweet smell of victory. And victory only comes when you've accomplished a goal—accomplishing it together brings intimacy. It sets up a chorus begging for more victories.

To become a team, take on projects together. Church projects are particularly well suited for couples. Teach a class together, or work on a food or toy drive, or visit nursing homes. Such projects bring a double blessing. You not only have the sweet aroma of success when you're done, but you also have the wonderful feeling of knowing that together you've been of some help in God's kingdom.

After working to bring you closer together, this next topic may seem contradictory. It's not. However, it is paradoxical.

Create Healthy Separateness

First the obvious: Each partner is an individual with personal likes and dislikes, special talents and weaknesses, unique emotions and background. Each responds differently to any given situation and has different buttons that can set him or her off. And, although each may be saved, each will undoubtedly have a unique personal relationship with the Lord and may view Him very differently.

Now the not so obvious: A healthy oneness not only respects all those differences but also revels in them. Your spouse's uniqueness—particularly his or her talents—creates excitement. And at no time does oneness dominate that uniqueness. Domination reveals a lack of respect, and respect is key to intimacy.

A healthy oneness also allows each partner the space necessary to fill a reasonable need outside the marriage—like gaining an education or taking a hobby-oriented class. When it doesn't hurt the overall goals of the marriage, such space increases the personal and marital satisfaction of both partners.

Healthy separateness gives partners the opportunity and the freedom to be who they are while continuing their obligations to the marriage. Now, frankly, I don't like the word *obligation*. It sounds a bit heavy-handed. But it is appropriate. Marital intimacy, in a very real sense, is the obligation of both partners. However, it's one of those obligations that is tantalizing, rewarding, fulfilling, and hardly off-putting. If one partner's separateness begins to impact the couple's oneness, if it ceases to uphold the marital obligation, then it ceases to be healthy and needs to be cut back or somehow reshaped. Balancing the two takes a lot of careful work.

Move in Together

As intimacy grows and you move frequently across the bridge between your islands of me, you'll very naturally want to set up housekeeping on the island of we, a beautiful island ringed by white sand beaches, caressed by warm ocean breezes, fed by warm tropical rains, and planted with sweet jungle fruits. It's a paradise I want for you. So work at intimacy and allow it to bloom in your hearts.

A Final Word

So now you know how to create your island of we. In the next chapter, we're going to discuss what should be a natural expression of your love—sex.

Twenty-Six

Sexual Intimacy

The greatest erogenous zone in a woman's body is her heart.
—*Ingrid Trobisch*

*I*t's difficult to think of a human activity more personal than sex. There may even be some people who are so embarrassed or put off by the subject that they'll be tempted to skip this chapter altogether. That in itself is telling. Sex is personal; it's to be confined to the marriage bed, but it's not forbidden. God put a strong emphasis on sex in the Bible: Song of Solomon, 1 Corinthians 7, Hebrews 13:4. And He portrayed it as a natural human interaction that's blessed when practiced within the marriage covenant.

But you know all that.

You also know that sex is often a barometer of your marriage's health. When things are going well, the sexual experience is usually satisfying. When things are not, the beauty, of the sexual experience is the first to decay. It's all but impossible to be fully intimate with someone you're angry at, someone you think is willing, if not already trying to hurt you. You may still have intercourse, but it's not making love. Sex becomes something else altogether.

Of course, now you're beginning to look at your spouse differently—love is growing, an intimate knowledge of your spouse is on the rise, and trust and respect are deepening. You may again be making love, which may be better described as expressing love,[1] and beginning to taste the sweet fruit of sexual intimacy again; or maybe you're tasting it for the first time. If you are only beginning to walk cautiously down the path of becoming sexually active again, this chapter may help you take those steps.

A Personal Issue

What gives us sexual pleasure is a very personal matter. There might be images involved, particular spots and activities. It's easy to become embarrassed and guarded. Because we want to minimize embarrassment, it's natural, at least in these early stages of coming back together, to keep your guard up. But it's also important that as your spouse gains your trust, you begin to let your guard down to reveal more about yourself and what pleases you. As you feel increasingly accepted, your sexual relationship with your spouse will become more intimate, rewarding, and exciting.

Of course, I do not intend to intrude into your bedroom, but I do hope to give you some general guidelines that will help you achieve a satisfying intimate sexual life together.

A Safe Zone at Its Safest

In chapter 18 we began the task of building a safe zone, a place where you two could be yourselves, protected from the onslaught of an uncaring world. Now we need to bump the notion of safety up a notch. The marriage bed needs to be the safest place on earth—emotionally, physically, and spiritually—for both of you. When you think about expressing love to each other, it must become inconceivable that either of you would intentionally hurt or belittle the other.

Since you're coming out of severe turmoil, this may seem like a very tall order. Partners in turmoil often use the marriage bed as a place to subtly torture each other, a place where they can exercise control, where they can make themselves rulers. In those circumstances, sex becomes a weapon. And weapons can wound.

What's Good Is Good

How *do* you make the marriage bed the safest place on earth? You allow each other all the freedom you need to become all you both want to become as a sexual human beings.

That's a pretty sweeping statement, isn't it?

Many Christians put limits on the marriage bed—they believe that sex is great but that God only blesses certain types or certain positions. Others hold the attitude that sex is somehow a sin that God will forgive if they're married, but that while engaged in it, they still have to keep a lid on their passions. In doing so, they believe they are fulfilling some commandment to keep the sexual experience a controlled and very proper activity. Except for Hebrews 13:4, which tells us to keep the marriage bed pure from adultery and sexual immorality, I can find nothing in Scripture that limits the marriage bed.

Now, of course, certain activities might spill over and batter some of the other commandments, and you need to be sensitive to that, but I believe those situations are rare. Allow your partner to express love to you without fear of ridicule, disgust, or censure in any way. Such reactions are laced with arrogance and have no place in the marriage bed. That doesn't mean you have to go along with everything your mate suggests. You have a right to your own tastes, your own likes and dislikes, your own limits and boundaries.

Strive to keep what happens, sexually, or in any other area for that matter, strictly between you and your spouse. Your partner doesn't need to have something he or she told you in confidence come back in the form of a joke, or advice, or an admonition. He or she deserves all of you, and if you're giving even a small portion away, you're cheating your spouse. If you need to discuss something with a third party, make that third party your counselor.

Exploration—Allowed, Encouraged, and Full of Fun

It's time to explore your sexuality as a couple. Try new things. God doesn't limit our joy—we do.

And as you try new things, have fun. Laugh, tickle, bop each other with pillows, sneak off, and have a real giggle. The sexual experience between married couples can be the hoot of hoots. It can also be the most passionate, most consuming experience you'll ever have.

But remember, never have fun at your partner's expense. When you laugh, laugh together. When you tickle, stop when you're asked. This is never a time to force your will on your partner. It's a time for you to find mutually exciting and rewarding ground upon which to build a thrilling, rewarding, and very fulfilling relationship.

Guys, Especially: Listen, Observe, and Learn

When it comes to sex, many women believe that men just don't have a clue how to please their mates. Some believe men don't even *care* about pleasing them. For these women, this old adage rings true: When it comes to sex, women need a relationship, men often only need a place. Guys, let's prove them wrong.

Listen to what your spouse tells you and take mental notes; if you should forget, ask and make notes again. Then observe. As you two explore, you're naturally going to come upon little nuggets that make your mate respond. Again, take notes, draw yourself a mental map so you can revisit these spots, and if they don't elicit the same response later, keep looking and observing until you find others that do. And learn—learn all the time, not only when you're experiencing one another but also afterward. It's all right to talk about sex openly, erotically, frankly, in any way you're both comfortable. And as you grow closer, as you feel your freedom expand, those discussions will become more meaningful, sensitive, frank, and honest—and more tantalizing.

Tenderness, Gentleness—And Befores and Afters

The sexual experience is truly a time when partners can show each other unbridled tenderness, gentleness, and sweetness—in your touch, in your words, with your eyes. It's a time when all reasonable wishes and desires should come true. In the end your sexual appetites should be satiated.

But that's the physical experience. For men, that's often enough. But for many women, it's not. They like the *befores* and *afters*, sometimes even more than they like the *durings*.

The "Befores"—Sex Starts Before Bed

For some the "befores" are a time of wooing, of slowly and tenderly stoking passion's fire. Draw your mate in, break down and overcome inhibitions, revel in the promise and anticipation. Others also include playfulness, coyness, maybe a bit of teasing. They spend time making the experience fun, even entertaining. Still others see it as strictly a time of passion.

No matter what form your "befores" take, allow them to be everything you *both* want them to be. Guys, take your time, stoke the fires patiently and gently. Let your wife guide you. And even if it takes longer than you would like, never let her see your impatience. She is your wife—you're to love her and give yourself up for her. And this is a wonderful time to do just that. Remember, sex is about joining with your mate as God designed for warmth, intimacy, and bonding. Do nothing that would jeopardize that divine goal.

Couples often have trouble expressing themselves about this time. Marriage partners may spend decades together without revealing their desires for this before time. And if neither speaks up, pretty soon the befores disappear altogether and making love becomes just the act— one that is far less satisfying and marked by emotional dryness. So talk about this before time and make this element of lovemaking as important, maybe even more so, as the act itself. You might want to go slowly at first and reveal yourself in small, less vulnerable increments. But take the risk; as the months unfold you'll be very glad you did.

The Afters

Again, men can be a little brief in their "afters." Don't be. Take the lead from your wife; most women prefer a little snuggling after, a little time to revel in and even relive the moment. Take the time to settle gently back to earth. This is also the time to express how much you appreciate each other, how much you mean to each other, and how empty life would be without each other. For it would be; you know it would be. Sexual intimacy involves giving far more than getting; take the opportunity to give as much as you can.

Build Each Other Up

Any time in the marriage, but particularly as you engage in physical love, work to build your spouse up. You have been sent by God to be your spouse's sexual partner; let him or her know you relish that assignment as one of the greatest ministries you could possibly have. Your job is to help each other become fully loved, absolutely satisfied, sexual beings.

Work to expand that privilege beyond the marriage bed as well. Expand it to playful patter, to random hugs and kisses, to love pats. Expand it to include just holding hands while walking—to those warm touches that say you're there and you love your spouse.

Sexual Dysfunction

Sometimes, in spite of all the commitment, things just don't go right. Sixty percent of couples will go through a period of sexual dysfunction in a given year.[2] If sexual dysfunction should happen to you, don't treat it as the end of the world. Often the worst thing you can do is make too big a deal out of it.

Of course, when sexual dysfunction does show up, you want to make sure it's not the tip of a large iceberg—a more severe physical, emotional, or spiritual problem. If it is, it may be God's way of bringing attention to the larger problem.

Problems That Lead to Sexual Dysfunction

Problems that lead to sexual dysfunction can generally be divided into three categories, physical issues, a painful past, and current sin. Let's take a look at the physical issues first.

Physical Issues

A number of physical problems can cause sexual dysfunction—diabetes, prostate problems, medications that suppress organ function or sexual desire, certain gender-related issues. All can be serious. Begin addressing sexual dysfunction by seeing a physician to rule out a medical reason. If all the tests come back negative, perhaps emotional scars from a painful past are involved.

Painful Past

Although the issues that follow might manifest themselves in sexual dysfunction, they can, and often do, also stand in the way of reaching full intimacy. So, if these issues have been part of your past, even only briefly, discuss them with your counselor. They might include sexual abuse—rape or incest. Or they could be hidden or buried secrets that have manifested themselves in anger and guilt.

One dear client, a woman in her mid-thirties, was in the process of recreating marital and sexual intimacy with her husband when she very suddenly became completely unapproachable. Her husband could no longer show her any form of affection. After a few weeks of counseling and emotional exploration, her secret came out. She hadn't always been the loving Christian woman she was now. Before her marriage she'd been quite promiscuous and had cultivated a pretty sordid reputation. But then the Lord saved her and she moved to another town and started a new life in Jesus. As she had begun to taste real sexual intimacy with her husband, she'd begun to feel herself unworthy of those wonderful feelings. Shutting down sexually was her way of punishing herself for past sins. She needed to forgive herself as God had forgiven her so long ago. After she learned to forgive herself, she resumed her journey to intimacy with her husband.

Perhaps there's a pregnancy that you've never discussed with your husband or never forgiven yourself for; perhaps you've even had an abortion. I once had a male client who had pressured a girlfriend to get an abortion and had never truly forgiven himself. If there are scars, take them to the Lord and to your counselor, and do the work necessary to keep yourself moving toward marital and sexual intimacy.

Current Sin

If the pain is rooted in a sin you're still involved in, the principles are the same. Conscious, unrepentant sin not only separates you from your mate, but it also drives a wedge between you and the Lord. If you're engaged in a current, conscious sin, you need to stop. Before the Lord takes your discipline into His hands, as He says He will in Hebrews 12:6, take your well-being into your own hands. Confess and repent of your sin, discuss the issues with your pastor or counselor as necessary, and begin to enjoy your forgiveness and freedom in Christ (1 John 1:9). If your sin might be construed by your spouse as an attack upon him or her, it's best to get it out in the open. Sins will be found out anyway, and by confessing, you can face the issue boldly and together.

A Final Word

Sexual intimacy is a God-given gift to married couples. And like all of God's gifts, it's a far greater gift than we can ever imagine. But it takes care and loving attention. Come together with great tenderness and passion, with great excitement and yearning, with hearts filled with one another and expressing all the growing love that lives within them.

As your physical, emotional, and sexual intimacy grows, you'll naturally take up residence on your island of we, that island you both protect from the outside world.

TWENTY-SEVEN

THE ISLAND OF THREE—
SPIRITUAL INTIMACY

*Trust in the Lord with all your heart, and lean not on
your own understanding; in all your ways acknowledge
Him, and He shall direct your paths.*

—*Proverbs 3:5–6*

How does the island of we feel? Do you feel a little crowded on an island that has twice the population of your island of me? I'd be surprised if you did. I have always found far more room there to be myself, to enjoy the space that comes with being accepted for who I am. I hope you're finding that true, as well.

But there's another population paradox coming. The population of your island is about to increase again. And when it does, you will find even *more* room to grow and prosper.

That other inhabitant, of course, is God. But hasn't God told us that He will never leave nor forsake His people? If that's true, it seems we shouldn't have to add Him; He's already there. Well, He is there and I don't want to minimize His presence. But in order for Him to be a true resident of the island of we, He needs to become an integral part of your marriage; He needs to be its focal point.

In this chapter, we'll explore how you can enjoy the fulfillment of the spiritual intimacy that embracing God will bring.

What Is Spiritual Intimacy in Marriage?

Webster defines intimacy as a "personal, confidential friendship gained by close study."[1] God defines marital intimacy as two becoming "one flesh." Intimacy is a close, personal tie. It is knowledge and understanding, a total commitment to another's well-being, concern for another's sensibilities. It's marked by the characteristic of being deeply invested, and there exists an overwhelming sense of safety between those involved. Intimacy is the highest expression of love and, therefore, is what God desires as a relationship with all His people.

Spiritual intimacy results when the Lord is so tightly entwined in every element of your marriage that your steps as a couple and His steps are wholly in concert. Somewhere along the way most found out that there is no true intimacy without God. Although we live in a society of decaying morals and values, a hunger for spiritual renewal seems to be sweeping this country. *Newsweek* recently reported that "millions are embarking on the search for the sacred in their lives."[2] The desire's there. But the flesh is weak. We're all sinners saved by grace—at war with the desires that wrestle inside us. And a large part of that sin involves our lack of faith. When we walk our own paths instead of the Lord's, make decisions based on our own wisdom instead of God's leading, barriers to intimacy with the Lord go up.

Just think how different your life would be—particularly your relationship with the Lord—if you fully believed that God only had your best interests at heart, that He rewards those who diligently seek Him. You'd seldom stray. You'd be right there arm in arm with the Lord doing everything He tells you. Most of the time, you'd make thoughtful and godly decisions, because every decision process would start with the question, "What would the Lord have me do in this situation?" Maybe you wouldn't waffle, rebel, or put yourselves first as often. Instead, you'd acknowledge the presence and power of God in every aspect of your marital relationship. When you put God in the center of your relationship, it will decenter you. Every twist and turn that you and your spouse make will be at the Lord's leading. His gentle, healing fingerprints would be all over your present and your future.

But above all, you would be building a strong relationship with Him, one marked by trust, understanding, and a deep, unfathomable love. In such a relationship, each partner strives to hold up the other and bring the other the very best possible. Within the context of such a relationship, you'd know beyond all doubt that if you loved and selflessly took care of your spouse, the Lord would take care of you.

With that kind of relationship with God, you would be a couple about the Lord's business—wonderfully bonded by the Lord's purpose and love, able to walk with beautiful confident assurance of each step.

How do we achieve such a relationship? Begin by tearing down as many barriers that exist between you and the Lord as you can and strengthen your faith to overcome the barriers that remain.

Barriers to Spiritual Intimacy

Stress

Just as the stress of everyday living drove a wedge between you and your spouse, stress drives a wedge between you and God. There's no time to pray, to have devotions, to read the Bible, no time to talk to one another about the Lord and what He's doing in your lives and in your marriage. Just as stress made it impossible for the two of you to relax together and whisper sweet nothings in each other's ears, stress robs us of time to be intimate with our Lord. When was the last time you and your spouse walked in a garden or on a beach and just thought and spoke about Him? Often stress keeps us from doing just that. We either skip the walks altogether or take them and spend the time talking about overdue projects, or money problems, or issues surrounding our kids or parents. It's also important to realize that failing to have time to commune with the Lord has a negative effect. You begin to believe such time is unimportant—after all, you've gotten this far without it. Godlessness stands just around the corner from such thinking.

Personal Sin and Selfishness

Second Timothy 2:19b says: "Let everyone who names the name of Christ depart from iniquity." We've already discussed how sin and selfishness can hurt your relationship with your spouse; it hurts your relationship with God even more. Deliberately sinning and not repenting of sin is like shaking a fist in God's face. It's like sticking your tongue out at Him. And there is a price tag (James 1:14ff). An intimate relationship with Him is impossible during times of sin. We all sin, and we often take our time admitting that we've really sinned. We usually like to spend a little time rationalizing before coming to grips with it. God understands all that. Certainly He might rattle our cage a little to wake us up, but He forgives when we come to Him in repentance (1 John 1:9, Ps. 51).

Unhealthy Learned Behavior

Most of us have scars of varying severity from our childhoods or from catastrophes that haunt our future relationships—an alcoholic parent can bring fear of commitment, sparse love from a parent can make one clingy, or worse yet, afraid of loving or of being abandoned. Such painful pasts often distort our perspectives on life and how we see our heavenly Father. Those who had parents—particularly fathers—who were unreasonably strict, or dour, or angry, or absent often see the heavenly Father as having some of their earthly fathers' characteristics. Such images of God make it difficult to have an intimate relationship with Him. We don't trust Him enough to rely on Him. Intimacy is built on a foundation of trust and love, and a distorted view of God makes intimacy with Him impossible.

Satan

The last thing Satan wants is for you to have an intimate relationship with the Lord. If you have such a relationship, Satan's opportunities for success in your marriage go way down. So, alive and active, he skulks around like a roaring lion looking for the slightest weakness in your relationship with the Lord to tear into an open wound (1 Pet. 5:8). Paul admonished us that our ability to stand firm is predicated on being strong in the Lord (Eph. 6:10). And, of course, as a couple your resistance is far stronger together. Ecclesiastes 4:9–12 confirms that when it says, "Two are better than one, because they have a good reward for their labor. For if they fail, the one will lift up his companion. But woe to him who is alone when he falls, for he has no one to help him up. Again, if the two lie together, they will keep warm, but how can one be warm alone? Though one may be overpowered by another, two can withstand him."

Therefore, when Satan attacks your marriage, stand firm as a couple in Christ. If one weakens, the other can pick up the slack. Satan's strategy is to divide you up, then conquer each of you separately. He'll try to raise old rages and battles by resurrecting issues long since resolved. In doing so, he'll hope to drive new and more resilient wedges between you. You must resist his efforts to split you again at all costs. If you don't, your journey to spiritual intimacy will be the first of many casualties that will litter that beach.

Now that we've identified the barriers to spiritual intimacy, we will take a good look at how to overcome those barriers.

Twenty-Eight

Overcoming
the Barriers

When a man's ways please the Lord, He makes even his enemies to be at peace with him.

—*Proverbs 16:7*

I hope you're beginning to crave the wonder of an intimate relationship with the Lord. Life is so much more fulfilling and joyful when we know that we are truly children of God. A significant step toward achieving spiritual intimacy in marriage is to deal with the barriers we named in the last chapter.

Have a United Purpose

I have learned that it is easier to serve God without a united purpose. Because when you do, you are not bothered by what God desires and requires. You decide what's necessary and important. The marital journey will *seem* more carefree if you never receive the directives of God for your marriage. But it isn't.

As you approach this issue of spiritual intimacy, don't come to God with the intent of changing your spouse or even yourself (although both will probably occur). Rather, come to build a loving and intimate relationship with Jesus Christ—together. Allow the Spirit of the Lord to work in you so that you can become more like Him. And ask what your partner's spiritual needs are. Commit yourself to the task of seeing him or her grow in the likeness of Christ. God has chosen to work through you to impact your partner for His sake.

Such purpose, though, requires discipline, the kind Paul encourages Timothy to have: "Exercise yourself toward godliness" (1 Tim. 4:7). Of course, we must do the same. Spiritual intimacy is intentional and requires daily investment through a variety of means, including praying, reading and studying Scripture, praising and worshiping, singing, fasting, and more.

Most important, know that spiritual intimacy doesn't come through a program or method, but rather with the cultivation of a relationship with Jesus Christ (Phil. 3). Remember, spiritual intimacy is not about *time* with God but rather about a *life* with God.

And such a life brings many wonderful benefits. When someone is connected with God and daily expressing or living out that relationship, change takes place. Spiritual intimacy can increase our level of communication, demonstrate a strong commitment to one another, and reflect our strong love toward each other.

Validate the Lord's Presence in Your Marriage

Remember the Robinson Crusoe story? Marooned on a desert island, he believed himself very much alone. How did he find out he wasn't? He saw another's footprints on the beach.

Similarly, when we see the Lord's footprints alongside our own, we have proof He's there, too, walking the earth with us. What, then, *are* the Lord's footprints? They're evidence of His faithfulness to us—times when we sought Him earnestly and He made a way for us. Or when he took our disobedience and taught us the right lesson *without* giving us the full punishment we deserve. Or maybe it took going through the very darkest hour to finally bring us to repentance. That, too, is evidence.

There are also His miracles. Perhaps the revitalization of your marriage might be considered a miracle. But there are probably others—anger that suddenly dissolves, fears that are suddenly overcome, people who wish you ill but end up doing you great good.

And finally, He blesses obedience—times when you did the right thing knowing that it would likely aggravate a worsening situation, but just the opposite occurred.

Look back together on those moments in your life—identify the evidence of God's footprints. Then marvel at the Lord's work and if you haven't already, thank Him. He is with you both and with your marriage; He's never left you alone once.

Do this every time you see a coming trial or problem. It'll help put the approaching problem in perspective and strengthen your confidence to deal with it.

Deal with Problems in a Godly Way

It is often said that there are three states of humans—we are either getting into trouble, in trouble, or getting out of trouble. What trials are you going through as a couple? Write them down. For instance, there may be problems that are still keeping you from being as close as you could be—old resentments that bubble up now and again, or scars that break into open wounds. Maybe there are problems at work that affect you both. Or problems with the kids. But whatever you write down, agree on what the problem is and how to define it.

In chapter 18, as part of establishing your safe zone, we discussed a method of solving problems in a way that wouldn't add stress to your marriage. I hope you've been using it. Now, though, let's be sure the Lord is an integral part of the problem-solving process. The basic steps will remain the same, but now we'll trace the spiritual core at the center of them.

Define the Problem

You've already made a list of the trials you and your spouse are going through, and before that would be enough. But now take a close look at them and pull out the spiritual issues that each stirs up.

Collect Data

As before, do your best during this step to understand everything you can about the problem. However, there's a new place you need to go for data—the Bible. Since each one of those issues is spiritual in nature, you need to understand and factor into your decision process what the Lord has to say. So, assemble the verses in Scripture that address each.

Look at Alternative Solutions

Add to what we said earlier concerning this step a discussion of those alternatives in light of the scriptural verses just found. Stick to what the verses say, and work hard to read nothing into the verses that isn't there. If you come to any conclusions that seem at odds with other verses you know about but haven't researched, do more research.

Get to Yes

Determine the godly response to each issue based on your search of Scripture. If necessary, consult with your pastor. If you find yourself in a situation you can't handle because you lack training or skills, ask a professional to intervene. And don't forget to pray as you get to yes.

As you put your plans into effect and see the Lord working within them to bring Himself glory and work things out for your good, the reality of the Lord will make more and more of an impact on your lives and your marriage. And the greater the Lord's impact becomes, the less of an impact Satan, the world, and your flesh will have. As you rely on the Lord for more of your life's activities, you and the Lord will become more intimate—which, of course, is the heart of *spiritual intimacy*.

Dealing with Your Childhood Issues

It could very well be that you have few or no scars from childhood. You were raised by loving parents in an Eden-like environment or the equivalent. But the likelihood is there will be issues, maybe major, maybe minor; if you find yourself dealing with any emotions that seem stronger than they should, or with moods that last longer and go deeper than one might call normal, again reach out and get some help from someone who knows and lives the Word—your pastor, a professional Christian counselor, or trained lay leaders who can give you wise counsel. Of course, if you've been journeying through a difficult marital situation, you're already either getting such counseling or thinking very seriously about it. If there are other issues to resolve, that should cinch your decision.

But first, look up to the Lord. God is still working amid His people. If you have anger, pray that it might be removed. If you need forgiveness, pray that you might be delivered from the desire for vengeance. If you feel pain, pray that it might be quieted. If you're afraid of abandonment, pray that God's promises might reach to you. God wants you to reach out to Him. He's eager for you to do so. (See Acts 17:26–27.) He's waiting there to help.

Dealing with Sin and Selfishness

Let's let Scripture speak for itself. James 1:14–16 tells us, ". . . but each one is tempted when he is drawn away by his own desires and enticed. Then when desire has conceived, it gives birth to sin; and sin, when it is full-grown, brings forth death. Do not be deceived, my beloved brethren."

Romans 7:14–18 makes the deceitfulness of sin plain, "For we know that the law is spiritual, but I am carnal, sold under sin. For what I am doing, I do not understand. For what I will to do, that I do not practice; but what I hate, that I do. If, then, I do what I will not to do, I agree with the law that it is good. But now, it is no longer I who do it, but sin that dwells in me. For I know that in me (that is, in my flesh) nothing good dwells."

Sin and selfishness bring a hollow life. Not only do they run contrary to the Lord's Word, which drives a wedge between you, but they also leave you with an unfulfilled life. You may end up surrounded by things, even a certain comfort, but it's a lonely, bitter comfort far from spiritual intimacy.

All that said, how then do you deal with sin and selfishness—particularly toward your spouse? Do so through love—for your Lord and for your mate. The Lord Jesus tells us in John 14:15 that if you love Him, you will keep His commandments. Sin offends Him, but worse than offends, it wounds Him. To trample His sacrifice beneath your feet by sinning hurts Him deeply. When the temptation to sin comes calling, and that includes selfishness, stop and ask yourself who you love more, Jesus or your sin. The more often you choose Jesus, the more intimate your relationship with Him will become.

Dealing with Stress

Even though you won't achieve perfect faith until you see Jesus face to face, you can try to live as Jesus did. After all, if you could truly comprehend Romans 8:28—"And we know that all things work together for good to those who love God, to those who are the called according to His purpose"—then there would be a lot more freedom in you. You'd know that God is working in your life and no matter how bad things look, they will work out to your good. But many don't completely believe that. A strong part believes if something looks like it's going to explode, it will—and it will destroy. The bigger the possible explosion, the greater the stress. So, until you do have perfect faith, behave as if you do. Look the situation that's providing stress right in the eye and tell yourself that no matter what happens, God is in control. Then do what's *godly*—secure in the knowledge that God is right there with you. Will this stop stress? Not right away, nor all of it, probably, but as you see God working, you'll taste freedom.

A Cherished Level of Connectedness

Spiritual intimacy in marriage brings a level of connectedness between you, your spouse, and the Lord that you will believe only when you've experienced it. And once you have, you'll find it so precious, I believe you'll work very hard to keep it. I wish such intimacy for you and your mate. It will not only bless your present, but it will also assure a continued blessing for the future as you set up permanent housekeeping on your island of three.

A Final Word

You and your mate have come a long way in a short time. Where you were thinking seriously about calling it quits and living with the excruciating pain of separation, I pray that now you're working on building a level of intimacy that may be more loving and enduring than you had ever achieved before. If not, my earnest prayer is that God has allowed this work to impact you in some way—to have an effect on your future. In the next chapter I have a few parting thoughts I'd like to share before bidding you Godspeed.

TWENTY-NINE

LOVE REMAINS

And now abide faith, hope, love, these three;
but the greatest of these is love.

—*1 Corinthians 13:13*

The brittle chill in the air was no match for the warm memories he had of her as he beheld her for the last time. The thoughts came like ethereal snapshots, haunting his heart, only to be replaced by ever warmer images—gentle hands soothing a child's tears, her own tears as she shared a friend's heartache, her tender expression as she nursed a sick child, her loyalty to her husband's ministry, her courage, her leadership, her unequivocal and undying love. She had graced and enriched his life with all of it—with all of her. And now, after only fifty years together, she was gone.

They'd met as teens. And overnight he went from not thinking much about girls to walking miles to spend what seemed like just a few minutes with her. By the time he was seventeen and had volunteered to serve in World War II, they were discussing love and marriage. They even talked about marrying before he shipped out with the Navy. But they both knew they were too young, and his future too uncertain.

"I remember the day I left," he said. "She stood there sobbing, rivers of tears running down her cheeks. I could feel her heart begging me to stay. Would I ever see her again? None of us who were going really expected to come back. But somehow I knew I would."

He, of course, was right, and the moment his feet hit home he grabbed her from among several other suitors and married her. "The day I slipped that ring on her finger was the happiest day of my life."

Then, for all those many years, they traveled a path together—hand in hand. Like every marriage, theirs had peaks and valleys. There were even times when the going really got rough, and they questioned their direction. But throughout the journey, they remained steadfast in their commitment to making it with each other. And they did.

And what they did together was build a strong Christian family. Their eight children came one at a time, each unique, each with a joy all his or her own, each reminding them of their special bond. As what might be called the backbone of the family, she invested heavily in each child. By day she nurtured, instructed, and disciplined. At night, she cried tears—sometimes of joy and sometimes of pain—while praying for and giving each of them over to God.

But with all that investment in the kids, she never faltered in her support of her husband. She struggled right beside him as he pastored several country churches. His constant encourager, she believed in him and what he did. And above all else, she believed in their Lord. Together, they touched thousands of lives in their small Pennsylvania town. Now, several hundred had gathered to join in the joy of her new life and the sorrow of their loss.

At the gravesite many remained, silent except for the tears and the occasional cough, as he stood beside her casket. Peering into it, he realized that this would be the last time they would be together on this side of the Jordan. With that he was both buoyed and crushed by an avalanche of memories and emotion. Then my father stood alone to spend one final moment with the woman who had made his life complete in every way. As he did, we eight kids and our wives and husbands and children stood by silently honoring our parents.

"I just have one regret about marrying her," he said to anyone close enough to hear his trembling voice. "I just wish that I had married her before I shipped out. I would have enjoyed three more beautiful years with her as my wife if I had."

I can think of no better way to end this book than with this story. During their fifty years together, my parents overcame many obstacles and faced painful challenges. Together, they made it through financial hardship, severe health problems, and the loss of close friends and family. They grieved together and laughed together, counted pennies and blessings together, and through it all managed to successfully raise eight children. But at that gravesite what mattered most—more than all the successes and failures, all the major and minor struggles of what had been their life—was their love for and commitment to each other. To me, their marriage exemplifies all that Christ has intended for a man and a woman. Their love remains.

How will it be for you? At the end of your life, will you be able to look back and see running through it that same iron thread of love and commitment? Will your mind be filled with cherished memories or deep regret? Believe it or not, these are choices. If I learned one thing from my father and mother, it is the importance of making each day a day of building, of moving forward, and of struggling to love.

It's living each day and bringing 1 Corinthians 13—the great love chapter—to life.

Life's too short to do anything else. James 4:14 calls life "a vapor." Any moment we may be called to Jesus' side. Think about that the next time you're tempted to become angry, disappointed, bitter, or unkind to your spouse. Love brings eternity—both your love for God and your love for one another. For in love there are no regrets, only hearth fire memories and better tomorrows. Love much.

NOTES

Chapter One

1. Janice Castro, "Simple Life," *Time* (8 April 1991), 58.
2. The Roper Center, "Conventional Men and Women in a World of Change," *Public Perspective 1* no.4 (1990): 24–28.
3. Richard Swenson, *Margin: Restoring Emotional, Physical, Financial and Time Reserves to Overloaded Lives* (Colorado Springs, CO: NavPress, 1992), 154–155.

Chapter Two

1. See Gary Smalley, *Making Love Last Forever* (Dallas, TX: Word, 1996); I first heard this concept at one of Gary Smalley's workshops in Gatlinburg, TN.
2. See Gary Oliver, *Real Men Have Feelings Too* (Chicago: Moody Press, 1993); Gary Oliver and Norm Wright, *Good Women Get Angry* (Ann Arbor, MI: Servant Publications, 1995).

Chapter Four

1. Lynn Gigy and Joan Kelly, "Reasons for Divorce: Perspectives of Divorcing Men and Women," *Journal of Divorce and Re-marriage* 18 (1992):169–87.
2. Judith Wallerstein and Sandra Blakeslee, *Second Chances: Men, Women, and Children a Decade After Divorce* (New York: Tickner and Fields, 1989) 3–4.
3. George Ohlschlager, "The High Cost of Divorce," unpublished manuscript; see also Julie Conneily, "Divorce: Getting the Best Deal," *Fortune* 127 (17 May 1993), 124–30.
4. Kenneth Kressel, *The Process of Divorce: How Professionals and Couples Negotiate Divorce* (New York: Basic Books, 1985), 4.
5. Judith Wallerstein and Sandra Blakeslee, *Second Chances: Men, Women, and Children a Decade After Divorce* (New York: Tickner and Fields, 1989), 29–30.
6. Paul Bohannon, "The Six Stations of Divorce" in *Divorce and After* edited by Paul Bohannan (Garden City, NY: Doubleday, 1970).

7. Lee Salk, quoted in Archibald Hart, *Helping Children Survive Divorce* (Dallas, TX: Word, 1996), 19.

8. Judith Wallerstein and Sandra Blakeslee, *Second Chances: Men, Women, and Children a Decade After Divorce* (New York: Tickner and Fields, 1989).

9. Tom Whiteman, "Children of Divorce." Radio interview, October 1997.

10. Quoted by James Dobson, *Straight Talk to Men and Their Wives* (Waco, TX: Word, 1978), 44-45.

11. See Archibald Hart, *Helping Children Survive Divorce* (Dallas, TX: Word, 1996); Judith Wallerstein and Sandra Blakeslee, *Second Chances: Men, Women, and Children a Decade After Divorce* (New York: Tickner and Fields, 1989

Chapter Five

1. James Cordova and Neil Jacobson, "Couple Distress," in *Clinical Handbook of Psychological Disorders: A Step-by-step Treatment Manual,* 2nd ed., edited by David Barlow (New York: Guilford Press, 1993), 482.

2. Quote by "Megan," from personal correspondence by a former client.

3. Robert Coombs, "Marital Status and Personal Well Being: A Literature Review," *Family Relations* 40 (1991): 97–102.

4. Nina Donnelly, *I Never Know What to Say* (New York: Ballantine Books, 1987), 123

5. Judith Wallerstein and Sandra Blakeslee, *The Good Marriage: How and Why Love Lasts* (Boston: Houghton Mifflin, 1995), 15.

Chapter Seven

1. H. McCubbin and J. Patterson, "Family Transition: Adaptations to Stress," in *Stress and the Family*, vol. 1, edited by H. McCubbin and C. Figley (New York: Brunner/Mazel, 1983), 10.

2. Richard Swenson, *Margin: Restoring Emotional, Physical, Financial and Time Reserves to Overloaded Lives* (Colorado Springs, CO: NavPress, 1992).

3. See Mark Karpel, *Evaluating Couples: A Handbook for Practitioners* (New York: Norton, 1994), 31.

4. Gary Smalley, "Treat Her Like a Queen," *New Man* (Jan./Feb. 1996), 31–33.

5. Dan Allender and Tremper Longman, *Intimate Allies* (Wheaton, IL: Tyndale House, 1995). This is the strong theme that flows throughout their work— an excellent resource for couples to build a solid spiritual basis to love and marriage.

6. James Cordova and Neil Jacobson, "Couple Distress" in *Clinical Handbook of Psychological Disorders: A Step-by-step Treatment Manual,* 2nd ed., edited by David Barlow (New York: Guilford Press, 1993), 498.

7. Judith Wallerstein and Sandra Blakeslee, *The Good Marriage: How and Why Love Lasts* (Boston: Houghton Mifflin, 1995), 12–13.

Chapter Eight

1. William James, *The Principles of Psychology, vol. 1.* (New York: Henry Holt, 1890), 293.

Chapter Nine

1. John Gottman, *Why Marriages Succeed or Fail . . . And How You Can Make Yours Last* (New York: Simon & Shuster, 1994), 68.
2. Ibid., 76.
3. Ibid., 79.
4. Ibid., 95.
5. Aaron Beck, *Love Is Never Enough: How Couples Can Overcome Mis-under-standings, Resolve Conflicts, and Solve Relationship Problems Through Cognitive Therapy* (New York: Harper & Row, 1988), 108–9.
6. Developed from James Cordova and Neil Jacobson, "Couple Distress," in *Clinical Handbook of Psychological Disorders: A Step-by-step Treatment Manual,* 2nd ed., edited by David Barlow (New York: Guilford Press, 1993), 498.

Chapter Ten

1. Frank Pittman, *Private Lies: Infidelity and the Betrayal of Intimacy* (New York: Norton, 1989), 121–25.

Chapter Twelve

1. Gary Smalley and Greg Smalley, *Bound by Honor: Fostering a Great Relationship with Your Teen* (Wheaton, IL: Tyndale House, 1998), 14.

Chapter Thirteen

1. Charles Stanley, *Enter His Gates: A Daily Devotional* (Nashville, TN: Thomas Nelson, 1998), 4.

Chapter Fourteen

1. Clifford Notarious and Howard Markman, *We Can Work It Out* (New York: Putnam, 1993), 18.

Chapter Fifteen

1. See Mark Karpel, *Evaluating Couples: A Handbook for Practitioners* (New York: Norton, 1994), 42.
2. John Trent, *Life-Mapping: Workbook Edition* (Colorado Springs, CO: WaterBrook Press, 1998), 211ff.

Chapter Sixteen

1. Stephen Grunlan, *Marriage and the Family: A Christian Perspective* (Grand Rapids, MI: Zondervan, 1984), 216–17.

Chapter Seventeen

1. From love survey, in Paul Chance, "The Trouble with Love," *Psychology Today* (February 1988), 44–47.
2. Developed with E. Glenn Wagner, personal correspondence, 1998; see also E. Glenn Wagner, *Strategies for a Successful Marriage: A Study Guide for Men* (Colorado Springs, CO: NavPress, 1994), 65ff.
3. Gary Chapman, *The Five Love Languages* (Chicago: Northfield Publishing, 1992); see also Gary Smalley and John Trent, *The Language of Love* (Colorado Springs, CO: Focus on the Family, 1991).
4. See Willard Harley, *His Needs/Her Needs* (Grands Rapids, MI: Fleming/Revell, 1986); see also Clifford Notarious and Howard Markman *We Can Work It Out* (New York: Putnam, 1993), 65ff; a wonderful resource at this phase is James C. Dobson, *Straight Talk* (Dallas: Word, 1991).

Chapter Eighteen

1. John Gottman, *Why Marriages Succeed or Fail . . . And How You Can Make Yours Last* (New York: Simon & Shuster, 1994), 57–61.
2. Ibid., 173ff.
3. Howard Markman, Scott Stanley, and Susan Blumberg, *Fighting for Your Marriage* (San Francisco: Jossey-Bass, 1994), 38ff.
4. This technique is derived from Scott Stanley, Daniel Trathen, Savanna McCain, and Milt Bryan, *A Lasting Promise: A Christian Guide to Fighting for Your Marriage* (San Francisco: Jossey-Bass, 1998), 59–69.
5. Oswald Chambers, *My Utmost for His Highest* (Urichsville, OH: Barbour Books, [1935] 1963), 86.
6. Henry Cloud and John Townsend, *Boundaries* (Grand Rapids, MI: Zondervan, 1992), 33.
7. Frank Datillo and Christine Padesky, *Cognitive Therapy with Couples* (Sarasota, FL: Professional Resources Exchange, 1990), 428–843; see also Aaron Beck, *Cognitive Therapy and the Emotional Disorders* (New York: International Universities Press, 1976); Aaron Beck, *Love Is Never Enough* (New York: HarperPerennial, 1988).

Chapter Nineteen

1. Excellent resources on forgiveness include: Michael McCullough, Steven Sandage, and Everett Worthington, *To Forgive Is Human* (Downers Grove, IL: InterVarsity Press, 1997); Chuck Lynch, *I Should Forgive, But . . .* (Nashville, TN: Word, 1998).

Chapter Twenty

1. C. S. Lewis, quoted in Dennis Rainey, *Lonely Husbands, Lonely Wives* (Dallas, TX: Word, 1989), 33